Eric F. Douglas, an award-winning management consultant and a graduate of Harvard University, is a partner in BMR Associates, a management and organization development consulting firm based in San Francisco. Clients include Time Warner, American Public Television, and the University of California. Douglas entered the publishing business in 1974 and spent twenty years as an executive in the media industry spanning newspapers, magazines, and electronic media. He was formerly vice president of the *Sacramento Bee*, where he helped achieve record circulation levels, and executive director of *Baltimore Magazine*, which he led to its first National Magazine Award. He was also associate editor of the *San Francisco Chronicle* and president of NeuroSonics, a media software company. He lives with his wife and three children in northern California.

D1416882

straight talk

TURNING

COMMUNICATION

UPSIDE DOWN

FOR

STRATEGIC RESULTS

AT WORK

Eric F. Douglas

Davies-Black Publishing
Palo Alto, California

Published by Davies-Black Publishing, an imprint of Consulting Psychologists Press, Inc., 3803 East Bayshore Road, Palo Alto, CA 94303; 800-624-1765.

Special discounts on bulk quantities of Davies-Black books are available to corporations, professional associations, and other organizations. For details, contact the Director of Book Sales at Davies-Black Publishing, an imprint of Consulting Psychologists Press, Inc., 3803 East Bayshore Road, Palo Alto, CA 94303; 650-691-9123; Fax 650-988-0673.

Cover photo: © Pierre-Yves Goavec/The Image Bank
Iconography and Matrix character designs: Studio Arno
02 01 00 99 98   10 9 8 7 6 5 4 3 2 1
Printed in the United States of America

Library of Congress Cataloging-in-Publication Data
Douglas, Eric
    Straight talk : turning communication upside down
  for strategic results at work / Eric Douglas
      p. cm.
    Includes bibliographical references and index.
    ISBN 0-89106-117-7
    1. Business communication. 2. Communication in organizations.
    3. Oral communication. I. Title.
  HF5718.D68   1998
  658.4′5—dc21
                        97-49444
                            CIP

FIRST EDITION
First printing 1998

For Susanna

Contents

Acknowledgments

This book is the result of many years of my own learning, thinking, writing, and teaching about organizational communication. Yet it is also the result of significant contributions from clients, colleagues, co-workers, friends, and family members.

First, for their professional counsel and wisdom, I am indebted to my colleagues at BMR Associates, particularly John Hershberger, Peter Kiers, and Susan Reich. For their invaluable insights, Katherine Benziger, Gerry George, Jack Jennings, David Katz, Nick Keefe, Jim Love, Ken Macher, and Bob Putnam. For her solid and painstaking research, Lisa Bohon. For inspiration and support, Lynda Applegate, Chris Argyris, Peter Drucker, Charles Handy, Dee Hock, Ray Miles, Bill O'Brien, and Peter Senge.

To all the people at Davies-Black Publishing, I extend my heartfelt thanks.

Above all, I wish to acknowledge my clients for their support, their patience, and their willingness to try new ways of communicating. They know who they are and how important they've been.

Finally, I want to thank my family. For inspiration, my parents, Peter and Alice. For their running commentary and support, my daughters Kate and Charlotte. For his counsel and wisdom, my father-in-law, Charles Cooper. And above all, for her steadfast and enduring love, my wife, Susanna.

Prologue: What Is Straight Talk?

In the middle of the journey of our life I came to myself within a dark wood where the straight way was lost.
—DANTE ALIGHIERI, *The Divine Comedy* (1320)

When we think of straight talk, we think of speaking candidly and openly. We imagine saying what we mean so that other people understand us perfectly. We imagine a world of insightful exchanges, where people from all backgrounds talk to each other in constructive ways. We imagine a world where everyone takes responsibility for clear, honest, and open communication.

This book is aimed at building such a world. It is aimed at building a world of competent communicators.

What do we mean by competent communicators? We mean more than the ability to use language well, or to articulate one's thoughts and feelings clearly. We mean more than knowing how to get a message across. We mean more than being able to listen well, although that too plays a part. When we talk about competence in communicating, we really mean three things.

First, we mean understanding that we all have our own styles of communicating—and that our different styles affect everything we hear and say. It means acknowledging that these different styles can lead to misunderstandings. In the long run, it means developing and expanding our repetoire of communication styles so that we can communicate easily and fluidly in any situation.

Second, we mean understanding and avoiding the *pitfalls* that lie in wait as we process and convey information. This means understanding that these pitfalls occur in a moment's time and that we are thus unconscious of them. It means acknowledging that how we process information can be changed and made more effective by challenging the way we think.

Third, we mean applying a set of *ground rules* that allows us, whether as two people or as a group, to acknowledge barriers to communication and overcome them. This means recognizing that competence in communication does not come easily. It means acknowledging that ground rules, like rules of the road, are necessary to avoid crashing into one another while we try to communicate.

Fundamentally, then, competence in communication means challenging and changing the ways we listen and talk to one another. It means turning some of our traditional ideas about communication upside down. At the heart of this book is the idea that competency in communicating is different from competency in any other field or endeavor. That's why it's so hard.

We've all experienced what happens when two unskilled communicators get in a room together and fling assertions back and forth like Ping-Pong balls.

Ping: **That's how we do things at XYZ Corp.**
Pong: Well, that's not how we did things at ABC Corp.
Ping: **Well, that's how we do them here.**
Pong: That's not the way it should be done.

Asking questions—especially good questions—is a sign of competence in communicating. Flatly stating your opinions is a sign of incompetence. Curiosity is a reflection of competence. Certainty is a reflection of incompetence. Good communicators realize that knowing all the answers isn't a sign of competence. It's most often a sign of incompetence.

This book is designed to help anyone who wishes to become a competent communicator. It is specifically designed for people in organizations and businesses, but the tools presented here are just as valid at home as they are at work. Part I lays out these tools and the principles behind them. First, you'll discover your particular style of communicating, and how it affects your daily interactions with other people. Next, you'll learn how to identify other people's styles, and how to apply that understanding to strengthening your communications. Then, through a series of exercises, you'll learn how to modify your style as the situation warrants.

Part I also lays out the tools needed to talk about typical organizational issues, such as marketing strategy, human resources, and production. It exposes the traps and pitfalls that undermine the way we process information and communicate our positions. You'll learn the kinds of assumptions that lead to breakdowns in understanding.

In Part 2, the focus of the book shifts from learning about the tools and principles of communication to applying them in specific situations. You'll discover how these tools can improve your life on a daily basis—whether organizing your time, making a decision, or supervising a project. You'll also learn how to apply these tools to run a meeting, solve a thorny problem, or resolve a conflict. And you'll get a set of basic ground rules that can improve the quality of your communications.

Finally, Part 2 also discusses the specific types of organizational culture that evolve from the way an organization communicates. You'll learn how to identify an organization's culture; you'll be able to predict an organization's habits, both good and bad. And you'll find out how to improve an organization's performance.

In sum, this book is designed to help you gain competency in communication as quickly and effectively as possible—and make you a stronger and more valuable contributor to your organization.

Several trends are making such competency more important today than ever before. First, the need to respond quickly to market changes creates the need for a less rigid and bureaucratic work environment. Information must flow up, down, and across traditional channels. No longer is it enough to have a few skilled communicators at key nodal points. The need for fast response time requires everyone to be a competent communicator.

Second, the emergence of teams as the basic unit of business requires people to communicate effectively and reach consensus quickly. They need to know how to work through complex issues on their own and how to resolve conflicts without relying on a boss.

Third, the increasing number of people working in global organizations drives the demand for more skillful communicators. When people collaborate on projects from offices separated by thousands of miles, when cultural differences can exacerbate shortfalls in communication, the standard opportunities to build trust and goodwill simply don't exist. Small misunderstandings can escalate into bigger conflicts. Knowing the tools for effective communication is therefore an essential—if not *the* essential—competency of the global corporation.

Fourth, technology is driving people toward new ways of communicating. More and more people are working in virtual offices, spread across multiple, sometimes moving, locations. At dozens of companies, teleconferencing and e-mail are replacing staff meetings. But virtual teams can grind to a virtual halt in a hurry if poor communication prevails. Technology has increased the volume of communications, but quantity has not improved quality. If the human software is not glitch-proof, technology will inevitably increase the number of communication snafus.

Fifth, there is wide recognition that the old ways of interaction among employees have simply reached the end of their useful life span. Today, new competitors arise so quickly that organizations that don't continually change and improve are left in the dust. Organizational thinkers like Chris Argyris and Peter Senge have laid out strong, persuasive arguments for "learning organizations" in which culture, structure, and interpersonal behaviors create a process of continual improvement.

This book is intended to provide a set of tools for people who aspire to be a part of a learning organization. It is for people who need to know how to challenge their own thinking—and to engage others in the search to find effective solutions. This book is intended to help build the social underpinnings of the twenty-first-century organization, where straight talk is the norm, not the exception.

That's the plan. Now let's go to work.

Part One
What Straight Talk Is All About

All great changes are irksome to the human mind.
—JOHN ADAMS, LETTER TO JAMES WARREN, APRIL 22, 1776

Consultants are usually hired to help organizations revolutionize their way of doing business. Sometimes the solutions are readily apparent: a lack of management strategy; a failure to be clear about job functions; a need to share information among employees. As outsiders, consultants can ask the questions that people don't ask: Why is this done this way? What is your reasoning? Did you consider other options? As outsiders, their job is to challenge the conventional wisdom.

And as outsiders, it's often easier to do so.

Consultants diagnose and treat these specific problems to the best of their ability. But organizations shouldn't depend on outsiders to ask challenging questions. Insiders should be able to ask those questions, too.

I have spent much of my career searching out the tools to help people engage in this kind of straight talk—tools that help bridge differences in style, tools to mediate conflicts, tools to help people understand one another, tools that enable change. The Communication Styles Profile, which appears in Chapter 1, forms the foundation of the tools designed to help anyone in an organization become a skilled, competent communicator.

Where we've succeeded in introducing the tools of straight talk, we've seen surprising results. Management teams become more adept at thinking and managing in innovative ways. Companies become more skilled in managing difficult projects. One organization experienced a 20 percent increase in profits the year after we introduced these tools— and its managers attributed the increase entirely to their new way of working together.

If straight talk were easy, there'd be no need to write a book about it. But straight talk is hard. Most people are lazy communicators even in the simplest situations—managing their time, laying out a task, setting goals. People communicate in clumsy ways because it's easier than communicating expertly.

If we communicate ineffectively in normal situations, imagine how we behave in a challenging situation. Imagine what we do when the topic is "Where is my business going?" or "What is happening to our industry?" In those situations, we're very likely to respond in ways that are exactly contrary to what is needed. In the situations where straight talk is most needed, it is most likely to be elusive.

Think of the costs of this inexpert communication. Think of the lost opportunities, misdirected resources, and underutilized human capital. One CEO totaled up the bill for his organization's ineffectiveness and put it at 15 percent of total revenues. In his case, that meant $45 million in lost revenues *each year* because his company didn't communicate about key issues head-on.

As you start to learn the tools and principles of straight talk described in the following pages, discuss them with your colleagues. Try them out in your meetings. Above all, trust these tools to work for you. This may mean changing your way of thinking. But at the heart of straight talk lies a willingness to accept that change is the only thing we can count on.

The spirit of this book is embodied, oddly enough, in a sign I once saw hanging in the customer service office at the Amtrak station in Los Angeles:

A Short Course in Productive Communication

The six most important words: "I admit I made a mistake."
The five most important words: "You did a good job."
The four most important words: "What is your opinion?"
The three most important words: "If you please."
The two most important words: "Thank you."
The one most important word: "We."
The least important word: "I."

Chapter One
It All Starts with Communication Styles

I know all but myself.

—FRANÇOIS VILLON (1431–1465)

In file cabinets, photo albums, and desk drawers, most of us have more photographs of ourselves than we will ever have time to sort through. Even if we did, these pictures wouldn't reveal all we wish we could know. They might remind us that our closest friend in childhood was the family dog. They might help us recall our first athletic exploits. But those flat, two-dimensional images can hardly tell the full story of who we are or how we relate to other people.

The Communication Styles Profile presented in this chapter is a sort of 3-D camera, one that captures a multidimensional snapshot of yourself. It enables you to see yourself as others see you. It reveals your particular style of communicating. And it will help you become a more successful communicator.

When people first discover their styles, it's often an epiphany. They turn to each other and say: "So that's why you love details!" Or: "Now I see why you and I get along so well!" People will spend hours talking about the insights they've gained. It's not unusual to see people huddled together, comparing their styles and saying, "If only I had known this when..."

One organization, a New York magazine publisher, took this response a step further. The president had baseball caps made for everyone, a different color hat for each communication style. We found the place swarming with green, red, yellow, and orange hats. On each hat was inscribed: "It's all a matter of style."

Reactions like these are typical. They show the excitement that comes with learning about communication styles. But along with the excitement comes a long list of benefits. You'll learn more about these as we go along. If you want to become a skilled communicator, this chapter is the place to start.

First Steps

Think for a moment about the people with whom you communicate easily and naturally. They are like your second self. You see things the same way they do. You share their thoughts and feelings—you can complete their sentences. Even when you have a dispute, you know they see your side of the story, just as you see theirs.

Some people, on the other hand, seem to be on a different wavelength. They never see things the same way you do. They don't tackle problems in the same way. Maybe you think there's something wrong with your relationship. Most likely, there's not. More likely, the differences are merely a matter of style.

Research shows that people communicate in measurably different ways that reflect differences in what they choose to hear and say. Some people focus on feelings. Some focus on tasks. Some focus on the big picture. Some on the smallest details. These choices determine how we relate to the world. So understanding our style is tantamount to understanding how we see the world around us. In a sense, our world is a reflection of our communication style.

Communication styles are a manifestation of our personalities. But they are not the same as personality. Scholars and researchers agree that personality is relatively stable, changing only subtly over time. Our style of communicating, on the other hand, is a learned behavior. We can modify it once we learn how. In fact, skilled communicators can modify their style on the spot, as the situation warrants. Just like reading a book, hitting a baseball, or diving into a pool, modifying your communication style is a skill. It doesn't come naturally. But once you learn it, it's a skill you can use all your life.

Why learn to modify your style? After all, shouldn't you be content to be who you are? That's a reasonable argument. But your world consists of many different types of people—including colleagues, bosses, employees, and customers—and it's to your advantage to understand exactly where they're all coming from.

At the same time, people have a basic need to feel understood, to feel listened to. When people perceive you as a competent communicator, when they know you understand their thoughts and feelings, something magical happens. People begin to look to you for leadership. They pay more attention to you, knowing that you respect them. In other words, there's a bonus that comes with understanding communication styles: It elevates all your relationships to a higher plane.

For managers and leaders, understanding communication styles is an indispensable skill. It enables them to translate differences in what people say. It enables them to mediate conflicts. And it paves the way for successful discussions about complex subjects. It's a truism that leaders and managers must be good communicators. But there's a difference between being articulate, which is what books about communication typically teach, and knowing the tools of straight talk.

Origin of Communication Styles

Anthropology helps answer the question of where our communication styles come from. Psychology, and particularly research into personality types, supports the idea that there are four distinct communication styles. Our research concurs that there are four basic styles of communicating, which affect all of our communications with other people.

Since these four styles have such an impact on our relationships, how can we learn more about them? Why do we have them in the first place? Why do we need different ways of communicating?

For some answers, we turn first to the science of anthropology. Claude Lévi-Strauss has noted the existence of four universal roles—or archetypes—that exist in societies around the world. These four archetypes may form the basis of our styles of communicating.

The first archetype is the ruler, the person who makes decisions, dispenses justice, divides wealth, and appoints successors. The ruler is omnipresent in primitive societies ranging from the Anasazi Indians to early Asian tribes. In primitive societies, there could be just one leader. In our society, there can be many: governors, presidents, CEOs. Regardless of title, their role is to lead.

The second archetype is the storyteller. His or her role is to entertain, to be a social mirror. The storyteller gives the tribe its memory, its cultural beauty, its intellectual life, its sense of humor, and its art. Through their stories and teachings, storytellers provide inspiration and wisdom.

The third archetype is the problem solver. They build, hunt, farm, cook, clean, scout, fight, and make crafts. They create tools, drive cattle, build skyscrapers, and design computer systems. They like to excel in a specific branch of knowledge or cultivate a particular skill.

The fourth archetype is the caregiver. Many can hold this role: doctors, nurses, midwives, religious leaders, therapists, counselors, and teachers. Their focus is predominantly in the realm of human relationships. They use their practical skills to care for people and to heal them. They endeavor to make sure that people feel loved. Where the storyteller may heal through inspiration, the caregiver heals through nurturing.

As you'll soon see, each of these archetypes corresponds to one of the four styles of communicating described in this book. The ruler is the Director, decisive and action oriented. The storyteller is the Expresser, animated and entertaining. The problem solver is the Thinker, meticulous and process oriented. And the caregiver is the Harmonizer, people oriented and nurturing.

This framework suggests one answer to the question of why we communicate in four fundamental ways. Our styles of communicating grew out of the needs of society. Carved out for us by our ancestors, and ingrained in our culture like ancient riverbeds, our styles of communicating naturally flow in one of these four directions because society needs them in order to thrive.

Personality Theory

Anthropology helps answer the question of where our communication styles came from. Psychology, and particularly research into personality, supports the idea that there are distinct communication styles.

One major branch of personality theory was developed by Carl Jung (see Jung, 1923). He based his work on the premise that it is the differences in how people perceive the world (through sensation or intuition), combined with how they make judgments based on these perceptions (through thinking or feeling), that creates their different personality types.

Perceives the World Through:	Focuses on:
Sensing	Facts
Intuition	Ideas

Makes Judgments Based on:	Focuses on:
Thinking	Logic
Feeling	Values

This resulted in four combinations, or personality types:

Sensing plus Thinking	Intuition plus Thinking
Sensing plus Feeling	Intuition plus Feeling

The work of Jung led to the development of the *Myers-Briggs Type Indicator®* (MBTI®) personality inventory. The MBTI, widely used in organizations today, separates people into sixteen distinct personality types, based on these combinations along with two additional dichotomies concerned with attitudes (extraversion or introversion) and with orientation (perceiving or judging) toward the outer world

Jung's work was inductive—it began with a theory. A second branch of personality theory, the Five Factors Model, is deductive, founded by empirical psychologists who examined the words we use to describe personality. They employed a series of statistical tests to categorize these terms into five separate factors. Adherents of the Five Factors Model disagree on the precise definitions of the factors. (One mainstream definition by E. F. Borgatta is assertiveness, likability, task orientation, emotionality, and intelligence.) But this school of thought contains the majority of scholars who work on personality typing today.

Both schools—the Jungian and the Five Factors Model—lend weight to one of the fundamental ideas of this book: that people have very different styles of communicating, and that understanding those styles is crucial for straight talk.

The Communication Styles Profile

It's time to discover your own communication style. Take a moment to find the Communication Styles Profile presented on pages 14 through 22. (An interactive version of the survey can be found on the World Wide Web. The address is www.Straight-Talk-Now.com.) Before you plunge in, here are some things to keep in mind.

First, the Profile helps you understand your style of communicating. We label each style in order to make the different styles clear and easy to understand. But don't confuse these labels with your personality. Your style of communicating can adapt and change as you desire.

Second, before you take the Profile, be open to making some discoveries about yourself. Put aside, for now, your assumptions about how you communicate or what you imagine your style to be. If you've taken other self-assessment surveys, put those out of your mind, too. There are no right or wrong answers here—just the answers that fit you best.

Third, take the Profile at a time when you know you can give it your full attention. The survey portion of the Profile should take only ten minutes to complete. The scoring will take another ten minutes or so.

Fourth, your style of communicating can vary depending on the setting. Your style at work may differ from your style at home. First answer the questions in the context of your work setting. Later you can take the survey again while you imagine yourself in a different setting.

Finally, before you take the Profile, make a master copy of it. You will probably want to use the Profile many times, both to track changes in your own style and to give copies to your colleagues and friends.

When you are finished, use the scoring sheets to determine your results. Then return to this section to discover what it all means.

The Four Basic Styles

When you take the Communication Styles Profile, the first payoff is discovering the styles of communicating you use most often—Director, Expresser, Thinker, or Harmonizer. We tend to favor two styles over the others, but we have within ourselves the ability to use any of the styles in different situations.

The Profile is designed to determine how often you use each style. For now, here are four key points to keep in mind:

1. Most people use two styles more frequently than the other two.
2. Your blend of styles determines the way you communicate.
3. It's especially important to understand your primary style, since this is the one you use most often.
4. No one style is better than the others, but it may be to your advantage to play up one style over another, depending on the situation.

14

InVision
Communication Styles Profile

Survey Instructions

These are the instructions for taking the written survey and scoring your results. The survey will take approximately ten minutes to complete and another ten minutes to score. If you would like a computer to do the scoring for you, you can take the survey on the Web, at http://www.Straight-Talk-Now.com.

STEP 1: Make Copies

Before you take the survey, make at least one copy of these instructions, the survey, and the five scoring sheets. Then set aside one set of copies in a safe place to serve as your master copy. That way, you will be able to take the survey again later.

STEP 2: Take the Survey

Find a quiet place to take the survey. The survey asks you to evaluate certain statements as they apply to you. Make sure you answer each one as honestly as you can. When you're finished, go to Step 3.

STEP 3: Score the Survey

To score your survey, fill out the worksheets for the Director, Expresser, Thinker, and Harmonizer, adding up the totals at the bottom of each page. Then transfer those totals to the appropriate boxes on the top of the Scoring Summary sheet. Continue following the steps on the Scoring Summary to find your specific communication style.

STEP 4: You're Finished!

Congratulations! You're ready to learn about your individual style of communicating. Please continue reading Chapter 1.

Taking the Survey

Carefully consider each of the statements below; then use a pen or pencil to fill in the appropriate circle on the survey that best describes you. When you're finished, use the Scoring Summary sheet to compute your score. Be as honest as you can in your responses. They'l be most useful to you this way; no one else needs to see them.

Your style of communicating may vary depending on whether you're at work or at home. To assess your style of communicating while at work, think of yourself in that setting. Similarly, if you're trying to assess how you communicate with your family, then picture yourself in that context.

You will be using the following key to respond to the survey, so take a moment to familiarize yourself with it.

A not at all like me
B not much like me
C somewhat like me
D a lot like me
E completely like me

You should fill in one circle—and only one circle—for each statement.

EXAMPLE:

	A	**B**	**C**	**D**	**E**
1. I follow instructions well.	○	○	○	●	○

Remember, there are no right or wrong answers. But you do need to fill out the survey correctly (meaning, only one circle per statement) to determine your style of communicating. When torn between two answers, go with your first response. It's more likely to reflect your true style.

Relax, and enjoy!

		not at all like me	not much like me	somewhat like me	a lot like me	completely like me
		A	B	C	D	E
1.	I'm not very precise.	○	○	○	○	○
2.	I'm reserved around strangers.	○	○	○	○	○
3.	I like envisioning big projects.	○	○	○	○	○
4.	I don't promote an atmosphere of harmony.	○	○	○	○	○
5.	I don't follow instructions.	○	○	○	○	○
6.	I'm courageous.	○	○	○	○	○
7.	I lack attention to detail.	○	○	○	○	○
8.	I mix easily with new people.	○	○	○	○	○
9.	I feel calm and relaxed most of the time.	○	○	○	○	○
10.	I'm not talkative.	○	○	○	○	○
11.	I like big challenges.	○	○	○	○	○
12.	I analyze situations carefully.	○	○	○	○	○
13.	I maintain a cheerful disposition.	○	○	○	○	○
14.	I'm shy with new people.	○	○	○	○	○
15.	I'm persistent.	○	○	○	○	○
16.	I'm soft-spoken.	○	○	○	○	○

	not at all like me	not much like me	somewhat like me	a lot like me	completely like me
	A	**B**	**C**	**D**	**E**
17. I pay attention to detail.	○	○	○	○	○
18. I'm quick to challenge the views of others.	○	○	○	○	○
19. I enjoy talking in front of a group.	○	○	○	○	○
20. I'm careful and deliberate in making a decision.	○	○	○	○	○
21. I'm not peaceful in my inner self.	○	○	○	○	○
22. I'm not confident in my abilities.	○	○	○	○	○
23. I'm a good team player.	○	○	○	○	○
24. I'm daring.	○	○	○	○	○
25. I'm focused on getting things done right.	○	○	○	○	○
26. I'm even-tempered under most circumstances.	○	○	○	○	○
27. I don't like taking risks.	○	○	○	○	○
28. I'm not generous with my time.	○	○	○	○	○
29. I make new friends easily.	○	○	○	○	○
30. I'm very cautious.	○	○	○	○	○
31. I'm trusting of others.	○	○	○	○	○
32. I'm not outgoing	○	○	○	○	○

Survey Scoring

Fill out the four worksheets for the Director, Expresser, Thinker, and Harmonizer, adding up the totals at the bottom of each page. Then transfer those totals to the appropriate boxes on the top of the Scoring Summary.

 Director Worksheet

Points

_____ For item #3, give yourself 1 point for A, 2 points for B, 3 points for C, 4 points for D, or 5 points for E.

_____ For item #6, give yourself 1 point for A, 2 points for B, 3 points for C, 4 points for D, or 5 points for E.

_____ For item #11, give yourself 1 point for A, 2 points for B, 3 points for C, 4 points for D, or 5 points for E.

_____ For item #15, give yourself 1 point for A, 2 points for B, 3 points for C, 4 points for D, or 5 points for E.

_____ For item #18, give yourself 1 point for A, 2 points for B, 3 points for C, 4 points for D, or 5 points for E.

_____ For item #22, give yourself 5 points for A, 4 points for B, 3 points for C, 2 points for D, or 1 point for E.

_____ For item #24, give yourself 1 point for A, 2 points for B, 3 points for C, 4 points for D, or 5 points for E.

_____ For item #27, give yourself 5 points for A, 4 points for B, 3 points for C, 2 points for D, or 1 point for E.

_____ **Total Director score equals the sum of item points**

Expresser Worksheet

Points

_____ For item #2, give yourself 5 points for A, 4 points for B, 3 points for C, 2 points for D, or 1 point for E.

_____ For item #8, give yourself 1 point for A, 2 points for B, 3 points for C, 4 points for D, or 5 points for E.

_____ For item #10, give yourself 5 points for A, 4 points for B, 3 points for C, 2 points for D, or 1 point for E.

_____ For item #14, give yourself 5 points for A, 4 points for B, 3 points for C, 2 points for D, or 1 point for E.

_____ For item #16, give yourself 5 points for A, 4 points for B, 3 points for C, 2 points for D, or 1 point for E.

_____ For item #19, give yourself 1 point for A, 2 points for B, 3 points for C, 4 points for D, or 5 points for E.

_____ For item #29, give yourself 1 point for A, 2 points for B, 3 points for C, 4 points for D, or 5 points for E.

_____ For item #32, give yourself 5 points for A, 4 points for B, 3 points for C, 2 points for D, or 1 point for E.

_____ **Total Expresser score equals the sum of item points**

Thinker Worksheet

Points

_____ For item #1, give yourself 5 points for A, 4 points for B, 3 points for C, 2 points for D, or 1 point for E.

_____ For item #5, give yourself 5 points for A, 4 points for B, 3 points for C, 2 points for D, or 1 point for E.

_____ For item #7, give yourself 5 points for A, 4 points for B, 3 points or C, 2 points for D, or 1 point for E.

_____ For item #12, give yourself 1 point for A, 2 points for B, 3 points for C, 4 points for D, or 5 points for E.

_____ For item #17, give yourself 1 point for A, 2 points for B, 3 points for C, 4 points for D, or 5 points for E.

_____ For item #20, give yourself 1 point for A, 2 points for B, 3 points for C, 4 points for D, or 5 points for E.

_____ For item #25, give yourself 1 point for A, 2 points for B, 3 points for C, 4 points for D, or 5 points for E.

_____ For item #30, give yourself 1 point for A, 2 points for B, 3 points for C, 4 points for D, or 5 points for E.

_____ **Total Thinker score equals the sum of item points**

Harmonizer Worksheet

Points

_____ For item #4, give yourself 5 points for A, 4 points for B, 3 points for C, 2 points for D, or 1 point for E.

_____ For item #9, give yourself 1 point for A, 2 points for B, 3 points for C, 4 points for D, or 5 points for E.

_____ For item #13, give yourself 1 point for A, 2 points for B, 3 points for C, 4 points for D, or 5 points for E.

_____ For item #21, give yourself 5 points for A, 4 points for B, 3 points for C, 2 points for D, or 1 point for E.

_____ For item #23, give yourself 1 point for A, 2 points for B, 3 points for C, 4 points for D, or 5 points for E.

_____ For item #26, give yourself 1 point for A, 2 points for B, 3 points for C, 4 points for D, or 5 points for E.

_____ For item #28, give yourself 5 points for A, 4 points for B, 3 points for C, 2 points for D, or 1 point for E.

_____ item #31, give yourself 1 point for A, 2 points for B, 3 points for C, 4 points for D, or 5 points for E.

_____ **Total Harmonizer score equals the sum of item points**

Scoring Summary

Step 1: Transfer the totals from the four worksheets to the appropriate boxes below.

☐	☐	☐	☐
Director Score	**Expresser Score**	**Thinker Score**	**Harmonizer Score**

Step 2: Circle the two highest scores you received. If your highest score is 10 points or more above your next-highest score, then go to Step 4. If your two highest scores are identical, go to Step 5. Otherwise, proceed to Step 3.

Step 3: Using the following table, circle the style in the first column receiving the highest score. Circle the style in the second column receiving the second-highest score (or identical high score). Then circle the corresponding style in the third column (follow the arrows). That is your specific communication style. Use the example on page 25 for reference.

My highest score +	My second-highest score (or identical high score)	→	My specific style
Director +	Expresser	⟶	Initiator
	Thinker	⟶	Explorer
	Harmonizer	⟶	Persuader
Expresser +	Director	⟶	Charmer
	Thinker	⟶	Diplomat
	Harmonizer	⟶	Socializer
Thinker +	Director	⟶	Investigator
	Expresser	⟶	Organizer
	Harmonizer	⟶	Supporter
Harmonizer +	Director	⟶	Counselor
	Expresser	⟶	Nurturer
	Thinker	⟶	Provider

23

Step 4: If your highest score is 10 points or more above your next-highest score, use the table below to discover your specific style. In the first column, circle the style receiving the highest score. Then circle the corresponding style in the second column (follow the arrows). That is your specific communication style.

My highest score	$\longrightarrow$	My specific style
Director	$\longrightarrow$	Dictator
Expresser	$\longrightarrow$	Entertainer
Thinker	$\longrightarrow$	Analyzer
Harmonizer	$\longrightarrow$	Pleaser

Step 5: If your two highest scores are identical, you are a blend of styles. Choose one to be your highest score, and follow the instructions in Step 3. Then choose the other as your highest score and follow the same process. You should end up with two specific styles. For example, if you received the same score for both Harmonizer and Thinker, then you'd calculate two combinations: Harmonizer + Thinker = Provider, and Thinker + Harmonizer = Supporter. Your communication style is a blend of Provider and Supporter.

Step 6: Write down your specific communication style (or styles) in the box below:

Your name _____ Date _____

Survey Example

My highest score + My second-highest score ⟶ My specific style
(or identical high score)

Director	+	Expresser ⟶	Initiator
		Thinker ⟶	Explorer
		Harmonizer ⟶	Persuader
Expresser	+	Director ⟶	Charmer
		Thinker ⟶	Diplomat
		Harmonizer ⟶	Socializer
Thinker	+	Director ⟶	Investigator
		Expresser ⟶	Organizer
		Harmonizer ⟶	Supporter
Harmonizer	+	Director ⟶	Counselor
		Expresser ⟶	Nurturer
		Thinker ⟶	Provider

Follow the arrows to find your specific communication style. In this example, a person's primary style is Thinker and her secondary style is Harmonizer. Thus her specific communication style is Supporter. If you have questions about scoring the survey or finding your specific style, please refer to the *Straight Talk* Web site at www.Straight-Talk-Now.com.

You may wonder whether men or women favor a particular style. There's no evidence that they do. Some styles may strike you as more "male" or more "female"—or as more consistent with our traditional stereotypes of male and female behavior. But research shows that gender has no correlation to a particular style.

You may also wonder whether people from different countries or places of origin prefer certain styles. Our research shows that the styles are universal to all people. Yet certain cultural tendencies may favor one style over another, and a full appreciation of communication styles must factor in the particular habits of each culture.

As you read the following descriptions of the four basic styles, write down any thoughts that occur to you. You may want to take notes in the margins.

Directors

Imagine someone who likes to get things done—whether it's building a new product or starting a new company. This person is a Director, one of the four basic communication styles.

The Director talks about actions. Directors don't have much time for small talk, or for social niceties. In fact, they can be a little uncomfortable around people. They're quick to make decisions, quick to assign tasks, always on the move. Imagine Orson Welles in *Citizen Kane* and you've got a good mental image of the Director.

Directors tend to focus on doing, not listening. They don't tell long stories or inquire into the health of your children. But they do talk about goals, about getting a jump on the competition, about the importance of getting the job done. That's the key for the Director: completion; getting it done. Now, not later. "Give me the bottom line"—that's one of the Director's favorite phrases.

Directors take risks. They're willing to make tough decisions and gamble. Directors like to be in charge. Because Directors focus on getting things done, not on people, they can at times appear insensitive—even intimidating. We'll explore later how to deal with this.

In sum, Directors emphasize action and results. They're great at setting goals. Without the Director's drive, vision, and decisiveness, the world would be a much more static place.

Expressers

Now imagine people whose modus operandi is expressing themselves, talking about their ideas and opinions and feelings and experiences. These people—the Expressers—are great talkers. They like to gesture and use animated facial expressions to make a point. You'll find them describing what they felt when they bought their first new car, or dreaming up a clever advertising campaign. Unlike Directors, Expressers like to tell stories. In fact, they're so animated and expressive when they tell stories that they may make other people feel limp. But give them credit: Expressers are entertaining to have around.

Imagine David Letterman or Carol Burnett. Expressers have lots of ideas and thoughts going on at once, sometimes so many that the ideas tumble out of their mouths before they've had a chance to edit them. In fact, thinking aloud is one trademark of the Expresser.

Expressers are creative, always trying to find new ways to do things. They're willing to take chances, especially if their creative reputation is on the line. They're fun to invite to a brainstorming meeting—they're always coming up with an out-of-the-box idea. Yet they can also be disorganized and lack follow-through.

Expressers have a hard time focusing on one topic and listening. They lack a long attention span for something that doesn't involve or interest them. This can be frustrating for the people around them. So Expressers can demand a lot of patience. At the same time, Expressers tend to be sensitive to other people's feelings, and they'll express great embarrassment once they realize they've said something that hurt someone else.

In short, Expressers are dynamic, dramatic, exciting, engaging, and entertaining. They may not always be organized. But without them the world would be a much less interesting place.

Thinkers

Now imagine people who like to solve problems. They like the process of working through all the details, the nuances, the ramifications and implications. These people—the Thinkers—are focused on getting things done right. Their exacting sense of detail drives them to ask lots of questions.

If a Thinker is considering buying a new computer system, for example, she'll ask for all the comparative data. She'll make sure she has all her facts exactly in order. She'll make a list of the features she wants (the list is a trademark of the Thinker). Often she'll postpone making a decision until she's certain she's got every piece of information she can find—much to the frustration of Directors, who'd like things to move more quickly.

Problem solving is of paramount importance to Thinkers. Imagine the character played by Jeff Goldblum in *Jurassic Park* and *The Lost World*. The Thinker possesses a marvelously honed ability to focus entirely on the problem at hand—often to the exclusion of the bigger picture. Thinkers can seem tedious at times. But details are not tedious to the Thinker. All those questions are crucial to getting the job done right. And their attention to detail can make Thinkers very valuable to have around.

As you might surmise, Thinkers tend to be more cautious than either Directors or Expressers. They play out scenarios in great detail in their minds, thus they're likely to consider other people's needs and feelings before acting. They like to discuss these details with others, to make sure they've considered every angle.

Thinkers tend to underestimate the amount of time they need to complete a project. Unlike Directors, who rarely miss a deadline, Thinkers will give themselves "extensions" in order to make sure the project is done correctly the first time.

In sum, Thinkers are the world's problem solvers. They ask questions and revel in details. They may miss an occasional deadline, but no one is more superbly equipped than the Thinker to think things through.

Harmonizers

Now let's meet the fourth major style of communicating. Picture someone who listens to other people's problems, someone who is steady and dependable, someone who will offer sympathy when your child catches the flu. Picture Ingrid Bergman in *Casablanca* or Gregory Peck in *To Kill a Mockingbird*. Or better yet, Mother Teresa.

These people—the Harmonizers—are caregivers and healers. They bring muffins to work in the morning. They give special presents at holidays. People naturally turn to them for comfort in times of trouble. They speak warmly and lovingly to other people, who in turn speak warmly and lovingly of them. Harmonizers may not be decisive or daring, but they keep people working happily together, often in subtle ways.

Harmonizers are attuned to people's feelings, and they like to talk about people—not in the same animated or aggressive way Expressers do, but more quietly, with less attention drawn to themselves. They're focused on the group's well-being; one of the Harmonizer's trademarks is being a team player. At lunch or at a company picnic, you'll see the Harmonizers sitting together talking quietly—or not talking at all. Harmonizers aren't trailblazers. In social situations, they'll rarely say anything inflammatory or unconventional. Harmonizers prefer to fit in, not stand out.

Harmonizers seek to avoid conflict. When a stranger comes into their midst, they are careful, guarded. You can only get to know them gradually, not right away. Because they like to please other people, they'll say "yes" to something even though it would be better all around if they declined. As a result, Harmonizers can take on too much and feel overwhelmed.

In short, Harmonizers are quiet, caring people whose words express pride in the accomplishments of the team. Without them, the world would be a far less caring place.

Conclusion

One of the earliest efforts at understanding human nature was led by a school of Greek philosophers who maintained that people's characters were determined by four special "humors." Each humor was concentrated in a particular bodily fluid. High levels of blood resulted in an enthusiastic type; an excess of black bile resulted in a melancholy character; high amounts of yellow bile caused one to be irritable; and an excess of phlegm created a slow, apathetic personality.

In this chapter you've learned about the four communication styles—a modern counterpart of the four humors. By training yourself to identify and understand each style, you'll quickly learn to appreciate some of the subtleties in people's communications—the hidden meanings behind their words, the types of things they pay attention to. This, in turn, will lead to more satisfying and more successful interactions.

More important, as you begin to appreciate how people see things in four very different ways, you will begin to appreciate how around us revolve four different worlds—the worlds of the Director, Expresser, Thinker, and Harmonizer.

EXERCISE: GUESS YOUR COLLEAGUES' STYLES

This exercise will help familiarize you with the four basic communication styles. Using the information from this chapter, guess the styles of the members of your immediate work group. This will just be a guess at this stage, because you haven't learned all the techniques for interpretation. But it will be fun to have a record of your early impressions later on.

Look at the four squares below. First, put your initials in the square that represents your primary style (refer to your survey results). Then write the initials of each member of your work group in the square that you think best describes him or her.

Director	**Expresser**
Talks in action verbs.	Speaks rapidly.
Cares about the "bottom line."	Uses animated gestures.
Always on the go.	Entertaining.
Speaks crisply.	Thinks out loud.
Talks about goals.	Talks about ideas.
May seem insensitive.	May be imprecise.
Thinker	**Harmonizer**
Talks about details.	Talks about people.
Inquiring.	Sensitive to others.
Often makes lists.	Avoids conflict.
Speaks carefully.	Dedicated and loyal.
Wants things done "right."	Speaks softly.
May procrastinate.	May overcommit.

Chapter Two
Zeroing In on Your Own Communication Style

A wonderful fact to reflect upon, that every
human creature is constituted to be
that profound secret and mystery to every other.
—CHARLES DICKENS, *A Tale of Two Cities* (1859)

Understanding your style of communicating would be relatively easy if you limited yourself to one of the four basic styles. However, depending on the situation, you may alternate between one, two, or even three styles. It's like walking. You naturally walk at a certain pace. But then you shift gears to match the pace of someone next to you.

It's the same with communicating. People prefer to use one style. Our "primary style" is the one we're most comfortable with. But we also have a backup style. Typically, this second style is dictated by our situation—the demands of our particular job if at work, the demands of domestic life if at home.

We refer to the backup style as our "secondary style." Most people vacillate frequently between their primary and secondary styles. As a result, our overall or specific style becomes a combination of these two styles. It's like mixing lemon into tea: The concoction has a flavor all its own.

In this chapter, you'll start to learn about your unique flavor. For example, if the Profile revealed your primary style to be Thinker and your secondary style to be Expresser, then this creates an identifiable pattern of communicating called the Organizer. This specific style is highlighted on the Matrix of Communication Styles shown in Chart I.

The Matrix can be somewhat confusing at first, but it's a very useful tool once you understand how it works. In fact, once you instill in your mind a mental image of the Matrix, you can use it to identify another person's communication style, even if he or she hasn't taken the Communication Styles Profile. (Identifying another person's style is covered

CHART 1: THE MATRIX OF COMMUNICATION STYLES

DIRECTORS   **EXPRESSERS**

Dictator	Initiator	Charmer	Entertainer
Explorer	Persuader	Diplomat	Socializer
Investigator	Organizer	Counselor	Nurturer
Analyzer	Supporter	Provider	Pleaser

THINKERS   **HARMONIZERS**

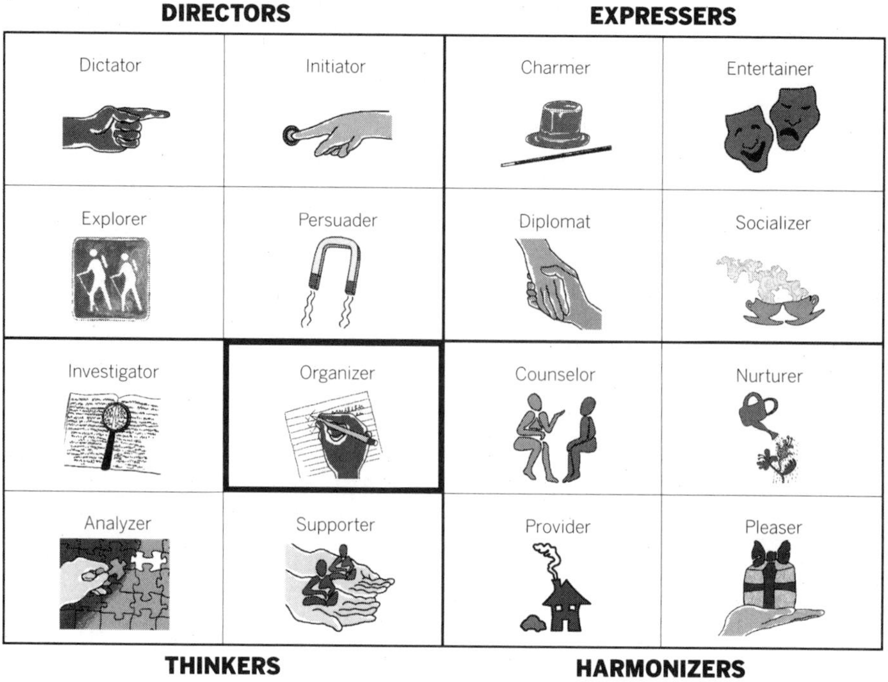

in detail in Chapter 3.) So take a moment to read through the following explanation of how to use the Matrix of Communication Styles.

The Matrix is based on the four basic styles we've already discussed. If you split the Matrix into equal quarters, or quadrants, then each quadrant illustrates a primary style—Director, Expresser, Thinker, or Harmonizer.

Each quadrant contains four more squares. Your secondary style determines your particular square within each quadrant.

Here's how it works, using the Organizer as an example:

Step 1. Your primary style governs your placement in one of the four quadrants of the Matrix. Directors are in the upper left of the Matrix, Expressers are in the upper right, Thinkers are in the lower left, and Harmonizers are in the lower right. Since the Organizer's primary style is Thinker, he's in the lower-left quadrant.

Step 2. Once you've located your quadrant, cover up the other three. Pretend they don't exist. In this case, you would cover up the top half of the Matrix and the lower-right quadrant. The only quadrant visible would be the Thinker quadrant.

Step 3. The Thinker quadrant is divided into four smaller squares. Each has a label, like Investigator or Supporter. Use the same rule of thumb as in the first step. If your secondary style is Director, then the upper-left square is your square (Investigator); if your secondary style is Expresser, then the upper-right square (Organizer) represents you; if your secondary style is also Thinker, then the lower-left square is yours (Analyzer); and if your secondary style is Harmonizer, then the lower-right square is yours (Supporter). In this case, the secondary style is Expresser, which makes this person an Organizer.

The Matrix is a very helpful tool because it lets you see the relationship between all sixteen styles at a glance. As you familiarize yourself with the Matrix and work through the various exercises in this book, you'll find that the Matrix helps you bring all of your relationships into sharper focus.

Some people—approximately one in a hundred—are so-called "corner styles." The four corner styles are Dictator, Entertainer, Analyzer, and Pleaser. Corner styles occur when a person's score for one basic communication style is ten points higher than his score for any of the other three. For example, a person who scores 38 for Expresser, 25 for Director, 12 for Thinker, and 15 for Harmonizer would be an Entertainer because his highest score is thirteen points above his next-highest score.

Corner styles have particular challenges to face in developing their communication skills. Because they don't regularly use a secondary, backup style, their communications tend to be less adaptable and flexible. These challenges are discussed under the description for each corner style in this chapter.

Blended Styles

Some people truly have two styles and occupy two places on the Matrix. We call these people "blended styles." A blended style occurs when a person's high score is identical for two of the basic communication styles. For example, a person who scores 35 for both Thinker and Director would be a blend of Investigator and Explorer.

If you have a blended style, don't worry. It's a perfectly natural out-growth of the way the survey is constructed. Taking the survey again might slightly alter your score, and thus give you a neater fit within a particular square on the Matrix. But your score the first time you take the survey is typically the truest reflection of your style. And a person who has a blended style can get just as much out of this book as some-one who occupies a single square on the Matrix.

After you read the descriptions of each specific style in this chapter, it may be readily evident which specific style is yours. If so, adopt it as your own. But if you are still wavering between two styles, accept your fate. The purpose of the Matrix is to help you improve your communi-cations, not to shoehorn you into a particular category or give you a label.

The Sixteen Specific Communication Styles

The first thing you'll want to do in this section is read the description of your particular style (or styles). Then you should read the descriptions of all sixteen styles, since this will help you become familiar with the full range of possible communication styles.[1]

Dictator

The Dictator thrives on being in control. He bristles when someone else is in charge. When the Dictator is talking, it's usually to discuss things he wants to accomplish. Personal issues and emotional situations are awk-ward for the Dictator. He'd rather talk about a new business venture.

At work, the Dictator seems to have amazing energy to get things done. But he can also seem insensitive and manipulative. He's valued for his leadership skills and "take charge" attitude, but he tends to make decisions quickly—much more quickly than other people. So not every-one may agree when he says, "This is what we're going to do."

---

1. The male pronoun and female pronoun are used interchangeably throughout this book. However, there is no gender bias or correlation in these styles; each description applies equal-ly to women and men.

The Dictator has a hard time with interpersonal communication. He talks in abrupt sentences and doesn't offer a lot of information. The way he's perceived makes it hard for people to open up to him. He enjoys dealing with other "bottom-liners," but he doesn't like to waste time on idle chitchat.

To be a more competent communicator, the Dictator needs to be much more patient and inquiring about other people's ideas and feelings. Since this is difficult, a Dictator should try to set aside a specific time and place to talk about a problem. He should imagine how much time people will need—and then double it. He should start by talking about how he feels about a particular situation, but emphasize that his mind is open. Then he should give other people plenty of time to talk it through. Above all, he should ask questions and listen. But he shouldn't conduct an interrogation! A Dictator needs to make people feel he's really interested in their point of view, not just in collecting evidence against them. Dictators should practice active listening, by paraphrasing what people say. Once he learns to temper his instinct for snap judgments, the Dictator is far more likely to find his troops behind him when he yells "Charge!"

Initiator

The Initiator is happiest when she's leading a group of people or is on her own—she's not happy when someone else is in charge. Her energy and ingenuity inspire admiration, but her desire to make others conform to her way of doing things can undermine the respect she desires. She tends to be private with her own feelings. In her best moments, the Initiator is charismatic and enthusiastic; in her worst moments, arrogant and bossy.

At work, the Initiator can display great vision about the needs of an organization. She may undertake too much at times, yet she somehow manages to get the job done. She is often regarded as having impossible standards and making snap judgments about people. This can make the people around her feel uneasy and anxious.

The Initiator has the potential to be a good communicator. She likes people and prefers a direct, honest approach. But she tends to jump to conclusions about what people mean without checking the facts. To be more successful as a communicator, the Initiator needs to soften her style, to ask more questions. Because the Initiator is perceived as aggressive, her questions can appear patronizing or demanding. She needs to make it clear that she wants to increase the level of understanding for everyone involved, not gain the upper hand. She should try to restrain herself from drawing conclusions too quickly. It also might help to control her body language and reduce the amount of direct eye contact. She should show respect for other people by paraphrasing what they say. They'll respond much more positively once they see she's willing to take the time to understand what they're saying.

Explorer

Complex challenges are what the Explorer enjoys most, whether it's manipulating a three-dimensional spreadsheet or climbing a mountain peak. The Explorer prides himself on how much he can accomplish compared to other people. People view the Explorer as logical and independent. They also think of him as unemotional. In relationships, he tends to be a perfectionist. He's not always an easy person to get along with.

At work, the Explorer is known for doing things on his own and conceiving new theories or solutions. He enjoys taking the long-term perspective and meeting large challenges. At the same time, the Explorer can become lost in the theoretical, forgetting about other people's emotional concerns.

To communicate better, the Explorer needs to remember that his natural instinct is to hide his feelings and look at everything logically. So he should focus on people's feelings more. At times he is prone to jumping to conclusions about the solution to a problem before he's gathered all the facts. He may be right about the solution—but he needs to pay more attention to the process of getting buy-in, of letting other people talk through the problem. Expressing frustration at how much time it takes to reach a solution won't help. He should practice putting himself in someone else's shoes and feeling what they feel—and not worry about being wrong or looking foolish. By focusing his attention on other people's feelings, he'll find they respect and respond to his insights far more readily.

Persuader

The Persuader possesses a pragmatic, people-oriented approach that enables her to get other people to do the things she wants. For the most part, she can be warm and friendly. But when her back is up against the wall, she can seem cold and dictatorial.

At work, the Persuader likes to run and organize activities. She makes a good leader because she tends to consider everyone's point of view, not just her own or a select group's. Her pragmatic approach enables her to communicate effectively and honestly—though sometimes with a degree of cynicism. While balanced in her approach to people and the requirements of a situation, she can be imprecise in spelling out exactly what she wants. This can make her weak on follow-through.

Most of the time the Persuader communicates effectively and honestly. To communicate better, she needs to work on two things: First, precision. The Persuader tends to leave out crucial details, leaving her audience uncertain about what to do next. She should organize her thoughts in advance and make sure everyone has the same information. Second, while she recognizes the need to listen and gather input, she tends to make assumptions about what needs to be done before this process is complete. This can undermine the input-gathering process and cause people to respond cynically when she calls a meeting. The Persuader will benefit by making it clear that her mind is open to suggestions and alternative strategies. Only after the input is gathered should she try to be persuasive. Given her ability to listen, this will make her a very effective communicator.

Charmer

The Charmer is happiest when he's expressing himself or doing something creative. He's not happy with humdrum day-to-day chores. Details are not the province of the Charmer. Instead of preparing in advance for important situations or meetings, he tends to rely on his personality to carry the day. This can make him popular and well liked, but can also make him appear inconsistent or superficial. He especially likes people he's just met, revealing to them his innermost feelings and secrets. This can vex the people closest to him, who wonder why they don't get such special treatment.

At work, the Charmer is well suited to providing a creative spark to an organization and its people. At the same time, he may not be patient enough, or sufficiently well organized, to provide the necessary structure and stability. Because he tends to be assertive and demanding, he can appear insensitive to others. But in fact the Charmer is tuned in to how other people feel.

The Charmer tends to leap to conclusions, especially about people's intentions. He's quick to feel slighted if people don't communicate with him. He's sensitive to any apparent sign of disrespect. This can make him seem difficult to get along with.

The Charmer has the potential to be a competent communicator, especially if he can learn to pay more attention to details and process. When important situations arise, he should give himself plenty of time for preparation, and focus his attention on the details of planning. He should decide on two or three objectives. He should rehearse and allow other people to critique his presentation. In meetings, he should ask more questions and paraphrase people's responses. And he should tell people when he's thinking aloud. It helps them to distinguish his finished thoughts from "works in progress."

 Entertainer

The Entertainer is happiest when the spotlight is on her—and least happy when someone else is getting all the attention. The Entertainer is good at public speaking and sales presentations, maybe even one of the performing arts. But her sensitivity and desire to be liked make it difficult for her to deal with awkward situations and make tough decisions.

At work, the Entertainer's strength is expressing herself to other people. She is at her best in a creative environment that requires improvisation and imagination. Brainstorming meetings are where the Entertainer shines, not analyzing financial reports or preparing a work plan.

To communicate better, the Entertainer needs to listen more carefully, ask more detailed questions, and think more analytically. She should avoid assuming that she needs to be the center of attention. Instead, she should try to listen, gather data, and analyze what additional information is needed before drawing a conclusion. When she has the spotlight on her, she should try to talk about someone other than herself. Thinking aloud can get the Entertainer into trouble, so she should rehearse what she's going to say—especially in sensitive situations. This can help prevent her from developing a sudden case of "foot-in-mouth disease."

Diplomat

The Diplomat is a bit of a contradiction: fun loving and jovial, yet aloof and analytical. He revels in pleasurable things, people, and places—and loves talking about them, which makes him a magnet for other people. Yet he can be very analytical and sober-minded. Taken together, this can make the diplomat something of an enigma. People can interpret him as masking his calculating nature with his social skills. Such a double-edged sword can cause people to resent him.

At work, the Diplomat is perceived as personable, versatile, and analytical. He is drawn to situations and organizations where his people-management skills can be used. He is competent at leading people through complex projects. At times the Diplomat's focus and determination can be overwhelming to others, especially those less articulate. The Diplomat may need to learn to temper his drive for perfection with a sensitivity to other people's feelings.

The Diplomat can be a skilled communicator. His ability to ask detailed questions is a nice complement to his expressive side. To communicate better, he may need to allow other people to contribute equally to the discussion. He may need to remind people that his mind is open—that he's genuinely looking for ideas and input. He should remember to begin persuading only after everyone has had a chance to say their piece. And he may need to temper his drive for perfection with a sensitivity to other people's concerns.

Socializer

The Socializer is happiest with other people, engaged in animated conversation; least happy when she's alone. She loves social activities—going to parties, attending meetings, engaging in conversation. To her friends, she's loyal to the end. But when she feels unappreciated, she can become depressed and withdrawn. In relationships, the Socializer is a true friend, sensitive to others' needs. Her only downside is that the Socializer may not examine a situation logically, and therefore may make decisions without considering all the information.

At work, the Socializer is a born team member, always looking to inject a creative idea and motivate people. When inspired, she can work endless hours. Socializers typically know how to make people around them feel appreciated. The Socializer may need to work on handling conflict more directly by remembering that conflict is natural in any organization.

To communicate better, the Socializer needs to be more logical and analytical in her communications. She should work on asking logical questions and pursuing a rational line of inquiry, especially in disagreeable situations. By avoiding painful feelings and situations, the Socializer is only half a communicator—the easy half. She should try to analyze a difficult situation in terms of the missing information. What does she know that other people don't? Or what could she be missing? It will also help if she rehearses what she's going to say. The more practiced she gets at addressing the things that don't feel right, the more effective a communicator she will be.

Investigator

The Investigator likes to be viewed as an encyclopedia of information, a walking expert. He's happiest when someone asks him to answer a question or perform a complex analytical task. He's not very focused on people's feelings, preferring to observe life and all its curious ways with an air of detachment. His logical, forceful personality is at its best during times of crisis, when he's known for calmly analyzing the situation and keeping his head while all about him are losing theirs.

At work, the Investigator is perceived as cool, calculating, and competent. He may make an excellent engineer because he likes dissecting things, figuring out how they work, and using his knowledge to improve them. He enjoys being called on to provide solutions on the spot; as a result, he makes a good troubleshooter.

To communicate better, the Investigator needs to curb his desire to dissect everything and everybody. He is by nature a good listener and communicator when the subject is a task, or a process, or a piece of equipment. But he may resist using the same skills of inquiry when it comes to people. By being more willing to expose himself to other people's feelings and points of view, he'll find that he can solve organizational problems, too. To counter his naturally cool demeanor, he might try using facial expressions and hand gestures more often to make his points. Above all, he should train himself to think about how other people feel. If he succeeds, he'll make a great communicator.

Organizer

The Organizer enjoys getting people to do things together, which makes her effective in almost any situation. At times she appears single-minded because of her analytical approach. But her compassion and dedication to other people is apparent. The Organizer is comfortable talking about other people, but not particularly comfortable talking about herself. Her relationships tend to be varied and well-rounded—if a bit lacking in passion. Her style of communicating is to avoid trouble spots, which may make her less of a leader than she could be.

At work, the Organizer is respected for her principled and conscientious way of doing things. Compassionate toward people, she enjoys helping them interact and work together, which makes her a good manager. At times she needs to go someplace where she can be focused and alone.

The Organizer has the ability to be a strong communicator. She knows how to ask questions and analyze a situation. She also knows how to say things in a sensitive, understanding way. Her challenge is to communicate when there's a potential conflict. She may be reluctant to take a position or raise an issue that she feels may be a magnet for controversy or criticism. She needs to be willing to step in and find out what people think and get their opinions. By asking for input, she can build ownership in the decision. By beating around the bush, she'll only leave everyone feeling frustrated.

The Analyzer

The Analyzer is painstaking and thorough with detail, valued for following a logical process and getting tasks done the correct way. He is happiest using his logical abilities to solve problems; least happy when forced to engage in social activities. To others, the Analyzer can be viewed as something of a social misfit. He tends to avoid showing his feelings or asserting his own desires. This makes him an enigma to those around him, who don't know how to get close to him or offer help when needed.

At work, the Analyzer can be counted on to respond positively to accomplishing a specific task—as long as it falls into his area of expertise and can be tackled using a tried-and-true approach. The Analyzer is adept at collecting information, but not at seeing the bigger picture. So in his communications, he may appear to be prematurely focused on details when the goal remains unclear. At times his style may appear too conservative and inflexible, and he may expect others to behave the same way.

To become a more effective communicator, the Analyzer needs to be willing to open himself up to outside input and ideas. His biggest barrier to being an effective communicator is holding back too much. He should try expressing his logic and asking other people whether they see the situation the same way—or whether there's another equally valid interpretation. He should try to force himself to listen to a full spectrum of opinions. As he opens up and people feel more comfortable around him, the Analyzer will discover he's apt to become a far more comfortable communicator.

Supporter

The Supporter's patience with people and innate kindheartedness make her an ideal person to turn to for help. She can be analytical when the situation requires it, but she is always looking out for other people. Cautious and conservative by nature, the Supporter prefers that someone else take the risks. In her communications, she displays a high level of loyalty and caring for other people. But she should be on guard that her low-risk approach doesn't land her in hot water—she may stick with something or someone far too long.

At work, the Supporter is patient and kind, preferring to blend a cautious approach with a desire for harmony among her colleagues. She is valued for knowing the rules and traditions, and for paying close attention to the consequences of a given decision on the people involved. She makes a good peacemaker or negotiator. However, she's not likely to be known for her innovative thinking, which may limit her in certain types of jobs.

The Supporter is a natural communicator, especially when discussing an issue or concern outside herself. But she can be reluctant to assert her own feelings and ideas. When she wishes to communicate something about herself, she should try the same patient approach she takes with others. She should preface her remarks by saying she wants to speak plainly—then say exactly what she feels. She shouldn't worry about appearing too blunt or cold. She runs little risk of being thought insensitive. Once she has expressed her views, she'll find that doing so breaks the ice for others to speak honestly about the same issue.

Counselor

The Counselor's strong suit is finding out what other people need and then helping them get it. He's better than most at mediating disputes. He may even have played matchmaker. The Counselor is something of a dual personality: happy to go along for the sake of the group, yet at times feeling a strong urge to express his own feelings. He operates from a deep sense of loyalty to his friends and loved ones. In relationships, he is perceived as low-key, caring, and competent. He tends to take criticism personally.

At work, the Counselor is likely to be someone people turn to for help. As a communicator, he is gifted in being able to articulate people's concerns and needs. His ability to empathize with other people's points of view makes him a trusted and respected figure. Because he operates from a deep sense of loyalty to the cause and is rarely seen as operating out of his own self-interest, he can be effective at mediating disputes.

To communicate more effectively, the Counselor needs to make sure to take the time to figure out his own priorities and goals. His tendency not to reveal himself makes it difficult for other people to open up and state their goals. This can lead to a dilemma—everyone spending time being nice; no one saying what's really on their minds. As a starting point, the Counselor should practice stating his thoughts and feelings, couching them in terms like: "It's important for us to be brutally honest with each other, regardless of how other people will react." In exchange, he'll have the standing to ask people to express their viewpoints more openly. The Counselor should also guard against being overly optimistic in his communications. He should try to be honest and clear about potential problems, not mask them.

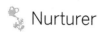 Nurturer

Easygoing, accepting, friendly, the Nurturer is both a good listener and a good talker. People tend to turn to her when they're down. In social situations, the Nurturer is always looking to create cooperation. In relationships, she's viewed as sweet-natured, warm, and enthusiastic. She likes any kind of social activity involving friends and colleagues, whether it's going to a meeting, planning a party, or attending a convention. At times she may let socializing get in the way of achieving her goals.

At work, the Nurturer is an open-minded and congenial communicator. She gets included in a lot of committees, because her enthusiasm and cooperation make her effective at bridging different people and groups. She's perceived as someone who knows the latest gossip, so people turn to her for information. She tends to be happiest in jobs that allow her to use her considerable people skills. Her weakness is not focusing sufficient energy on the analytical side.

The Nurturer can be an effective communicator, especially as a go-between when people need to understand each other's feelings. To communicate more effectively, the Nurturer needs to spend more time thinking through the financial and pragmatic ramifications of a particular decision or course of action. She should communicate a desire to make sure that all information is considered before a decision is reached—even if this means making a tough decision in cases where it's tempting to take the easier course. In her communications, she should talk about the negatives, not just the positives. People will still like her—even if they don't like some of the information she brings to the table.

Provider

The Provider is in his element doing things for others. He loves figuring out just the right gift to buy for someone's birthday, or solving other people's problems. The Provider is a traditionalist; no one would accuse him of being too daring. Sensitive and careful of others, he is likely to have many friends. In relationships, he's loyal and steadfast—maybe even when it's not in his best interest to be so. He prefers someone else to take the lead. He's very aware of other people's behavior and can show a judgmental streak—especially of people not like him.

At work, the Provider tends to succeed by a combination of people skills and dogged determination. He's very good at figuring out what motivates other people. This can make him effective in preparing sales presentations—though not in presenting them (he tends to be uncomfortable in front of a crowd). Not showy or flashy in temperament or style, he's valued for his steady contribution to the team. However, he has to keep his judgmental streak under control.

To communicate more effectively, the Provider needs to be more willing to assert his own opinions and feelings. When he's being assertive, he may think he's gone overboard. Not to worry! He can be even more so. An excellent listener, the Provider could easily become a very effective communicator if he would demand for himself some of the listening time he's so willing to give others.

Pleaser

The Pleaser is quiet and shy. Her loyalty, patience, and concern for others are her greatest strengths. She lives for the comfort of relationships with other people. She is likely to do anything to avoid a scene or an argument, which is why she wouldn't dream of forcing her opinions on others—unless she knows they're shared. The Pleaser's happiest moments are spent in quiet conversation. In relationships, she is modest, cautious, and conventional. She prefers to let someone else take the lead, as long as that person is mindful of her and doesn't cause any embarrassment!

At work, the Pleaser likes to spend her free time building relationships with other people. With regard to accomplishing tasks, she most likely has a set way of doing things, and may not be easily swayed to another—perhaps more suitable—method. This can make the Pleaser seem stubborn and rigid. She can have strong opinions, but because she doesn't like conflict, she withholds her opinions from others. This may limit the Pleaser in the long run.

Communication is a dance in which partners need to alternate taking the lead. To communicate more effectively, the Pleaser should learn to lead. She should ask a friend to give her fifteen minutes of serious, undivided listening time. She should rehearse what she's going to say, then state exactly how she feels about someone or something. Then she should ask the friend to paraphrase what she said: "Do you understand what I mean?" Through this process, she may come to realize that she can rely on her friends as much as they rely on her.

Conclusion

As you begin to familiarize yourself with each style, certain themes begin to emerge about what constitutes a competent communicator: The importance of asking good questions. The need to assert one's own beliefs and feelings clearly and honestly. The importance of getting all the facts before you draw conclusions. The need to distinguish between asking pertinent questions and conducting a self-serving interrogation. The value of active listening—paraphrasing what another person says to confirm your understanding of the situation.

Once you start to appreciate the full spectrum of styles, you can also begin fitting your colleagues and friends into the Matrix. You can start to appreciate the dynamic shifts between communication styles. You can see how the styles at the top of the Matrix are the most assertive, while those at the bottom are the least so. How those on the left side are the most analytical, while those on the right are the most intuitive.

One time I was teaching a seminar of twelve MBA students. In my introduction, I told them that "we each have a style, and each style has strengths and weaknesses." I went on to say that "being conscious of those strengths and weaknesses will be useful to you as managers."

One of the students raised his hand and said he didn't see the value of this information. "You're saying that we need to be conscious of our behavior. But what if we simply can't do that? I don't want to be aware all the time of what I'm saying or doing."

"It's true that there are different levels of self-awareness," I said. "But right now you're asking a question about your level of awareness. Do you see that you have to be somewhat self-aware to ask that?"

"Yes," he admitted. "But I still don't see how the information can be particularly useful."

"It's no different from math class," I said. "You learn from your mistakes there. This can help you identify your mistakes—so you can train yourself to behave differently the next time."

"I still don't get it," he said. "You're asking me to change my behavior."

I asked him his style.

"Initiator," he said.

"What do you remember about Initiators?"

"They leap to conclusions before they've gathered all the data," he said. "They need to be more open to understanding other points of view."

Then he paused.

"Oh, I think I get it now."

EXERCISE: CONSIDER A COMMUNICATION LINK

Put your initials in the square on the Matrix below that corresponds to your specific style. Now imagine your boss or someone you work closely with. Based on the descriptions in this chapter, make a guess as to his or her style and put that person's initials in that square. Now draw an arrow between the two squares.

DIRECTORS		EXPRESSERS	
Dictator	Initiator	Charmer	Entertainer
Explorer	Persuader	Diplomat	Socializer
Investigator	Organizer	Counselor	Nurturer
Analyzer	Supporter	Provider	Pleaser
THINKERS		HARMONIZERS	

Consider your two communication styles. If you were communicating with that person, what would you do to make the communication more productive? If that person were communicating with you, what should he or she do? Jot down your thoughts below.

1. Things I should do differently:

■

■

■

2. Things the other person should do differently:

-
-
-

Chapter Three
Communication Styles
at Work in Other People

A friend is, as it were,
a second self.
—CICERO (106–43 B.C.)

Several years ago, the CEO of an executive recruitment company called me out of the blue.

"I've heard about how you teach people straight talk," she said. "I think we could use you. Could you be here next week?"

Immediately I knew I was dealing with a Director. She was looking for results—the sooner, the better. So I put on my Director hat.

"Can't do it next week," I said. "But three weeks from Monday I could manage a one-day session." I told her the cost. "How does that sound?"

"Let's do it," she said. "I'll have my assistant arrange the details."

"Fine. I look forward to it." I hung up the phone. The call lasted no more than three minutes.

Had she been a Thinker, of course, I would have put on a different hat. I would have drawn her out, asked her to describe the specific problems she was experiencing. Then I would have explained to her how our programs could address each specific issue. I would have displayed the utmost patience in answering any lingering questions. The call would have lasted a minimum of fifteen minutes.

Had I used that style with her, however, I wouldn't have made the sale. She would have been bored by all the details. She'd wonder why I wasn't getting to the bottom line and closing the deal. She'd start to question my competency.

Her company turned out to be very profitable for our firm. More important, she became a convert to our program—so much so that she has modified her approach and now works as one of our trainers.

You may already have reached conclusions about other people's styles of communicating. In this chapter, we'll provide you with techniques to confirm your interpretations. These tools are fun to use. They're especially helpful when used in conjunction with the tools described later for modifying your own style. The skills you acquire in this chapter will be essential for mastering the art of straight talk.

It's exciting when you first use these skills. And it never ceases to be exciting. Meeting new people is more enjoyable. Your colleagues are more responsive. Managing your boss becomes easier. Team members feel that you relate to them better. Your own strengths emerge to their full advantage. It can make every relationship more interesting and productive. Why? Because you're *tuning* yourself to maximize the quality of your communications.

The Role of Attention

To become proficient in identifying other people's styles, you need to understand how communication styles work.

Of the nearly infinite things we could be aware of at any one time, we focus on only a few. At the center of this selection process sits our attention. It is the roving lens of the mind, constantly scouring the environment and choosing in a nanosecond which things to concentrate on. For example, when you walk down the street, do you pay attention to the buildings or focus on people's faces? In a restaurant, do you get engrossed in the menu or observe the people in the room? In a meeting, do you pay attention to people's remarks or think about what you're going to say? Attentions differ, which dramatically alters the way people see and respond to the exact same situation.

This is an important point. Because if one person pays attention to people and another to buildings, or if one person focuses on tasks while another focuses on feelings, their conversations have the potential to misfire. Although they're sitting in the same room or discussing the same topic, they'll interpret what they're hearing in radically different ways and draw very different conclusions. If they don't recognize and acknowledge their different ways of thinking, their communications will whiz by each other with little chance for a connection.

In our work with organizations, we've studied these different styles. We know, for example, that some people approach a decision wanting to get as much data as possible. Others make decisions swiftly. Still others want to generate as many ideas as possible. In case after case, we have found that people can communicate far more effectively once they understand their different styles.

Filters and Frames

Two concepts help us interpret the different styles of communicating. One relates to what people pay attention to. The second relates to how people respond.

The first is called "filtering." Filtering yields those things to which we pay attention. This invisible and largely unconscious process is always at work. To a large degree, we are our filters, and they are us.

To visualize how this works, imagine a large lake. A stream flows from it to a clear pool many miles away. This system is analogous to the areas of your brain that process sensory inputs. The lake is filled with the stimuli you receive at a given moment. The river contains the filters, many thousands of them. The clear pool is your attention—what you're actually aware of at a particular moment.

Now imagine walking along a crowded street. Thousands of stimuli assault you each millisecond, but you're aware of only a few. What's going on?

Your filters are sorting and eliminating most of what you unconsciously perceive. One set of filters eliminates the male adults passing you on the street. A second set removes all sounds—except for a baby crying. A third set eliminates all smells. Yet another reduces your visual field to the sidewalk in front of you. Finally, after hundreds of filters have been passed, you're left with the thing that actually catches your conscious attention: a woman pushing a baby stroller.

All this in a nanosecond.

Now if you could somehow remove all of these filters and view the world in an unfiltered way, the result would be a mind-boggling gush of data. Nothing would make sense. Our filters literally bring order to the chaos. We are a process of elimination—in this case, elimination of data.

Interestingly, we routinely make the assumption that we all see things the same way. We assume that the "facts" we see are the same as the "facts" that other people see. We assume we have the ability to interpret for others what they see, because we are viewing the same pool of data. In fact, the filtering process guarantees just the opposite. It guarantees that we each respond in different ways, even if we're in the same room listening to the same conversation.

Our differences aren't a result of pigheadedness or stupidity. They are a result of the way we communicate.

The second key to understanding different styles of communicating is how we frame incoming data. To visualize how this works, cup your fist into a narrow tube and hold it up to your eye. Now look at something in the room so that you cannot see it in its entirety, but only a detail. How confidently can you describe what it is? How much additional data would you need to complete the picture?

Now open your fist so that you see the entire scene. Clearly, the larger the frame, the more confident our interpretation. The more we see, the more we feel empowered to speak out about it.

The way we frame a situation constricts and dilates in the same way. It depends on our level of experience with the situation, our state of mind, and the role we are asked to play. As the situation varies, our frame shifts.

Our filters and frames are connected in a dynamic way. The filtering system determines which data we see; framing determines our response to those data. A small frame means we're going to hesitate, to ask questions, to inquire for more data. A big frame means we're going to draw conclusions. The size of our frame determines whether we tend to assert ourselves in a given situation or gather more information. In other words, it dictates our levels of assertiveness and inquiry.

The combined workings of these filters and frames—both of which occur within our subconscious—help us define the four basic styles of communicating. Some people set their filters so that more attention is placed on facts; some set them to allow more feelings to come through. Some people set their frames so that their responses are more assertive, some set their frames so that they respond with questions.

Using filters and frames, you can distill the four basic communication styles down to the following terms:

Directors: Filter for facts and respond assertively.
Expressers: Filter for feelings and respond assertively.
Thinkers: Filter for facts and respond by probing.
Harmonizers: Filter for feelings and respond by probing.

CHART 2: FILTERS AND FRAMES

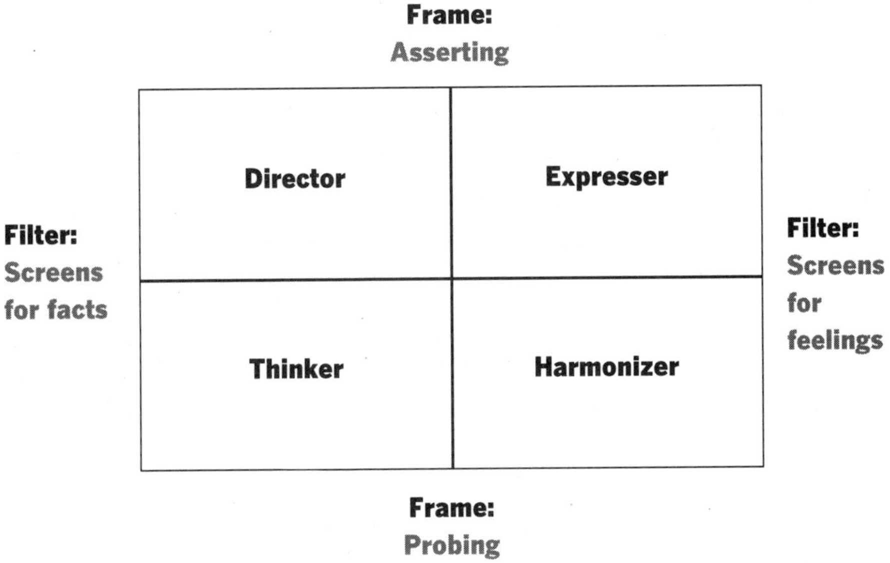

Frame:
Asserting

Director	**Expresser**
Thinker	**Harmonizer**

Filter:
Screens
for facts

Filter:
Screens
for
feelings

Frame:
Probing

Chart 2 shows this relationship.

This is not to say that the only thing that distinguishes Directors from Expressers is that one filters for facts and the other for feelings. The behaviors of each communication style are more complex and varied than that. But certain behaviors are "markers" for each style, and these markers can help us identify a person's style. A marker is simply a specific behavior we look for in another person—and in ourselves.

For example, one marker would be sensitivity to people's feelings. That's a clue that the person's filters are set for feelings. A second marker is how often someone cites specific facts. A third marker is one's level of assertiveness. And a fourth marker is the extent to which one probes and inquires for more information. Each marker is a clue to help you determine a person's style.

Chart 2 helps you sort out these markers. It links the four marker behaviors to the four basic styles. By studying the chart, you can see how the various combinations of filters and frames are linked to the four basic communication styles. Understanding these markers is the first step to interpreting the styles of people around you.

EXERCISE: CONFIRM YOUR COLLEAGUES' STYLES

Let's practice identifying the various styles. Refer back to the exercise at the end of Chapter 1, where you guessed the styles of your immediate work group. Let's see if those same guesses stand up when you factor in the information we've learned in this chapter.

For example, if you identified someone as an Expresser, ask yourself: Does the person typically filter for feelings more than facts? Is he or she more likely to respond by being assertive? If so, then you've confirmed your earlier choice.

For each set of initials in the exercise at the end of Chapter 1, determine whether you still agree with your choice, based on your new understanding of filters and frames. Use the four squares in this exercise to change your assessments.

Asserting

Director	**Expresser**
Talks in action verbs.	Speaks rapidly.
Cares about the "bottom line."	Uses animated gestures.
Always on the go.	Entertaining.
Speaks crisply.	Thinks out loud.
Talks about goals.	Talks about ideas.
May seem insensitive.	May be imprecise.
Thinker	**Harmonizer**
Talks about details.	Talks about people.
Inquiring.	Sensitive to others.
Often makes lists.	Avoids conflict.
Speaks carefully.	Dedicated and loyal.
Wants things done "right."	Speaks softly.
May procrastinate.	May overcommit.

Facts (left) **Feelings** (right)

Probing

Case Study Diagnosing the Ad Agency

The parent company of a midwestern advertising agency hired us to help reengineer the agency's sales processes. The CEO wasn't meeting revenue goals. More important, there were rumors that the three top account representatives were about to leave and start their own firm. Armed with that limited background, we flew to meet the CEO in person and try to get a sense of things.

We arrived a bit early, and while we sipped coffee in the first-floor reception area we focused on the room's decor. The walls were a bright shade of blue, with photographs of the agency's personnel hanging on one wall. A trophy case filled another wall. In the corner a television was on.

A secretary ushered us into the CEO's office, past desks that were mostly empty. As we walked through the room, we could see people in twos and threes clustered around desks in the back of the room. We couldn't hear what they were saying, but the conversations seemed pretty lively. People were laughing and having a good time.

Dan, the CEO, met us with a warm handshake and asked us to sit down. He immediately launched into a description of a new radio campaign the agency was planning. He spoke very rapidly about the prospects of attracting younger buyers, a key concern for this particular client.

We asked a couple of questions about his agency, and he told us that everything was going great. The staff was "on fire," and the competition was "getting creamed."

We asked why he thought the parent company had called us in.

Dan took off his glasses and moved around to the front edge of his desk. He punctuated his comments by jabbing at the air in front of us with his glasses.

"Our parent company wanted us to use you, and so you're here. We think it's probably a pretty good idea to take stock. But we've got a great team here, and everything's going great. We've got a few problems in a few departments, and one department has some problems, but we've never been better, and we're really looking forward to this next year."

Stop here, and ask yourself what style of communicator we were dealing with. If you said "Expresser," you're absolutely right. Dan's rapid-fire delivery, his disjointed stream of logic, and his emphatic gesturing with his glasses were all clues. So we responded with the following:

"One of the things we perceive in general about business," I said, "is how disorganized things can get. Especially in your type of business, where people are so focused on juggling multiple clients and deadlines. People aren't clear on the bigger goals, managers don't set priorities, people come up with a million ideas but they don't have time to take one and execute it carefully.

"We can help your organization learn how to discipline itself to do things in a more carefully thought-out manner. The result will be better performance."

"I guess corporate spelled it out for you pretty well," he responded. "You've got a good handle on our problems here."

"Actually," I said, "we didn't get it from corporate. That comes from picking up clues in the twenty minutes since we got here. It's a bit of a lucky guess. But we knew what to look for."

To Dan, what seemed like clairvoyance was simply the result of analyzing his communication style and knowing its likely impact on the organization. All it took was using the tools of straight talk—and a little observation.

Identifying a Person's Primary Style

You've already begun to learn the basic markers for identifying a person's primary style. The box on page 58 provides a useful summary. In brief:

- Directors enjoy challenges; they like to get things done quickly and move on to the next task.

- Expressers like being the center of attention; they enjoy expressing their thoughts and feelings.

- Thinkers like to focus on details; they like to understand precisely what needs to be done.

- Harmonizers like being part of a group; they enjoy making small talk and looking after others.

There are a number of additional tricks for figuring out a person's primary style. This section focuses on the subtleties of the art.

When meeting someone for the first time, there are three things to do: Ask questions, observe reactions, and listen actively. My goal is to size someone up within five minutes. Ask a question like: "What do you do to stay current with trends in your business?" Or: "What kind of person is successful in your field?" Then watch for clues.

An asserter will instantly give a response, and typically won't ask whether you agree. An inquirer, on the other hand, will say what he or she thinks, and then ask a genuine question: "That's just my sense of it. What's your opinion?"

A person who focuses on feelings will talk about the quality of the people he or she works with and their ability to meet whatever challenges lie ahead. A more fact-oriented person will talk about studies or numbers or industry trends.

You can't rely on just one question. You've got to ask two or three to be sure. Weigh the number of times the person talks about feelings. Weigh the balance of inquiry and assertion. Here are some questions that work well:

How do you spend your free time, when you have some?
What do you like to read?
What did you study in school?

Watch how people interact with you. Do they engage in small talk? Or do they cut to the chase? Do they tell stories? Do they break an issue down into its constituent parts? Do they ask questions? Each of these is a trademark of a particular style.

In assessing a person's style, observe the role that person is playing. A manager may feel she has to be assertive. It's her job. But is she assertive by nature, or just playing a part? The balance of inquiry and assertion will tell you. The same thing is true of someone in a subordinate role. Is he probing by nature or because it's required of him? There's no simple key that will yield the correct answer every time. You simply have to practice observing.

Another trick is learning to recognize the assertive questioner. Some people temper their nature by disguising statements as questions. Take the CEO we mentioned at the start of this chapter. She didn't ask: "When would your schedule permit?" She said: "Could you be here next week?" She laid out her desire very clearly—but tried to soften it by asking a question.

You'll also learn to recognize the opposite: the passive asserter. "We've got a really good team here, and it's taken a long time to build it.

EXERCISE: IDENTIFY A COLLEAGUE'S PRIMARY STYLE

The chart below will help you sort through another person's style. Circle each behavior that applies, then total the number of squares you circled in each column. The two columns that get the highest scores will tell you that person's preferred styles of communicating.

Speech	opinionated	questioning	"right" "wrong"	"good" "bad"
Body language	fast moving, dynamic	poised	tentative, cautious	relaxed
Eye contact	direct	indirect	distant	inviting
Response to crisis	risk taking	risk averse	analytical	empathetic
Total				
	Assertive	**Probing**	**Factual**	**Feeling**

Once you've circled two styles at the bottom of the chart, use the next chart to determine a person's primary style.

If a person is:		His or her communication style is:
Assertive and factual	⟶	Director
Assertive and feeling	⟶	Expresser
Probing and factual	⟶	Thinker
Probing and feeling	⟶	Harmonizer

It's very important here at XYZ Corp. that we have a good team." On its own, that statement means relatively little. Certainly no one's going to challenge it. It is utterly safe and benign. It is a passive assertion.

Asserters like to run the show; probers defer to others and ask questions. Asserters leap to conclusions and take risks; probers look for confirmation and safety in numbers. Be attuned to the situation. An asserter may appear passive at first. But put him or her in a situation that requires someone to take charge, and a different style may emerge.

Observe where people invest their attention. Do they talk about their family, or about their new car? If they tend to say things are "good" or "bad," that's the mark of a feeler. If their judgments are cast more in the words "right" and "wrong," that's the sign of a factual style.

Again, you have to be careful not to be tricked by the situation. A person you know from church may have an entirely different style at work.

Identifying a Person's Prevailing Styles

There's no fail-safe way to pinpoint a person's secondary style short of having him or her take the survey. That said, you can still figure out which two styles a person uses most often—information that is almost as useful as knowing his or her exact position on the Matrix. This is called identifying a person's "prevailing styles."

Let's assume you're trying to understand your boss. You're pretty sure she's either an Expresser or a Harmonizer. She exhibits many of the traits of an Expresser: she's an animated speaker, she loves to brainstorm ideas, she has a capacity for meeting new people that frankly amazes you. But she also has a lot of the qualities of the Harmonizer: she's good at making small talk, at putting people at ease, at making people feel part of the team.

Moreover, she isn't one who painstakingly pursues a particular task to the finish line—a key trait of the Thinker—nor does she take on big challenges and risks like the Director. So you're pretty confident of your diagnosis: Expresser or Harmonizer.

If you stop and think about it, you're already 90 percent finished. She must be either an Expresser/Harmonizer, which makes her a Socializer, or a Harmonizer/Expresser, which makes her a Nurturer. Review the profiles for these two styles in Chapter 2. You may figure

EXERCISE: IDENTIFY YOUR COLLEAGUES' PREVAILING STYLES

This exercise will help you become more skilled at quickly identifying people's prevailing styles and placing them on the Matrix. Remember, however, that taking the survey is the only way to *guarantee* an accurate portrait.

Step 1: List four people whose communication styles are important to you in your work—your colleagues, boss, key customers, or others with whom you work closely. Based on what you've learned so far, think about the two styles you think each person uses most frequently. Write them down in the chart below: If you think a person relies on a single style, then write it down in both squares—for instance, Expresser, Expresser. Use the example as a guide.

	Example	1	2	3	4
Name	Will Jones				
Most-used style #1	Expresser				
Most-used style #2	Thinker				

Step 2: Using the chart below, find in columns A and B the two styles you listed in Step 1. It doesn't matter in which columns the styles appear. To the right, find the two specific communication styles that result from that combination.

Column A	Column B	Specific communication style(s)
Director	Director	Dictator
Director	Expresser	Initiator, Charmer
Director	Thinker	Explorer, Investigator
Director	Harmonizer	Persuader, Counselor
Expresser	Expresser	Entertainer
Expresser	Thinker	Diplomat, Organizer
Expresser	Harmonizer	Socializer, Nurturer
Thinker	Thinker	Analyzer
Thinker	Harmonizer	Supporter, Provider
Harmonizer	Harmonizer	Pleaser

EXERCISE: IDENTIFY YOUR COLLEAGUES' PREVAILING STYLES (cont'd)

Step 3: For each person you listed in Step 1, write down the specific communication styles from Step 2 in the table below. Follow the example

	Example	1	2	3	4
Name	Will Jones				
Specific communication style #1	Diplomat				
Specific communication style #2	Organizer				

Step 4: For each person you listed, go back to Chapter 2 and reread the descriptions of the specific styles you wrote down under his or her name. Decide which description is a better fit. Once you decide, put that individual's initials in the appropriate square on the Matrix below. If you can't decide, put his or her initials in both squares. Put your own initials in the appropriate square, too.

DIRECTORS		EXPRESSERS	
Dictator	Initiator	Charmer	Entertainer
Explorer	Persuader	(WJ) Diplomat	Socializer
Investigator	Organizer	Counselor	Nurturer
Analyzer	Supporter	Provider	Pleaser
THINKERS		HARMONIZERS	

EXERCISE: IDENTIFY YOUR COLLEAGUES' PREVAILING STYLES (cont'd)

Step 5: Now think about what you could do to improve your communications with each person you listed. Write down your thoughts in the space below.

1. To improve communications with Person 1, I should:

-
-
-

2. To improve communications with Person 2, I should:

-
-
-

3. To improve communications with Person 3, I should:

-
-
-

4. To improve communications with Person 4, I should:

-
-
-

out right away which description is the better match. Even if you don't, you'll have enough information to make some very informed decisions about how to improve your communications with your boss.

As your understanding of communication styles grows, you'll learn how to detect which two styles prevail in any individual. If circumstances allow it, you can, of course, ask the other person to take the InVision Communication Styles Profile. When you do, be sure you give him or her the complete instructions, along with the scoring sheets.

By the way, even after you confirm your assessment by asking the person to take the Communication Styles Profile, don't assume that his or her style is permanent. People's styles change. One colleague's style changed three times in three years (from Initiator to Charmer to Provider).

Of course, he changed jobs three times, too.

Perimeter and Center Styles

Many people have what we call "perimeter styles," meaning they are located on the outer edge of the Matrix, as shown in Chart 3 on page 68. There are twelve such styles. You can usually identify them by using the framing and filtering markers described above.

Other people have "center styles"—Persuader, Diplomat, Organizer, or Counselor. A center style is somewhat more difficult to decipher because his or her secondary style is the *opposite* of his or her primary style.

How can you tell if someone is a center style? Again, it's a matter of observation. Here are some questions to ask as you observe someone's behavior:

> **Does he or she show a pattern of unpredictability?**
>
> **Does he or she veer from discussing ideas to discussing details?**
>
> **Does he or she veer from expressing curiosity about people's feelings to strongly advocating his or her own agenda?**
>
> **Does he or she demonstrate a capacity to communicate in many different styles?**

If you answer yes to any of these questions, that's strong evidence that the person has one of the center styles.

CHART 3: LOCATING PERIMETER AND CENTER STYLES

DIRECTORS		**EXPRESSERS**	
Dictator	Initiator	Charmer	Entertainer
Explorer	Persuader	Diplomat	Socializer
Investigator	Organizer	Counselor	Nurturer
Analyzer	Supporter	Provider	Pleaser
THINKERS		**HARMONIZERS**	

Case Study The Bank Manager's About-Face

People change their styles of communicating over time. Most of the changes are for the better, but sometimes the change can be for the worse.

In one case, we gave the Communication Styles Profile to the managers of a midsized bank in New England. A year later, we returned to chart the bank's progress. We gave the Profile again to the management team. We then compared the results to see whether people's styles had changed.

Naturally, some people had changed. A manager who'd previously been a Dictator was now an Investigator. A marketing manager had moved from Provider to Organizer. Typical changes.

The one surprise was a woman named Trish. She had changed her style over the twelve months from Supporter to Initiator. That's a dramatic shift. Trish had gotten a major job promotion, and was now responsible for a team of fifteen salespeople. It was understandable that she would modify her style.

But in Trish's case, she'd gone too far.

When we interviewed her sales staff, we could see that they weren't happy with the change. "Trish seemed like such a nice person before she got her promotion. Now she keeps everyone walking on eggshells," one person said.

Another staff member said that Trish had stopped allowing copies of a key industry newsletter to be circulated to the staff. "She makes us all feel like idiots," this person recounted.

When we gave this feedback to Trish and pointed out that her team was wondering what had happened to the old Trish, she reacted defensively by saying that she had no choice if she was to succeed. She said she was only doing what her boss had asked of her.

We were puzzled by this change. We'd seen countless examples of newly promoted executives changing their styles to be more assertive, thinking that was the key to success. But Trish's leap on the Matrix from a Thinker/Harmonizer to a Director/Expressor was extreme. And the evidence that her staff was unhappy didn't seem to matter to her. Something else seemed to be going on.

Out of curiosity, we took it upon ourselves to probe a little deeper. We interviewed Trish's boss and asked him if he'd been surprised by Trish's change of behavior. "No," he said. He had told Trish that he was going to continue to promote her so long as she "delivered the numbers. She's a real up-and-comer. She'll be running things one day if she keeps doing what she's doing."

That explained why Trish didn't care. Her boss was giving her positive feedback about her new, more assertive style. It didn't bother him that this was causing a problem with her staff. As to whether the boss's boss (in this case, the bank's board chair) realized there was a time bomb ticking away at the bank, we didn't know.

Nor were we asked to address that particular problem.

A year later, we read that the bank had been sold. Now the boss's strategy made sense. Driving up the numbers at the expense of morale was logical if he knew the bank was on the selling block.

Case Study **A Charmer Turns Persuader**

One of our assignments was with a company that sold paging equipment. The manager was an expert in telecommunications named John. He asked us to help him work with his sales manager, a woman named Sandy.

Sandy was smart, and she had experience, John told us. But she wasn't meeting her sales goals. John was frustrated in his attempts to get her to change her ways—and frustrated by his inability to get her to see what he wanted.

After getting the results from their Communication Styles Profiles, we found that John was an Initiator and Sandy a Charmer. That was in keeping with John's diagnosis of her major weakness: She tried to get prospective customers to like her, and then to like the product.

We described to John how the tools of straight talk could help him manage Sandy more effectively. We coached him in modifying his style to work with Sandy more productively.

After the coaching, we joined John in a meeting with Sandy. He began by admitting that his own style of communicating might have caused her to be baffled by what he wanted. He admitted that he was prone to making blanket assertions and not providing enough detail. He revealed to her the things he was working on to improve his communication.

Then he asked her, with a note of genuine curiosity in his voice, what she felt she needed from him in order to improve her performance.

She answered with the following statement: "I need to believe that when I don't know something I can ask you, and that you'll be genuinely interested in helping me. Otherwise, I just feel alone out there. I need to feel that I won't be judged because I need help."

John told her that he would try. He invited her to challenge him if he failed to show that level of support. They shook hands, and Sandy left the room.

Within the next year, Sandy became a new force in the sales department. She saw her role as helping her clients identify their business needs ahead of their competitors. She learned to ask her clients expert questions to help them to do this. Her sales figures nearly tripled that first year.

We came back the following year to do a follow-up survey. Sandy's style had shifted from Charmer to Persuader. We asked her whether she felt more successful in her job.

"I know I am," she said, "and it's all because I've changed the way I see my role when I sell. I don't see my role as getting the business, but asking good questions. The business seems to come naturally."

Conclusion

Learning to identify another person's prevailing styles without relying on the Communication Styles Profile is a key skill in becoming a competent communicator. As your skill and confidence grow, you'll discover that you'll quickly be able to determine the two communication styles others use most frequently. Then it's a relatively simple matter to place them on the Matrix.

Once you understand how your style differs from another person's, you can see how you might modify your communication style to be on the same—or a more similar—wavelength. As you'll see in the next chapter, by subtly adapting your style to that of another person, you'll more quickly reach a level of common understanding—and be able to make decisions that will satisfy you both.

EXERCISE: REASSESS YOUR COLLEAGUES' STYLES

Using the skills discussed in this chapter, place the initials of the people in your immediate work group (the same people you identified in the exercise at the end of Chapter 1) in the appropriate squares below. Then write down specific behaviors you could look for to confirm your assessment.

DIRECTORS		EXPRESSERS	
Dictator	Initiator	Charmer	Entertainer
Explorer	Persuader	Diplomat	Socializer
Investigator	Organizer	Counselor	Nurturer
Analyzer	Supporter	Provider	Pleaser
THINKERS		HARMONIZERS	

Notes:

EXERCISE: CHART YOUR LIFE ON THE MATRIX

If you think about the changes in your own life, you know that the people around you have influenced your style of communicating in significant ways. You've had to live up to the expectations of your various teachers and bosses. You've had to learn how to adapt as your work and responsibilities have changed. You've had to learn how to work with different styles of people, with different work teams, in different industries. Over time, you've accumulated a wealth of experience about how to interact effectively with other people.

It's a valuable exercise to chart the course of your life across the Matrix. What was your style when you were at school? When you took your first job? What journey have you taken around the Matrix as you've grown and changed? In the Matrix below, write your initials in the squares that reflect the styles you've used in the past. Use arrows to trace your journey to where you are now.

What does this tell you about yourself? Are you more comfortable with your style today? Or were you more comfortable with your style in the past? Why? Take some time to write down your thoughts in the space on the next page.

DIRECTORS		EXPRESSERS	
Dictator	Initiator	Charmer	Entertainer
Explorer	Persuader	Diplomat	Socializer
Investigator	Organizer	Counselor	Nurturer
Analyzer	Supporter	Provider	Pleaser
THINKERS		HARMONIZERS	

Notes:

Chapter Four
Different Communication Styles at Work Together

Take the tone of the company you are in.
—THE EARL OF CHESTERFIELD (1694-1773)

When I worked as a marketing director for a newspaper company, I was often called on to talk to our biggest customers. But I never saw my role as selling. My goal was to communicate. I would ask the clients about their business strategy, I would inquire what might be missing from their current marketing, I would help them examine their options, and I would inform them about our products. Then I would help them draw conclusions.

One example was a large computer company in northern California that purchased millions of dollars' worth of advertising from us. The company was threatening to turn to one of our competitors because we were more expensive. And on paper, we were.

The CEO of this company was Randy Grant, a man in his early fifties. He had an engineering degree and good rapport with people. The meetings took place in his office, elegantly furnished with a black conference table, matching leather chairs, and an oriental carpet. His collection of model racing cars stretched along one wall. Along a second wall were three original photos by Ansel Adams. The third and fourth walls were sheer glass, looking over the city.

We had three meetings together—all of them focused on the company's needs. They consisted of Randy and Doug, his chief financial officer, plus myself. At the initial meeting, it was clear that Randy and Doug were Investigators. They liked data; they liked following a clear line of logic to its conclusion; so I modified my style accordingly. I was Mr. Data.

Unfortunately, when talking about strategy, there is no pure data. There's extrapolation, interpolation, curve jumping. You can utilize data, but you have to make assumptions about the future.

At the third meeting, we finally agreed to make three assumptions about the future of their company based on the data:

1. First-time buyers of computers were going to buy used computers in increasing numbers, with that percentage of the market growing to 28 percent by the year 2000.
2. Computer buyers over the age of fifty were going to lease computers in greater numbers than ever before, with that percentage increasing to 25 percent by the year 2000.
3. Competition from abroad was going to continue to be ferocious for the least expensive machines. The opportunity for American-made computers was in more expensive machines priced from $2,000 to $5,000.

As the third meeting got under way, I inquired whether Randy or Doug could draw any vision from these assumptions. "Based on nothing but these three assumptions, what would your strategy be?" I asked.

Randy spoke: "My vision would be to align ourselves with one hell of a financial partner, develop stores all across the country, and promote the best financing terms available, while at the same time pushing used computers to first-time buyers. I'd be very aggressively competing on leasing terms and the value of used machines. Just like the automobile business."

Doug agreed. "What I'd give up, if I had to, is the sale of new machines priced under $2,000. It's not going to be a major chunk of our profits. That has all sorts of ramifications for how we control our inventory and pay our sales force."

"Okay," I said. "So to be able to compete on the best possible financing terms, what do you need?"

"Volume, pure and simple," Randy said. "Guaranteed volume that would enable us to offer lower interest rates while amortizing the risk."

"And as a strategy, that implies what?" I asked.

"We get bigger," Randy said. "We become much bigger."

Doug spoke: "Which means finding a way to raise the capital to do so."

Randy added: "Which means a public offering, or finding one hell of a wealthy individual."

I inquired: "What does going public require?"

"Public disclosure and quarterly earnings growth and lots of hassles," said Randy. "We've always said we didn't want to do that."

Doug: "Then where does that take us?"

Randy: "It leads me to think about selling the business."

"Okay," I said. "Let's stop for a moment. Let's decide if that's the logical strategy based on these assumptions."

Randy and Doug took a fifteen-minute break and returned to the office.

"The surprising thing to me," said Randy, "is that selling the business is what I really want to do. I'm getting tired. This is just the first time I've stated it quite so clearly."

"It's Randy's decision," said Doug, pondering his boss. "I happen to agree with the strategy. But he owns it. It's his baby."

"If that's the logical strategy," I said, "then what are the next logical steps?"

Doug spoke: "It implies making our balance sheet look as good as possible."

"Right," said Randy. "It means pumping sales like crazy over the next year."

"The strategy you've come up with sounds good," I said. "Obviously you need time to think it over. I'm available any time you need me."

Two weeks later, Randy renewed his contract with our company, with a 12 percent increase in volume. Our sales manager was ecstatic.

"How did you do this?" he asked me.

"By modifying my style," I said.

Now that you've learned about your style of communicating and how to identify the styles of the people around you, how can this knowledge help you become a more competent communicator? The answer should be obvious by now: communicate in a mode that will make other people feel more comfortable relating to you. In other words, modify your style so that it takes the tone of the company you keep.

In this chapter, we're going to look at specific ways that you can do this without appearing unnatural or phony. You're going to learn a few simple tools to help you communicate in a style that more closely resembles others', without forsaking yours.

To know other people, walk in their shoes. To be an effective communicator, try to see the world as they do. Immerse yourself in their way of thinking. Imagine the world through their filters and frames. Try to understand how their communication style influences the way they live. Study their language.

The following sections are designed to help you understand the ways that each style communicates—the body language, specific words and phrases, and favored topics. In essence, language is the secret pass code for each style. Use this pass code, and you'll be able to enter another camp undetected.

The Language of Directors

The Director speaks in short, crisp sentences, often quickly. Directors like to talk about results. "Our goal is to achieve a 10 percent increase in market share. Let's focus on what we need to do to accomplish that."

The Director typically thinks the conversation is over before it really is. You may find yourself puzzled about what he expects you to do. "Just do it" is a phrase that personifies Directors. They naturally assume that everyone else wants to "just do it"—and the quicker, the better.

The only snag is: You haven't a clue what exactly it is that needs to get done. Simply inquire. "I don't follow what you're saying. Could you explain it in more detail?" Or: "Can we spend five minutes talking about specific steps?" By giving it a finite period, you allay the Director's concerns about wasting time.

Sometimes even the goal isn't clear. Clarify it. "I'm not clear on what the goal is, what the intermediate objectives are. Can you clarify that for me?" Or if time is running short (as it always is with Directors), say: "I'll put together a memo spelling out what I think our objectives are and run it past you, okay?"

Directors are typically comfortable talking the language of numbers. They may forget the details, but Directors love the bottom line. If you want to make a persuasive case to a Director, the best way to do it is with numbers. And emphasize the return, the bottom line, the profitability.

The best way to communicate with anyone whose style differs from yours is to put into words the dilemma you feel. For example, if you're talking to a Director, a frequent dilemma is this: "I know you're pressed for time, yet I need you to explain what you mean."

By putting this dilemma into words, you show sensitivity toward them. "I'm in a dilemma here. I feel you don't have time to go into this more thoroughly right now. Yet I need you to take more time to explain it. Is that okay with you? Should it be now, or sometime later?"

The Language of Expressers

Expressers love to talk, and talk they will, sometimes so quickly and on so many different topics that it's hard to keep up. They'll wave their hands, point their fingers, squeeze your arm—all to make a point. They love imagining what's possible, whether it's a new use for technology, a better way to organize the office, or a budding romance. They imagine everyone else likes to talk, too, and will seemingly talk for the sake of talking. That's why brainstorming is such a pleasure for Expressers: It's their natural form of communication.

Expressers, unlike Thinkers or Harmonizers, often talk before they think. Much of what they say is a "work in progress." If they're aware of their style, they'll say, "I'm thinking aloud here."

The best way of communicating with an Expresser is to brainstorm for a while. Let your spontaneous, creative side show. Tell him or her: "You know, it's just occurred to me while we're talking that . . . " Or: "That idea you have is really interesting. Imagine what would happen if . . ."

Sometimes you need to get Expressers to be more grounded in the concrete reality of things like budgets, tasks, and results. It helps to frame the conversation for them so they know you're shifting gears. "If everyone agrees, let's shift from brainstorming to how we're going to make this decision. I'd like specific suggestions from each of you."

Make sure you get the Expresser to commit to the decision by writing down specific agreements on what he'll do by when. Otherwise, the hours you spend together may be wasted, because when you return to the same subject, the Expresser will say: "You know, I've been thinking about a better way to do that."

However, if you've reached an agreement, you can say: "Since we already decided that, how about we move on to the next agenda item? Unless you feel your idea really warrants reopening this decision."

Expressers don't particularly like the language of numbers. Numbers are too precise and immutable and dry. Ideas are exciting and stimulating. So in speaking the language of finance, don't assume that Expressers are able to track your thinking. One of the most difficult tasks you can give an Expresser is to create a budget. Give him or her a template of exactly what you expect. Illustrate the backup information you need. And make it clear you're available if the person has any questions, regardless of how trivial.

If you're talking to an Expresser, a frequent dilemma is this: "I know you value brainstorming and coming up with new ideas, but a decision has got to be made." So put it like this: "I feel that I'm in a dilemma here. Your ideas are creative and good, yet we need to come to closure. How can we decide that it's time to pick one option and go with it?"

The Language of Thinkers

Thinkers talk in slow, precise, concrete terms. This is the language of the Thinker: "After we reviewed the language in Section D, we proceeded to Section E. We dealt with five issues, most of which we were able to resolve; however, I want to bring to your attention two subparagraphs in Section E having to do with . . ."

Thinkers revel in details. All those details can be wearying, especially to people with different styles. But Thinkers need to explain their reasoning and logic carefully. As we'll see in Part 2 of this book, that style of communicating can be very appropriate when you're dealing with tough, complex issues. But the Thinker's style may not be as appropriate when a deadline looms, or when you're trying to brainstorm.

Thinkers like to talk about things, especially subjects about which they may have accumulated some special knowledge. So you'll find Thinkers talking about their collection of Eartha Kitt records, or their boxes of baseball cards, or their interest in antique vases. The topic will be specific and grounded. Thinkers like to solve real-world problems.

As long as they feel comfortable, they will ask questions when faced with something they don't understand. They are most comfortable, in fact, when they are getting information they need to solve a problem. And that's a sign that your relationship with a Thinker is going well.

Like the Director, Thinkers are happy to focus on a task. But their approach to solving a problem is to slow down and understand every step along the way. The process is as important to them as getting results. They want to make sure they understand things the first time, so they don't make any mistakes.

To communicate effectively with Thinkers, simply remember to answer their questions thoroughly, ask them questions in return, and be patient. If time is a problem, tell them that you're going to have to resume the conversation at a later point. But be sure to schedule the time—and then give yourself a little extra. Expect the Thinker to use all of it.

Unlike Expressers, Thinkers are comfortable with the language of numbers. They enjoy financial discussions, and find it easy to think in concrete mathematical terms. Many accountants are Thinkers.

If you're talking to a Thinker, a frequent dilemma is this: "I know you want as much detail as possible, yet I can't give you all the detail you want." So put it like this: "I feel that I'm in a dilemma here. I understand and appreciate your desire to get all these things nailed down, yet I don't have the time (or all the answers) you need. Are there other sources you can use? Can you think of other people to turn to?"

The Language of Harmonizers

Harmonizers like to make small talk. Sports, weather, social gossip—any kind of small talk is their bread and butter. Harmonizers use language to loosen people up—to make sure that others feel included, a part of the conversation. This is the Harmonizer's goal: to make those with whom he or she is communicating feel comfortable and safe.

The Harmonizer is the neighbor who talks about his fishing trip, the friend from work who asks about your daughter's school play. She is friendly to all, incapable of giving offense, not boisterous or outgoing like the Expresser, but quiet and somewhat shy. Speaking of a Harmonizer in our office, one of my colleagues said: "She is the glue that holds this place together."

The Harmonizer's strategy is to enhance social interactions. As you might guess, Harmonizers spend a lot of time listening, engrossed in what other people are saying. "Tell me about your children. What are they doing this weekend?" It's typical of a Harmonizer to know more about what's going on in other people's lives than someone with a different style of communicating.

Harmonizers are reluctant to talk about tough issues or sensitive subjects. New business strategies or entrepreneurial ventures are not natural fodder for them. When those subjects come up, Harmonizers typically are silent. Even if you ask them a direct question about a challenging topic, Harmonizers will try to duck it. They'd prefer to talk about people and places they've seen or things they've done. Anecdotes are the natural province of the Harmonizer, not analysis.

Harmonizers tend to speak more patiently than those with other styles. They're trying to communicate, not just talk, and this makes them effective communicators. They deeply care whether someone hears what they're saying. And they love to participate in a two-way conversation—they enjoy listening as much as talking.

The language of numbers may or may not be of interest to the Harmonizer. Typically, he or she will prefer to work in an environment where tasks are well-defined, without risks or controversy. So if the number crunching is methodical and routine, the Harmonizer will feel comfortable. But if it's pie-in-the-sky forecasting, the Harmonizer may feel out of his or her element.

To communicate effectively with Harmonizers, always start off with small talk. Let them know how you're feeling about the weather, or last night's ball game. Approach them gingerly if you need to broach a sensitive issue. Cast your conversation in terms of what's good for everyone involved. The Harmonizer will always respond to questions that allow him or her to speak on behalf of the whole group, rather than as an individual.

If you're talking to a Harmonizer, a frequent dilemma is this: "I know you value the good of the team, but I feel you would get more done if you paid less attention to the needs of the rest of the staff." So put it like this: "I feel that I'm in a dilemma here. I fully appreciate how valuable you are to making people feel cared for and looked after, yet I feel that some of that prevents you from getting on with your work. How can we strike a reasonable balance between the two?"

Chart 4 presents a set of rules to help you speak the language of each style. Learning these different languages is a matter of practice. So start putting these techniques to work and watch how people respond. You'll find that people seem to relax when they hear you speaking their language. Pretty soon you'll start getting messages from them saying: "Hey, that was a really good meeting we had yesterday. Why don't we do it again soon?"

A Game Plan for Modifying Your Style

"The longest journey begins with but a single step." So spoke Confucius. Communicating more effectively with another person can be viewed as taking a single step as well—a symbolic step on the Matrix.

CHART 4: ALTERING YOUR LANGUAGE TO MATCH
ANOTHER STYLE

Speaking to Directors	**Speaking to Expressers**
Adopt a direct, serious tone.	Express your ideas, regardless of
Give information in "bottom-line"	how fanciful.
terms.	Show that you understand their
Keep meetings short and succinct.	feelings.
Assert your own ideas.	Talk about your own feelings.
Don't wait for them to invite	Use gestures; get excited.
feedback.	Let yourself "think aloud."
Don't misinterpret their abruptness	Touch them lightly on the arm or
as a sign of disrespect or criticism.	shoulder (but only if appropriate).[1]
Speaking to Thinkers	**Speaking to Harmonizers**
Be precise in giving information.	Lighten up and relax.
Break problems down into	Make them feel comfortable;
specific parts.	engage in chitchat.
Take time to review every point	Give them information in the form
thoroughly.	of questions whenever possible.
Ask them questions and solicit	Converse in a quiet manner.
their advice.	Avoid saying "no"; find a more
Keep a moderate tone and	gentle way of putting it.
body language.	Keep your distance; touching
	isn't okay.

This symbolic step, once you've figured it out, can mean the difference between communication that struggles and communication that achieves your goals.

The nature of effective communication between two people is that people prefer a balance, not extremes. Two assertive people will have difficulty getting along. An assertive person and an inquiring person will do fine. Couples work best when they are in balance—when each

---

1. Appropriate touch is always defined by the recipient. Look for clues in how they interact and respond with other people. Any type of contract that could be misinterpreted must be avoided.

person senses that his or her strengths are appreciated. Opposites do attract—but only if they're willing to work together.

The purpose of this section is to help you learn how to use the Matrix to modify your style with another person. Think of the Matrix as a game board, and effective communication as a game with the following rules.

The Matrix Game

Limit: two people
Object: to occupy neighboring squares—but not the same square

- Begin on the square that represents your style.
- Each person makes only one move.
- Each person tries to move to a square adjacent to his or her own, and closer to the other player's.
- The goal is to occupy neighboring squares—but not the same square.

How does this work? Let's say you're a Provider and your colleague is a Charmer. Look at your positions on the Matrix in Chart 5. According to the rules, your goal is to move one square up, and hers is to move one square down. If you succeed, then your two pieces will sit on adjacent squares.

You, the Provider, take your step by modifying your style: First, acknowledge that you have different styles. Then say that you want to speak openly and candidly and disclose what you really think and feel—even though that doesn't come naturally to you. Tell her that you value her way of thinking and that you value your relationship enough to want to make it work better.

The Charmer takes her step by acknowledging that she, too, recognizes the differences in your communication styles. She says that to communicate more effectively with you, she'll try to listen more carefully and patiently, and be more thoughtful about her reactions. She says that she really values your style, and values the relationship enough to want to make it work better.

As you both begin your conversation, balance the level of inquiry and assertion in your conversation. Pay attention to how much of the

CHART 5: CHANGING YOUR POSITION ON THE MATRIX

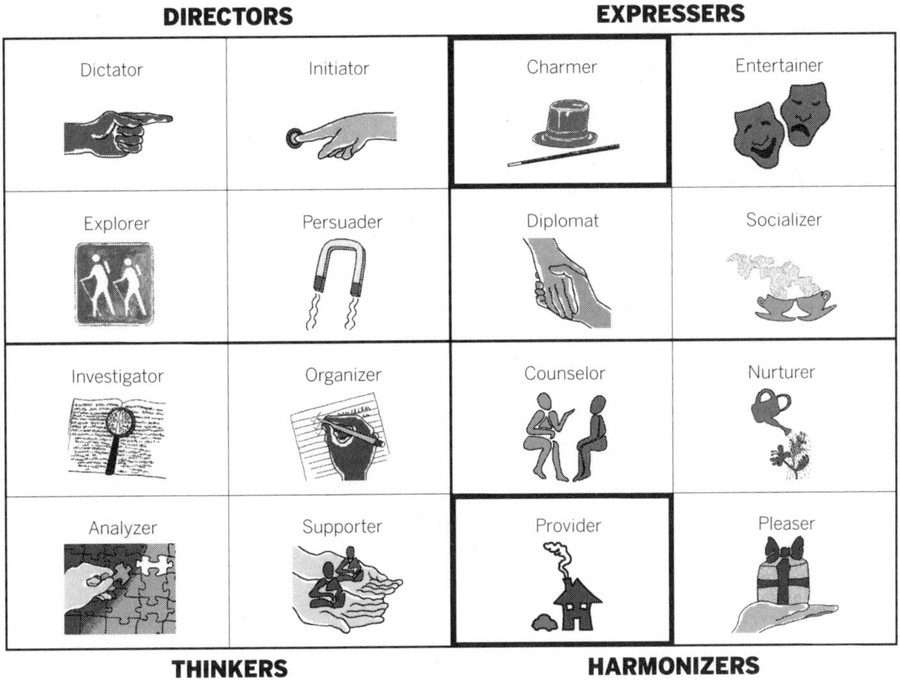

DIRECTORS		EXPRESSERS	
Dictator	Initiator	Charmer	Entertainer
Explorer	Persuader	Diplomat	Socializer
Investigator	Organizer	Counselor	Nurturer
Analyzer	Supporter	Provider	Pleaser
THINKERS		HARMONIZERS	

time each of you shows real curiosity about the other's intentions, ideas, and motivations. Answer every question as honestly as you can—even if you fear it will embarrass you or make you look weak.

This process sounds hard, and it is. If it weren't hard, we'd all be doing it. Start to practice using the Matrix to modify your style. Then you'll start to appreciate the benefits of the Matrix Game.

Ground Rules with Other People

Once you've begun to reap the benefits of using straight talk with another person, ask him or her if you can both agree to modify your behavior permanently. You, the Provider, might ask the Charmer to be more inquisitive and more patient. The Charmer might ask you, in return, to be more forthcoming about your feelings and thoughts. This type of agreement can be written down—or it can be a simple oral understanding. Then, whenever you meet together, you can practice.

When you need to have an important conversation, you can take a few minutes to review the ground rules you've established.

Certain styles find these ground rules easy to make. Persuaders, Diplomats, Organizers, and Counselors—the center styles—are used to juggling a mixture of styles. Other people may have more trouble shifting styles, and may therefore find the process more of a stretch. The bigger the stretch, of course, the tougher it is to stick to your ground rules. Some people can't undo old habits of communicating. They may be able to modify their style for a brief time, but then snap back into their old styles.

No one can force you to modify your style. But given a chance, these tools will work for you. Most people enjoy the feelings that come with being a more effective communicator. Once you put straight talk into practice, you'll find yourself getting hooked.

When starting out, it's useful to remember an axiom of psychology: "People act first, and their actions build and reinforce a set of beliefs." In its most pithy form, this axiom can be rephrased: "People act themselves into a state of believing." In other words, our values follow our behaviors, not the other way around.

So if you're a Charmer who loves to express yourself, force yourself to act like a Thinker for a period of time. Wrap a rubber band around your wrist to remind yourself of your elasticity. Practice filtering and framing like the other styles. As you develop these new communication muscles, you'll discover it's not such a stretch as you thought.

Case Study A Well-Rounded Communicator

One of the best communicators I know is a woman who heads up a major business school. I first met Alice when I was trying to get her to join a campaign to help a national nonprofit organization. She had valuable insights, and I wanted to enlist her help.

Naturally, when we first met, I wanted her to feel as comfortable as possible. So I set out to analyze her style.

After a quick introduction, she began talking about her career. How as an executive at a Detroit automotive company, she'd been stalked by a gunman. How she had been hit with a major union strike her first day on the job. How she had received her doctorate in organizational development at an age when many executives start to look toward retirement. She told these stories in an engaging, entertaining manner. I was already zeroing in on her style—Expresser.

Alice then asked me to talk about myself. While I was talking, I sensed she cared deeply about who I was. Was my initial diagnosis off? Was she a Harmonizer, I wondered?

As I started to describe the complex challenge our firm was being asked to solve, her mode of communication changed again. Her face hardened, she narrowed her eyes, she studied with intense concentration the diagram I placed before her. She asked several probing questions; she related comparable situations she had dealt with. Well, I thought, she's a Thinker.

After a half hour had elapsed, she suddenly stood up. "I've got a class in two hours that's expecting a course outline," she said. "I'm going to have to kick you out."

Well, I thought, she's a Director, too.

She shook my hand warmly and told me what a pleasure it had been talking together. She agreed to join the project. We laughed about her busy schedule. As I left, her door closed softly behind me.

"So, what's her communication style?" I wondered as I walked back to my car. I went through all the markers and checked them off. Finally I reached a conclusion. She was consciously shifting her styles. She could be a Director one moment, a Harmonizer the next, an Expresser the next, and a Thinker the next, as the situation dictated.

Since that initial encounter, Alice and I have become close colleagues. I admire Alice in many ways, but I most admire her communication skills. She is able to relate fluidly and effortlessly with everyone she meets. Invariably, they go away knowing they've made a valuable friend.

She's a master communicator, and this skill is a key to her enormous success.

The Rule of the Center

The Greek philosopher Aristotle espoused a simple philosophy of life. "All things in moderation," he said. Being too courageous meant you were foolhardy. Being too talkative, you were a gossip. If you were too quiet, you were a recluse. The best course lay in the center.

The Matrix has a law of the center, too. Here's how it works:

Put your finger on one of the four center styles shown in Chart 6. You'll see that your finger is surrounded by eight different squares. Therefore, if your style is one in the center, you are automatically adjacent to eight different styles.

CHART 6: NUMBER OF STYLES ADJACENT TO EACH SQUARE ON THE MATRIX

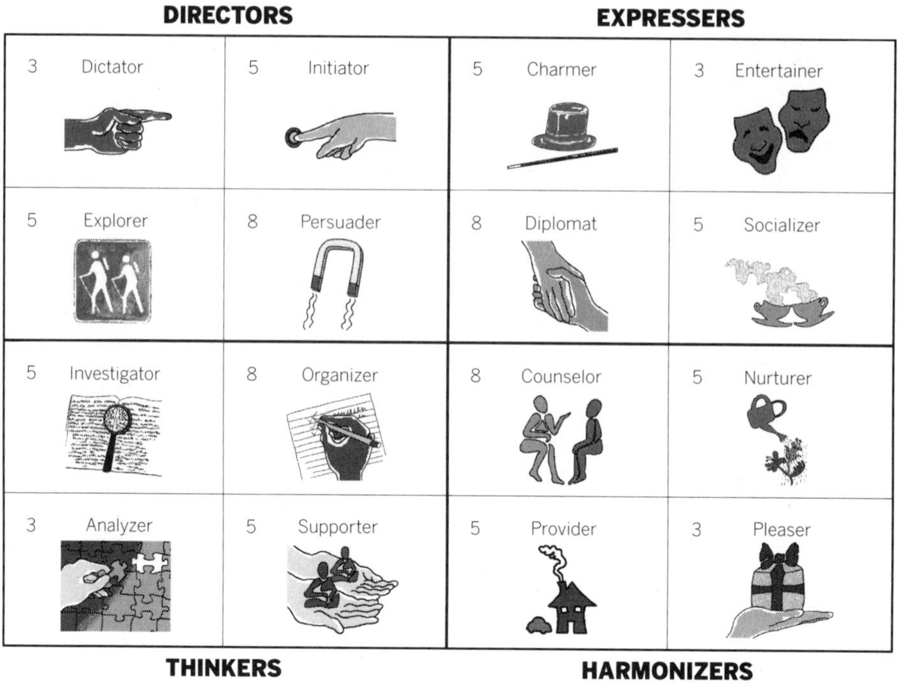

DIRECTORS   **EXPRESSERS**

3 Dictator	5 Initiator	5 Charmer	3 Entertainer
5 Explorer	8 Persuader	8 Diplomat	5 Socializer
5 Investigator	8 Organizer	8 Counselor	5 Nurturer
3 Analyzer	5 Supporter	5 Provider	3 Pleaser

THINKERS   **HARMONIZERS**

Now touch one of the corner styles. Your finger is surrounded by only three other squares. By touching the midperimeter styles, you'll see they border on five styles.

What does this mean? If you need to communicate frequently with many different styles, then it helps to modify your style toward the center of the Matrix. The Rule of the Center is simply a formula for being successful in many different settings with many different people.

If you're not already there, the Rule of the Center will seem uncomfortable initially. For example, if you are an Initiator who moves toward Organizer, there will be a period of adjustment. After all, it's contrary to your nature to think things over and ask questions before you speak your mind. But as your symbolic step begins to pay off, your inner discomfort will disappear. Chart 7 presents a set of rules to help you apply the Rule of the Center.

CHART 7: ADHERING TO THE RULE OF THE CENTER

Directors	Expressers
Be more personal and warmer in your delivery.	Be more precise and analytical in your approach to problems.
Ask more questions about other people.	Follow through and complete your projects.
Talk about your feelings	Learn to manage your time by planning daily.
Acknowledge and validate priorities other than your own.	Set your priorities and focus on them.
Show patience.	Avoid wasting time—yours or any-one else's.
Walk in other people's shoes.	Express the dilemas you feel.
Admit your fallibility.	
Express the dilemmas you feel.	

Thinkers	Harmonizers
Focus on the big picture, not just on the details.	Keep work issues separate from personal issues.
Ask only relevant questions.	Remember it's not always important to be liked.
Once a decision is made, put it behind you.	Learn to say "no" and to argue your position.
Focus on deadlines.	Prioritize your tasks.
Expect the unexpected.	Address problems in a "bottom-line" fashion.
Communicate the full scope of the problem, not just one aspect.	Express the dilemmas you feel.
Express the dilemmas you feel.	

Case Study The Transformation of a Dictator

One of the more interesting challenges we faced was working with a manager named Tom. Tom managed a staff of fifteen people at a radio station in New York. His employees resented him. They talked about him behind his back. His boss kept him around only because he had expert knowledge of the industry, and because he feared Tom would jump to the competition if he was fired.

So we were hired to try to rescue Tom.

Our first step, of course, was to interview Tom. Naturally, he viewed himself as a highly effective manager, who knew what he wanted and communicated it well. "That's what I was hired to do, and that's why I have a staff," he said. "They help me execute the goals we have as a company."

Yet as we saw Tom in action, we knew his style was that of a Dictator. And his Profile results confirmed this. He would express immediate and angry disagreement with his colleagues if they dared to suggest an idea different from his own. He wouldn't schedule staff meetings because he felt they were a waste of his time. He even stopped returning calls from the community, deciding that he had better things to do than answer complaints.

We worked for three days with Tom on modifying his style. We role-played. We went to meetings together. We videotaped him. We discussed the Rule of the Center. We agreed to focus on just three relationships to start.

The first was with the chief engineer, a man named Bill. His problem was that he worked very slowly and methodically in comparison to Tom. It was a classic conflict between a Supporter (Bill) and Tom's style.

The second relationship was with his boss, Randy. Randy knew that Tom was deeply insecure. Yet he didn't know how to get Tom to relax with other people and feel more comfortable. "If it weren't for the fact that he's the most talented guy in the business, I'd have fired Tom years ago," Randy said during our interview. "But I can't afford to."

Tom's most problematic relationship was with Sally, the marketing director. Sally was a Diplomat. She resented Tom. He resented her. Whenever he suggested a new program, she'd resist it. Whenever she came up with a new campaign, he refused to run it. The biggest blowup occurred at a meeting with the management team when Tom simply refused to sit through a presentation for a new advertising campaign that Sally had designed. When asked why, he said: "All our marketing is bad. Why should this be any different?" Sally got up and left the room. Later that day, she told Randy she was quitting. But Randy persuaded her to stay, pending the results of our work.

There was no single breakthrough with Tom. We asked him to put into words the dilemmas he felt, so that other people could understand his feelings. We coached him on how to talk to people who disagreed with him with more openness, more curiosity. We taught him that other people had a different lens and saw the same data differently than he did. We made him see that he was not 100 percent right all the time. In fact, we said, other people may have something to say that will actually make your work easier and better, if you'll only draw them out.

After we left, we got weekly reports on Tom's progress from Randy. Tom's relationship with the chief engineer, Bill, slowly improved. Bill saw that Tom was trying to soften his style, to ask more questions, to fire less from the hip. Bill spread the word to the other managers, and they slowly began to see the change in Tom, too. Randy also noticed a change for the better. "He's asking more honest questions," was the way he put it.

Six months later we returned to assist the company with a difficult plan of reorganization. We formed four committees to try to reinvent the various customer service areas. At the end of this monthlong process, Randy invited everyone to an Upper West Side bistro for pizza and beer. Typically, Tom didn't go to these events. But this time he did, and he found himself sitting between Sally and Bill. They started talking about the "new Tom," how he'd made such an impression that they were going to ask him to design the company float in the Macy's Thanksgiving Day parade.

Now, everyone knew this was absurd. Tom wasn't about to accept such an assignment—even if it was for real. But he dove into the banter, and began suggesting a number of parade committees. He appointed Sally head of the "post-parade-punch committee" and Bill head of the "keep-the-float-afloat committee"—all to much hearty laughter. Everyone was listening and smiling and enjoying themselves, thinking about Tom and his committees.

The nature of our work is that we spend an intense period with a client, and then we leave. In this case, Randy invited us back a year later to do additional training of the management team. Tom was still there. Everyone took the Profile again. There were new problems with the team's balance, resulting from a reshuffling of jobs. (Team balance and organizational culture are discussed in detail in Chapter 10.) But one thing was heartening: Tom's Profile now revealed him to be a Persuader. Tom had become quieter and more thoughtful, and his role on the team had changed from outsider to respected leader.

We congratulated Tom on his progress, and sent him a gold sticker in the mail. It read: "Master Communicator."

Conclusion

Modifying your style of communicating will ensure a clearer line of communication between you and another person. Once you know someone's place on the Matrix, a single step can mean the difference between a conversation that falters, and one that exceeds your expectations.

Some people find adopting a different style to be unnatural. And it can be. The trick is to act yourself into a way of believing. By adopting the body language, the style of speaking, and the mannerisms of a particular style, you will find modifying your style less of a stretch than you think.

People who learn how to modify their styles with each other can permanently change their relationship. Often it helps to codify the change with ground rules for each person. Most of the time, these ground rules need not be brought up; but if a touchy subject is on the table, it can benefit both parties to review the ground rules first.

Master communicators can flow easily from one style of communicating to another. Often their natural style lies somewhere in the center of the Matrix. While not everyone needs to be a master communicator, managers and leaders will invariably benefit by learning how to effortlessly shift from one style to the next.

EXERCISE: PLAY THE MATRIX GAME

Using the Matrix below, identify your square and the squares of three important colleagues by writing down their initials. Then play the following modified version of the Matrix Game described earlier in this chapter. Here are the rules:

Limit: for two to four people
Object: to establish a set of ground rules for all players that would create more effective communications

Step 1: Determine whether any one square touches all the initialized squares. If so, mark that square with a check and go to Step 4.

Step 2: Determine whether two squares touch all the initialized squares. If so, mark those two squares with a check and go to Step 4.

Step 3: Determine whether three squares touch all the initialized squares. If so, mark those three squares with a check and go to Step 4.

Step 4: Looking at the checked squares, have each player verbalize how to modify his or her style to improve communications among the players.

Step 5: Translate these behaviors into a set of specific communication ground rules. List these ground rules in the space provided on the following page.

DIRECTORS		EXPRESSERS	
Dictator	Initiator	Charmer	Entertainer
Explorer	Persuader	Diplomat	Socializer
Investigator	Organizer	Counselor	Nurturer
Analyzer	Supporter	Provider	Pleaser
THINKERS		HARMONIZERS	

Example:

Tom, Dick, and Harry are playing the Matrix Game. Tom is an Initiator, Dick is a Socializer, and Harry is a Provider.

Step 3: They check the squares for Persuader, Diplomat, and Counselor.

Step 4: Tom suggests that he needs to ask more questions before he jumps to conclusions. Dick says he needs to be more rigorous about basing his conclusions on facts. And Harry says he needs to be more assertive about his feelings.

Step 5: They agree to the following ground rules:
• Tom will ask more questions and wait until everyone else has spoken
  before stating his conclusions.
• Dick will probe for missing data he can use to support his arguments.
• Harry will be more assertive about what he thinks needs to be done.

The ground rules:

1.
....

2.
....

3.
....

4.
....

Chapter Five
The Tools of Productive Communication

The only wisdom we can hope to acquire is
the wisdom of humility: humility is endless.
—T. S. ELIOT, *Four Quartets* (1935)

I once asked the CEO of a New York bank to describe his communication style.

"When I started out as a manager," he said, "my style was to coach. That was the prevailing philosophy. So I'd tell my staff how to organize their client lists; I'd tell them how to sell our products; I coached them in handling complaints; heck, I'd tell them what to do with their personal lives.

"Then one day my boss invited me into his office. He said: 'You know, you're a very bright guy, but your staff doesn't seem to be responding to your style of management. They seem demoralized.'

"I was shocked. 'I'm trying to be a coach,' I said. 'I'm trying to teach people how to do their jobs.'

"'Yeah, I know,' he said. 'But how long do coaches last? One wrong answer, and you're wrong forever. Imagine instead if you taught them to learn from each other, not just from you. Stop trying to impress them so much. The best you can do is ask good questions. That sets the tone for everyone else.'"

After absorbing his boss's advice, he seized every opportunity to ask questions. If someone asked him what to do, he'd say: "What would you do? What do you need to know to make this decision?" Over time, people noticed the change. They saw that he was more open to other points of view. The quality of communication improved. Decision making grew more decentralized. And the bank's performance improved.

This story illustrates how people—in an attempt to be good managers—can become poor communicators. It illustrates our habit of elevating opinions to the level of expertise, our tendency to make snap judgments, and our instinctive desire to be on top of things. It shows how these habits are ingrained and reinforced by our culture—our desire to be in control, our trust in "expertise," our desire to be perceived as competent. Through our failure to question what we think we know, through our failure to get into the habit of asking good questions, we perpetuate a culture of poor communicators.

Three Tools

This chapter describes three tools that will help you relearn how you communicate. They are (1) the Circle of Assumptions, (2) Inner Scripts and Outer Scripts, and (3) the Chain of Missing Data. These tools will expose you to typical communication pitfalls and will also help you learn how to avoid such traps. In the process, you'll learn how to create a learning organization where competent communication is the norm, not the exception.

But first, a story. A major state university system wanted to start teaching business courses to adults via the Internet, but the culture needed changing. University administrators saw this new venture as a potential source of revenue, but professors viewed it as jeopardizing the quality of instruction, threatening their jobs, and tarnishing the reputation of the university. "What are we going to do, confer MBAs by e-mail?" one faculty member said.

Here was a classic case where the tools of straight talk could help. We were hired to facilitate a series of discussions between administrators and professors. We saw that both sides held a strong set of specific assumptions. We identified those assumptions, and then formed a small task force of influential administrators and faculty members to work through each of them.

Our first step was to lay out in the cold light of day everyone's points of view. We worked through a series of question, like "What are the core skills that business students must learn?" We analyzed what teaching methods were necessary to teach and reinforce each skill. We laid out the standards necessary for the university to uphold. Only after the task force had grappled with each of these issues did we ask whether an Internet-based method of teaching was appropriate.

After about three months of work, the task force felt it understood each issue fully, and understood how both faculty members and administrators could agree. The task force came up with a plan to launch the new service, and, in a series of informal meetings with other teachers and administrators, got them to buy into the plan.

After witnessing how we facilitated this change in culture, a senior vice president of the university said: "We should teach these tools to all our faculty members."

At which point, a member of our task force turned to me and half-jokingly said: "Unfortunately, our faculty might resist being told they don't know how to communicate."

Resistance to Change

Many people, when they're exposed to communication tools, react by saying: "We can't do things that way. It takes too much time." Or they say: "We can't do things that way. No one will go along."

Change is always resisted, of course. The best way to counter that resistance is firsthand evidence. In other words, personal experience. The reality is, someone has to feel what it's like to engage in straight talk. Often it begins with someone attending a seminar. That person may then begin pollinating other parts of the organization. Eventually, a pool of people will emerge as stewards of straight talk. Over time, they'll be instrumental in helping the organization change its way of interacting.

People also react by saying: "I don't have time for all this. The pressures of my job dictate that I make decisions quickly. I can't afford to analyze everything I do."

No one's asking you to. Again, the reality is that some of these tools can be used all the time; but others should be employed more sparingly, when the stakes are high, like at a strategic meeting. This chapter contains the basic tool kit; the examples will illustrate how each tool is best applied.

What exactly is the purpose of these tools? In two words, the goal is *shared understanding*. If you're discussing a business opportunity, these tools will help you get a clear sense of the relevant questions and what to do next. If it's a conversation about a personnel problem, they'll help you reach a consensus about how to address it. Bottom line, these tools can help your organization address tough problems—and in the process, learn how to value learning and change.

The Circle of Assumptions

Consider the following conversation between two people in the sales department of a database software company:

George: We can't afford to waste more time talking about this new sales promotion. Customers are already losing interest. They don't care about the sales promotion. All they want is our product.

Jim: I disagree. If we don't give them some incentive, they'll go with our competitor. Since this is a price-driven business, we have to offer a better incentive. Otherwise, we're going to get nailed on price.

George: All I hear is that customers want our product now. If we can deliver it, that's what they want. The promotion isn't going to be worth the time we spend on it. We'll lose money rolling it out; and we'll lose sales by taking the extra time.

Jim: I think we've got to give them something. Otherwise, we're going to see our market share slowly eroding. I don't think any of us wants that.

This conversation is typical of the way people talk. George and Jim have already reached different conclusions, and they are firing their conclusions back and forth like cannonballs. Each of them is articulate, well-spoken, intelligent. In fact, by most standards, they'd be viewed as good communicators.

But they have fallen into a trap. They aren't challenging their assumptions. As a result, they are poor communicators.

This trap will snare everyone. No one can avoid it. But if we learn to tune in to our assumptions, we can dodge this pitfall more times than not. Especially when the topic is critical to our organization's success, we owe it to the organization—and to ourselves—to engage in straight talk.

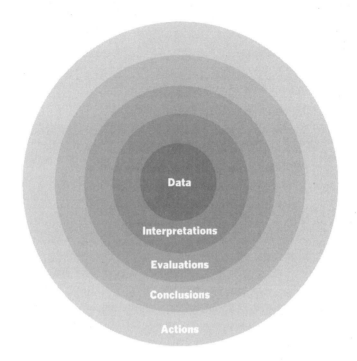

FIGURE 1. THE CIRCLE OF ASSUMPTIONS

People typically communicate on the outer rings of the circle—far from the data.

The Circle of Assumptions shown in Figure 1 is a tool that helps us tune in to our assumptions. By learning how to use this tool, your skill in communicating will increase dramatically.

Data

The Circle of Assumptions works like this: In the center of the circle are facts—hard facts that are accepted by everyone. These could be numerical data: sales figures, profits, customer retention levels. They could be data about events: "Three generators broke down yesterday because of the storm." Or they could be data about people: communication styles, past employment history. For our purposes, data are data as long as they're acknowledged as such by everyone else.

Perhaps there are no data that everyone can agree on. As one colleague maintains, data can support any outcome you choose. Mark

CHART 8: STANDARDS OF ASSESSING INFORMATION

Standard	Pros	Cons
Is it true?	Truth is indisputable.	Truth is elusive; the data collector always influences the data.
Is it reliable?	Standard measures of reliability exist; sampling errors can be minimized.	It's expensive to insist on reliability. Every twofold increase in inaccuracy results in ten times the cost.
Can we act on it?	If smart people agree on the data, then that's good enough. What counts is focus.	People err when their information is incomplete; how much can we afford to err?

Twain may have been hinting at a truth when he said there are three kinds of lies: "Lies, damned lies, and statistics."

People are funny about data, though. If you have a hand in planning how they're collected, you're much more likely to buy into the results. So letting all the relevant players partake in deciding what data are needed, and how they will be collected, helps when it's time to agree on what the data mean.

In the quest for data, people can get tripped up on standards of "truth"—What is it? How is it determined? This is especially true of industry or market research. People will ask: Is the information true? Can we rely on it? Are we able to go forward on the basis of what we've learned?

These questions are at the root of three different standards of assessing information. It helps to decide in advance which standard you'll use. Chart 8 presents a look at the pros and cons of each standard.

Despite the drawbacks, most organizations use the third standard—Can we act on it? It puts the emphasis where it belongs—on the people who are paid to make decisions.

Interpretations

In the next circle are interpretations of data. Interpretations are the first level in which we try to draw relationships between facts. "She didn't come to work today because her husband is very ill." "Complaints are down because we hired two additional inspectors." In these two examples, both sides of the equation are factual. Yes, complaints are down. Yes, we hired two inspectors. If someone challenges our interpretation, we will say that to the best of our knowledge, it is a solid interpretation based on the data.

Relatively speaking—that is, relative to the outer rings of the Circle of Assumptions—interpretations can be broken down into two assumptions: First, that our interpretation is the only valid interpretation of the data. If pressed, we would have to admit that there are other possible interpretations. It is possible, we might concede, that she stayed home because she was sick and tired of her job.

The second assumption is that events are linked in a single causality, that A happens because of B. Yet, increasingly, studies show that there are no simple causal relationships where "A happens because of B." If stated in a way that acknowledges this complexity, we would say: "Her husband is very ill; she didn't come to work today; and it's possible there's a relationship between those two events, but we can't be sure."

Note that we are already at a point on the Circle of Assumptions where your style of communication can influence your assumptions, and the group's assumptions. Directors tend to state their interpretations so forcefully and confidently that the group accepts them unquestioningly. Expressers tend to create "missing" data and argue for interpretations based on what they imagine is true. Thinkers tend to look for more data, and thus may be hesitant to make interpretations. And Harmonizers tend to think that, if they interpret the data differently from everyone else, then something must be wrong with them. So they just keep quiet.

Evaluations

In the third ring from the center are evaluations. These are judgments we make. "Sally is doing a good job attracting younger viewers." Or:

"The Receiving Department is doing a lousy job tracking our supplies." Adjectives like *good, poor, bad, worse, strong, slow, weak,* and so on are tip-offs to an evaluative statement.

Evaluations are based on one's own values. What makes you think it was good? How was it weak? Why was her performance better than her predecessor's? When people make evaluative statements, they should be open to challenging themselves, and challenges from others. If they can show a chain of reasoning that moves the conversation back toward the center of the Circle of Assumptions, that's good and healthy. If they cannot, then that's healthy, too, because people can see that the statement is really just one person's opinion.

In nonproductive discussions, evaluative statements are often used as arguments to support a conclusion. "The reason we don't need a new marketing information system is because *sales is doing a good job.*" "The reason we need another manager in the Receiving Department is because *they're doing a lousy job tracking our supplies.*" In each case, an evaluation, based on assumptions, is used to support a conclusion. This is like building a house on sand.

Often, when people make evaluations, they feel a sense of ownership. Once they pass judgment, their reputation is on the line. So if challenged, people are prone to justify their evaluations with defensive statements like: "It seems obvious to me." Or: "Clearly, this is the way it is."

Note how easily these types of statements shut down a conversation. One of my colleagues calls them "conversational hair balls." It's virtually impossible to respond positively once someone has said: "It's obvious to me." To challenge such a statement is to risk appearing stupid.

In these cases, it's useful to verbalize the dilemma. "My dilemma is, I don't want to appear stupid, but I don't understand your reasoning. Could you explain it to me again?"

Note how carefully the phrasing of that question attacks the issue, not the person. You've asked in very clear terms for a way out of a personal dilemma. If the response is defensive, or if you're attacked, it will be clear and obvious to everyone that a basic ground rule has been broken.

Which communication styles are most likely to use assertive statements to justify their evaluations? Directors and Expressers, of course. Thinkers and Harmonizers are slightly less prone to this particular trap.

Conclusions

The fourth ring in the Circle of Assumptions consists of conclusions. Note how familiar-sounding they are: "Those defective parts should never have gotten into the product line. They're doing a lousy job in the Receiving Department." Or: "Sales is doing all it can. Our new sales manager is really on top of things."

We're exposed to hundreds and thousands of similar conclusions every day. It's the standard currency of communication. Here's my conclusion. Here's yours. Here's another of mine. Oh, another of yours? Thanks!

Life is an endless whirling dance of conclusions.

For social purposes, that may be okay. But for the purpose of having a productive conversation, conclusions should be treated with the same delicacy as a rattlesnake in the refrigerator. Stand clear and seek help.

This is not an argument for eliminating strong advocacy. It's an argument for balancing strong advocacy with strong inquiry. Martin Luther King's "I Have a Dream" speech is entirely based on his conclusions about what the country needed at that time. Yet it was no less valuable because he was far out on the Circle of Assumptions. A meeting to discuss market positioning can be highly productive when several strong points of view emerge. But it will be even more so if everyone acknowledges the assumptions that underlie them.

Actions

In the outermost circle, beyond conclusions, are actions. People communicate all the time at the level of actions. Actions seem like the most natural and fluid things in the world. We are so swept up by action, that we neglect their often tenuous connection to facts. People who take action are seen as competent leaders. We forget that actions are based on conclusions, which are based on evaluations, which are based on interpretations, which are based on data.

"I placed the order today and they'll install it Friday. Everything will be back to normal then."

"In response to the competition lowering their prices, we have no option but to lower ours."

"I want you to fire that guy if it's the last thing you do."

By now, you should have a healthy appreciation of how many assumptions are buried beneath each of these action statements. By making too many assumptions, we trap ourselves into a false way of communicating.

"I placed the order today and they'll install it Friday. Everything will be back to normal then." Listening to this statement, it's very easy to take it at face value. It's communicated in such a way as to inoculate it against challenge. Who in their right mind would question something so obviously beneficial for the company? Yet it's really just an assumption. The speaker certainly hasn't made a convincing case. Perhaps the opposite is true.

The second trap is assuming you can see a situation clearly. The statement, "In response to the competition lowering their prices, we have no option but to lower ours," makes it seem as if all the facts have been examined, and that this is the only tenable course of action. By failing to acknowledge other possible perspectives, the speaker makes it difficult for communication to continue.

The third trap is assuming that you should conceal your selfish motives because they make you look bad. The statement, "I want you to fire that guy if it's the last thing you do," forces people to guess your hidden intentions. Is this a personal grudge? Or do you know something I don't? Unless you reveal all the data, including personal factors that may influence your point of view, it's impossible to have a clear communication about the issue.

Visually, the Circle of Assumptions can help you see how many different conclusions and actions can be drawn from the same set of data. As the diagram in Figure 2 shows, an almost infinite number of actions are possible by interpreting, evaluating, concluding, and acting on the same set of data. This is why a group can become so dysfunctional if it isn't attuned to its assumptions.

Inner Scripts and Outer Scripts

Another tool will help you learn how to make "undiscussable" ideas discussible. Organizations and groups are often plagued by an inability to discuss certain topics. Whether it's the boss's failure to listen, or rampant waste in the production department, all organizations have undiscussables. The question is, How do you get them on the table? And even more basic, Why should you?

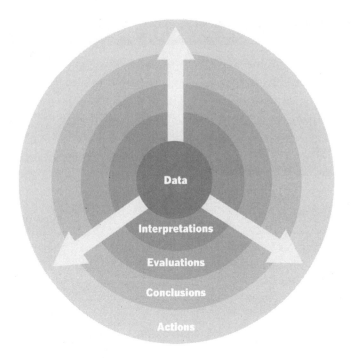

FIGURE 2. THE CIRCLE OF ASSUMPTIONS IN ACTION

The same data can give rise to dramatically different conclusions and actions.

Let's tackle the second question first. Why should a group try to get a taboo topic out in the open? Here's what we've discovered: While people may sincerely fear the repercussions of exposure, the turmoil an organization feels because of a taboo topic prevents the organization from dealing with other issues. People have a way of thinking that works like this: Since we're not tackling this sensitive topic, there's no point in spending any energy on any other issue. Because we're incapable of dealing with the real issues, why should I commit any energy to this charade?

One example always comes to mind. A general manager was known by many of his staff to harbor certain religious prejudices. He promoted people from his own church; people of other faiths got left behind. Of course, it's human nature to suppress such a taboo topic as religious prejudice. So no one in the organization ever asked him if, in fact, he was guided in his promotions by his religious faith.

EXERCISE: DECODE A DIALOGUE

Here's some practice to help you tune yourself to the Circle of Assumptions. The chart below contains the transcript of a dialogue from a meeting of two people, Abby and Bill. Cover up the right-hand side of the box and read each sentence. Then assess whether it is a fact, an interpretation, an evaluation, a conclusion, or an action. If the sentence is a question, decide whether it is a genuine question, or a statement masquerading as a question (and if so, what type of statement it is). After you analyze each sentence, uncover the answer.

Dialogue	Type of Statement
Abby: I wish we could get our customer service agents to pick up the phone after two rings.	Evaluation
We lose customers when they don't.	Conclusion
Bill: You're right.	Evaluation
But we also need a phone system that enables them to see how many callers are waiting.	Interpretation
Then they could make sure everyone got an acceptable level of service.	Conclusion
Abby: That's a good idea.	Evaluation
I've seen those types of systems.	Fact
But they're too expensive for us.	Evaluation
Bill: What do you mean?	Evaluation
Every call we lose means as much as $50 in lost sales. Multiply that times 20 a day, and 300 days a year, and you've got $300,000 in lost sales.	Interpretation / Evaluation
That buys a hell of a phone system.	Conclusion
Abby: You sound like you've already looked into it.	Conclusion
Why don't you bring it up at our next staff meeting?	Conclusion
Bill: I will.	Action
In fact, I'll call and get some quotes before the meeting so we can make a decision.	Action
Abby: Good idea.	Evaluation
It would be good to get someone other than Sally	Evaluation

to join us from Customer Service. I'm sure she'll try to put the kibosh on this idea.	Conclusion
Bill: I'll get back to you with some numbers on lost calls so we can play with a P&L before the meeting. Maybe we can get the boss to okay it right there.	Action Conclusion
Abby: Good idea!	Evaluation

We asked him privately: "Look, there are people who say you promote people based on whether they belong to your church. We're curious to know whether that has happened."

The general manager admitted that he'd made several promotions in the past of people who belonged to his church. "I thought they were the best people, but I can see how that might have gotten misinterpreted."

We advised him to meet with his staff and talk about his criteria for promotion. Be straight and open about it, we told him. Tell people that you can understand their concerns. Ask them what you could do to manage the process better in the future.

He did. And he was partially successful. Several months later, when the next major opening occurred, he again promoted someone from his church. This promotion turned out to be a disaster; the person was clearly unable to handle the job.

Two months later, both the newly promoted manager and the general manager were fired.

In helping people deal with these types of taboo topics, we use a mental model called Inner Script/Outer Script. Consider the following conversation, where Sally, an information systems engineer, is trying to talk to her boss about a project. This is the Outer Script.

Sally: I'm looking for feedback about how to ensure that this new system gets implemented effectively.

Joe: I'd suggest you look for clues about how involved people are: Are they feeling personally responsible to learn the system, or do they see it as an assignment for someone else to train them?

Sally: It isn't clear from the contract what the contractor has to do in the way of on-site training. I sent you a note about that.

Joe: How about talking to the contractor and asking directly what they are responsible for.

Sally: I'll give them a call if you like. But am I the right person to do it?

Joe: Yes, you're the right person to do it. Let me know if I can help you with anything.

The Inner Script/Outer Script model hinges on the idea that we keep sensitive thoughts and feelings to ourselves because we're afraid of the repercussions if we express them. Yet by failing to express them, we block communication because these sensitive thoughts and feelings usually lie at the heart of the problem.

So we ask people to express their Inner Scripts. Often this is best handled during a conversation: "What's your Inner Script right now?" someone will ask, thereby triggering a much-needed conversation. In essence, this tool enables people to express what is uncomfortable by acknowledging their Inner Scripts as a key element in productive communication.

Another technique is to diagram a conversation, showing your Inner and Outer Scripts. One organizational development firm calls it "left column" and "right column" thinking. The left column contains the things you think to yourself, but don't dare utter aloud. When we asked Sally to diagram this conversation showing her Inner Script, an entirely different conversation emerged. What she wrote down is presented in Chart 9.

As you can see, Sally's Inner Script contains a lot of taboo topics that need to be resolved. She's angry at her boss for writing a bad contract; she's angry at him for making her responsible; she's angry at him for not seeing that he needs to give her more support. This anger needs to be brought into the open. But how can she do this in a way that doesn't poison the relationship?

Here's the way out: Before she raises the issue, Sally needs to examine how she sees her boss. By going through this analysis, she may be able to identify certain assumptions she's making—assumptions that could be wrong.

CHART 9: DIAGRAMMING A CONVERSATION

Sally's Inner Script	Sally's Outer Script
So much pressure to get this on-line. Joe asked me to talk about it, but I wonder if he has anything to say that can really help me?	**Sally:** I'm looking for feedback about how to ensure that this new system gets implemented effectively.
Already now we're off on a tangent about their level of involvement. They've been very involved. Why is he assuming they're not?	**Joe:** I'd suggest you look for clues about how involved people are: Are they feeling personally responsible to learn the system, or do they see it as an assignment for someone else to train them?
I didn't write the contract, you did. And it's very poorly done. You didn't get a clear commitment about on-site training.	**Sally:** It isn't clear from the contract what the contractor has to do in the way of on-site training. I sent you a note about that.
How did this monkey get on my back? You screwed up initially, so why shouldn't it be your responsibility?	**Joe:** How about talking to the contractor and asking directly what they are responsible for.
Maybe he'll accept his role in it if I pose a question to him.	**Sally:** I'll give them a call if you like. But am I the right person to do it?
I just did let you know, and you didn't help me. This is typical of our relationship. You really aren't much use to me.	**Joe:** Yes, you're the right person to do it. Let me know if I can help you with anything.

How Sally sees Joe:

1. Joe is responsible for signing a bad contract.
2. Joe is not accepting his role.
3. Joe is not helping me in this situation.
4. Joe doesn't look after my interests in general.

CHART 10: REFRAMING ASSUMPTIONS

Assumptions	Possible Reframes
1. Joe is responsible for signing a bad contract.	He had good reasons for signing the contract that I'm not aware of. He did the best possible job under the circumstances.
2. Joe is not accepting his role.	He has thought about his role and he wants to give me as much leeway as possible so he's not perceived as micromanaging.
3. Joe is not helping me in this situation.	I haven't communicated clearly what I would like him to do to help me.
4. Joe doesn't look after my interests in general.	He's doing the best possible job he can and looks after my interests as much as he can.

These four statements frame Sally's view of the situation. If you apply the Circle of Assumptions and analyze these statements, you can see that they are far out on the circle. All four statements are conclusions.

Given what we know about the Circle of Assumptions, Sally needs to examine whether there are other equally valid interpretations. So we asked her to imagine other possible interpretations. This exercise may help her change the way she sees the situation. It's helpful to write the assumptions on a piece of paper and then list the possible "reframes," as shown in Chart 10.

The process of diagnosing one's undiscussables can be quite eye-opening. We build layer upon layer of assumptions about other people. Unless they're brought out into the open and examined, these assumptions can taint a relationship, triggering a downward spiral in the quality of conversation. In this case, Sally wanted help from Joe, but she may have prevented that from happening by assuming he didn't want to help. In other words, she placed herself in a Catch-22 that prevented her from getting what she wanted.

In most cases, we don't have time to work through our undiscussables and reframe our assumptions. But if you repeatedly feel inhibited in speaking openly, check your assumptions and figure out what's going on. Particularly with people important to your life and career, it's a good idea to check from time to time whether you're responsible for making your communication unproductive.

Here's another illustration of the importance of checking how you frame another person's intentions. I was asked to help one of our clients put together a project team to lead the company's foray into Internet commerce. There were six nominees for three places on the team. Two managers of the company and I were to judge these six candidates, none of whom was present during our discussions.

Of the six nominees, we rejected three unanimously. Two others were voted in unanimously. That left one more slot, and one more candidate. When the sixth nominee's name came up, two of us voted in favor and one was opposed. The final place had been filled—or so I thought. I turned to the other two panel members and said: "We appear to be finished. Before we move on, however, are there any undiscussables?"

An interesting thing occurred. The one person who had voted no said she had an undiscussable. "No one else in this room knows this man as well as I do," she said, "because I used to work for him. Let me say that I know things about Sam that I can never tell you about. If we are at all concerned about how this group is perceived by others, or about its ethical integrity, then we should not choose him."

This was a powerful speech, and we listened intently. We asked if it was possible she was making assumptions about him that should be examined before the group acted.

"It's fair to say that his past conduct has influenced the way I view him."

Was there sufficient evidence at the time to verify that his conduct was unethical?

She hesitated. "I don't think I should cite the specific cases. But I know of three separate instances in which he violated financial regulations."

This was enough data. The panel took another vote. The decision was reversed and another person was chosen.

This illustration shows why people need to be given permission to discuss their undiscussables. Otherwise, they may disguise or omit sensitive pieces of information. Giving people a mental model of how they frame taboo topics will help them exercise this right. By inviting undiscussables into the room on a periodic basis, there's a greater chance people will think about the things they keep private, and ask themselves whether they're inhibiting a productive conversation.

The Chain of Missing Data

The goal of straight talk is to reach agreements. Once your assumptions have been tested, once you've reframed how you view the situation, you can begin reaching agreements. This is where the Chain of Missing Data comes in. Imagine that you are trying to find some way to get a group of people to agree. Well, if nothing else, you can agree on what you don't know, but would like to know, in order to resolve the issue. Sure, the information may not be easily attainable, but if you can at least agree on the missing data, you will have started to forge a consensus.

For example, if your group is trying to decide whether to close a factory, you may be making financial assumptions about the impact of the closure on the company's financial performance. The plant manager may argue strongly that the group's projections underestimate future production capacity. Because of his production experience, people are reluctant to argue with him. So what data can you agree is missing? What if you had hard numbers on the costs and benefits of adding capacity somewhere else? What if the group did some scenario planning with projections of sales by specific product line? If you can all agree on the data you need in order to make a decision, then you've reached a point where the discussion should stop, and the information should be gathered.

You may find, of course, that the plant manager was right. In which case, you all will have benefited. Or you may find that you are faced with a dilemma. As the group digs down for the data it wants, it will ultimately be faced with a choice: Either agree that you have the data you need, or agree that the data are prohibitively expensive or time-consuming to collect. In the latter case, you may want to make some assumptions to unblock the path. Conscious assumptions, made with the agreement of the group, are far different from assumptions made unawares. Once a conscious assumption has been made, you can always retrace your steps after you see where the assumption leads.

Once you get the data—or agree to a set of assumptions— the process starts again. Define the focus of the discussion, clarify assumptions, inquire into missing data, push toward the center of the Circle of Assumptions, and agree on the data you need. The process can be pictured as an upward spiral. You use these tools to reach many agreements, and those agreements, over time, forge a lasting consensus.

If all of this sounds like hard work, it is. But the results are far more rewarding than what could be obtained without following this approach. Using this process, everyone is party to the conclusions reached. The organization will be stronger for it.

Case Study The Nonprofit's Conundrum

One of our clients is a nonprofit organization founded to help women make successful transitions in their careers. At its core was a self-evaluation tool to help people discover their appropriate career path. Unfortunately, the organization didn't apply the same standard of self-evaluation to its own strategic plan.

When it was founded, the organization was committed to helping women exclusively. Over time, however, its doors had been opened to men, who also found the programs very useful. The staff capitalized on this fact to win lucrative outplacement contracts with various corporations. Management was clear on the present-day mission: to serve both men and women with high-quality career transition resources. The board of directors, however, which consisted entirely of women, was divided: Some agreed with management; others saw the organization's mission as serving women only.

We facilitated an off-site retreat of the board of directors and top management. They readily defined the problem. As one board member said: "We've got an outdated mission statement that doesn't reflect the real mission of the organization or what we're doing today."

The board chair had warned that this was a divisive issue. Stay clear of it, she said. But we knew the organization needed to confront this problem, so we started a productive conversation. Or tried to.

We drew up a list of the assumptions people had. Here are some of them:

- Women's career transition needs are different from men's.

- The organization couldn't compete with firms that served men and women; its success lay in specializing in women.

- Women executives who supported the organization with their time, their counseling, and their cash donations wouldn't support the organization if it changed its mission.

- The special feeling of the organization would be lost if it opened its doors to men.

Each assumption was discussed. Data was presented showing that the organization's products and services were valued by men, and that the organization would benefit financially by eliminating the gender distinction. The data supported the new definition of the mission. Still, a small faction of the board wouldn't budge.

Two hours remained in the day. It seemed like the time was ripe for a breakthrough. So we asked the group to split into two camps, one that supported the new mission, and one that supported the old mission. We asked each group to list the logical reasons supporting its case and appoint a spokesperson. Then each side would present its arguments and try to sway the other.

The smaller group spoke first.

"We think women are different from men," they argued. "Women are intimidated by the old-boys network and they need their own network. We should be providing that."

The other side got up. "Serving the special needs of women in no way precludes serving the needs of men, too," they began. " We already have programs tailored to meet both needs, and they are working. We will lose major outplacement contracts to our competitors if we reverse our course. What value is there in clinging to our past when our future is already here, we're already doing it, and it's working?"

The first group rejoined. "No one who founded this organization would condone the mission this group proposes. No one supports this organization more than the women we serve. If we give up on them, this organization will be just another agency, lost in the shuffle, with no special character or identity."

The larger group spoke again. "We're in favor of keeping our identity of a caring, nurturing agency," they said, "bringing those values that women share to address a larger social problem: Both men and women are lost in their careers and need a place to turn for help. We can serve both genders in a distinctive way by capitalizing on the special caring character of our organization."

CHART 11: EVALUATING YOUR COMMUNICATION SKILLS

Tool	Yes	No
Do you know your communication style?	_____	_____
Do you know how to interpret other people's styles?	_____	_____
Do you know how to agree on the meaning of key words?	_____	_____
Do you understand how to inquire into your reasoning, and the reasoning of others?	_____	_____
Do you understand the Circle of Assumptions?	_____	_____
Do you understand how to identify missing data?	_____	_____
Do you understand how to analyze your Inner Script?	_____	_____

This back-and-forth lasted about thirty minutes. The competing logics were clear. But no one was shifting. The room was dead-locked. And we were running out of time.

It's clear, we said, that this is the central issue facing the organization. Both sides have argued well and persuasively. Let's take a break and, when we return, invite inquiry into both perspectives. Perhaps that process will shed additional light here.

Ultimately, it did not. The board remained divided. Operationally, the organization continued to open its doors equally to women *and* men, while at the same time the board retained a mission statement that called on the organization to serve the needs of women only.

When traditions are powerful, it takes more than logic to shake them loose—even in the face of overwhelming data. In hindsight, I wish I had had the time to ask each side one more question. It might not have changed things overnight. But it would have helped them reach consensus.

This is the question: "What data would you need to shift your position to the other point of view? What evidence would help you change your mind?"

I would have divided the board into groups of four and asked each group to discuss this question. The resulting discussion could have pushed the debate to its logical conclusion. By focusing on the missing data, the board could have reached agreement on what would be necessary to resolve this issue.

Conclusion

Part I of this book describes all the tools you'll need for straight talk. Chart II presents a quick summary. Check off each tool that you understand and can apply. Where you're unclear, go back and read that section again. You'll be using all these skills in Part 2, where we learn how to apply them to real situations. Suffice it to say that if you can answer yes to all the questions in Chart II, then you're already becoming a master communicator.

EXERCISE: PUT YOUR THOUGHTS INTO ACTION

Recall a difficult conversation you've had with a colleague, team member, or boss. Write the conversation down verbatim, or reconstruct it as best you can. Then follow these steps:

1. Using the Inner Script/Outer Script model, write down what you were feeling or thinking to yourself during the conversation.
2. Analyze the assumptions embedded in how you framed the other person. What motives did you impute?
3. Write down other possible frames of the situation. What different motives might explain the other person's behavior?
4. Write down what you'd like to say to this person, now that you've gone through this exercise. Try to express yourself as clearly as possible. Describe your assumptions. Then describe how you are willing to interpret the situation. Pose the questions you'd like answered.
5. Ask yourself what's preventing you from having this conversation.

Notes:

Part Two

Using Straight Talk to Work, Manage, and Lead

What one knows is, in youth, of little moment;
they know enough who know how to learn.
—HENRY ADAMS (1838–1918)

With all the talk about the global economy becoming one in which knowledge replaces capital and raw materials as the primary source of value, it's clear that tools that create knowledge are going to become very valuable. Silicon Valley and Wall Street are responding to this need by developing and investing in search engines that can connect people to the information they desire.

But lost in this quest for new software tools is the fact that people still need to turn off their computers and decide what to do with the knowledge and information once it's retrieved. An Internet browser may be able to reach out and snag a key piece of market data across cyberspace, but it's unlikely that a good browser program will ever become intelligent enough to make choices about how that information should be applied across a particular organization.

It may sound like heresy to some, but software and computers aren't the real source of value in the information age (except to computer and software makers). People are. That is, people who know how to communicate effectively about all this information—and transform it into real knowledge for their companies.

Going from company to company, we see glimmers of recognition of this fact. People decry the lack of tools to help them talk about information more effectively. They wish they had even the most basic tools to help them sort out what they know from what they don't know, and to build a set of shared insights into what's going on in their industries.

One of the most basic communication tools is language itself, and unfortunately English is woefully deficient when it comes to talking about communication. We have one word, *communication,* to describe several different things—a word that in Latin literally means "to make common knowledge."

Compare the words *engine* and *motion. Engine* describes a mechanism; *motion* describes a physical phenomenon. Engines result in motion. But engines are not motion. The words enable us to see the difference. If the two different words didn't exist, we might be confused.

We don't have words to distinguish between the *process* of communicating, and the *content* of what is communicated. To the untrained eye (or ear), they are one and the same. This book is a perfect example. It is a communication about communication. This lack of basic vocabulary impairs our ability to talk about how we communicate—or improve it. We talk about good communication and bad communication, but we have difficulty defining where the fault lies. Is it the content of what we say, or the process by which we say it? Our wimpy vocabulary is partly to blame.

For the sake of clarity, let's invent a new word. Let's agree that things that are said are *communits*—a blend of *communication* and *unit.* And agree that the process itself is *communication.*

For each communit, there's another layer of detail, stemming from the Circle of Assumptions. Is it data? An interpretation? An evaluation? A conclusion? These words can help us further understand how we communicate—and where we need help.

Let's see how this would work in real life.

A buyer at Starbucks Coffee says to four of his colleagues: "Don't be surprised if we get hit with a price increase from our suppliers. The crop is going to be poor this year."

First, we have the statement itself. It's a communit, an evaluation.

Those five people begin to discuss the range of possible company responses. That discussion is a communication. They decide to wait and watch the markets.

Elsewhere in the organization, the marketing director has gathered her staff into her office to talk about "the need to position Starbucks' prices as competitive." Her statement is a communit, a conclusion. The discussion that ensues is a communication. She decides to initiate a marketing campaign (a communication composed of communits) oriented to pricing and sends a memo to her staff. That memo is a communit, an action.

These two dialogues (communications) take place in separate places. A couple of days later, in a chance meeting (communication) in the hallway, one of the buyer's assistants mentions rumors of a possible price increase to the COO's assistant, who tells it to her boss. Both of these are communits (interpretations). The COO calls the marketing director (a communication).

"What's going on?" he says (a communit). "Aren't you working on a campaign on our competitiveness? Have you heard about possible price increases?"

The marketing director says: "Where did you hear that?"

The COO tells her.

"Damn," she responds. "This is a perfect example of how bad the communication is in this company." Her statement is a communit (a conclusion) about communication.

That afternoon, the buyer, the marketing director, and the COO meet to talk (a communication) about what went wrong with their communication. Angry words are exchanged. "Why wasn't I informed earlier?" the marketing director exclaims. "This is an example of really bad communication."

The buyer agrees. "I should have communicated to you. I'm sorry."

The COO says: "Look, the important point is this: We need to work on our communication. Will you both promise to do that?"

They nod. "Okay," says the COO. "Let's get to work on a new marketing campaign" (a communit about communicating to the market).

Case closed. No wonder there's so much confusion about communication.

In Part 2 you will learn how to apply straight talk to situations like this one. You'll learn how to separate the process of communicating from the content. You'll learn how straight talk can help you manage time, improve meetings, and solve tough business problems—even improve your organization's culture.

As you develop your understanding of these tools, remember to keep an open mind. By their very nature, they'll seem strange at first. Like learning to ride a bike, there's a leap of faith you'll have to make. It's counterintuitive to go faster to avoid falling. In the same way, it's counterintuitive, but no less true, that to learn these tools, you'll have to apply them in your daily life.

Chapter Six
Implications for Day-to-Day Business

*He got the better of himself, and
that's the best victory one can wish for.*
—MIGUEL DE CERVANTES, *Don Quixote* (1615)

A friend of mine insists on always being early to the airport. But he's invariably late to meetings—even those in his own office. The explanation? He's a Charmer. His attention gets easily distracted—by a drop-in visitor, an impromptu hallway discussion, or a phone call. People view him as having a double standard: one standard for him; a second for everybody else.

My college roommate was always trying to figure out how to sneak into his girlfriend's room after hours. He would draw elaborate diagrams. He would lay out plans to distract the security guards. Then, to his surprise, she dumped him. She said he wasn't paying enough attention to her. The explanation? He was an Explorer. He was so busy figuring out what ruse to use that he forgot the bigger picture.

A woman friend, the executive of an employment agency, always arrives at her office at 7:30 A.M. You can set your watch by when she clicks on her computer. But she has a hard time keeping projects on schedule. The explanation? She's a Provider. She's not comfortable confronting other people about deadlines. She holds herself to different—and higher—standards than her employees.

Everything you do, from managing your time to making a sales pitch, can be improved by using the information you've learned so far. Let's start with time management.

Time Management

Each style has a different way of viewing time. Simply by appreciating these differences, and being aware of them, you can manage time more effectively.

The Director sees time as a rare commodity, always in short supply. "There's no time" is one of the Director's favorite phrases. As a result, he has to do everything *now*.

The Director sees his time as more valuable than other people's. Directors run red lights, they cut into checkout lines, they complain about waiting in phone queues. A Director will tap his feet with impatience if you pause to sniff a spectacular rose. If you ask him, the Director will say he is a master of his time. But he is really its slave.

Harmonizers, on the other hand, can be blissfully unaware of time. Doing nothing is okay with them. They don't look at their watches before contemplating a rose, or a baby's smile. They do it naturally. Being limited by time is an affront to their sense of well-being. They focus on whatever it is that interests them, and time fades into the background. They are, indeed, masters of their time.

Daydreaming is one way we sever our connection to time, and Harmonizers like to daydream. It allows them to reflect on things at their own pace (even while those around them are losing sleep over tight project deadlines). Psychologists point out that daydreaming allows us to access our deeper feelings and intuitions. This may be one reason Harmonizers are easily able to empathize with other people.

Thinkers occupy a middle ground. They are cognizant of time, but they are not burdened by it as much as Directors. Doing the right thing is more important to the Thinker than doing it right now. Deadlines are important. But not supremely so. Thinkers can spend hours tinkering with a marketing report—just to make it perfect. Thinkers track time, but time is not their lord.

Expressers view time in two very different ways. While talking, they'll be oblivious to the clock. "Where did our time go!" the Expresser will say after talking extemporaneously for fifteen minutes. But when listening, the Expresser may grow impatient. He'll suddenly shift gears and say: "Hey, we better get to work on this," even if other people haven't had a chance to say what's on their minds. This double standard

CHART 12: USING THE MATRIX TO MANAGE TIME

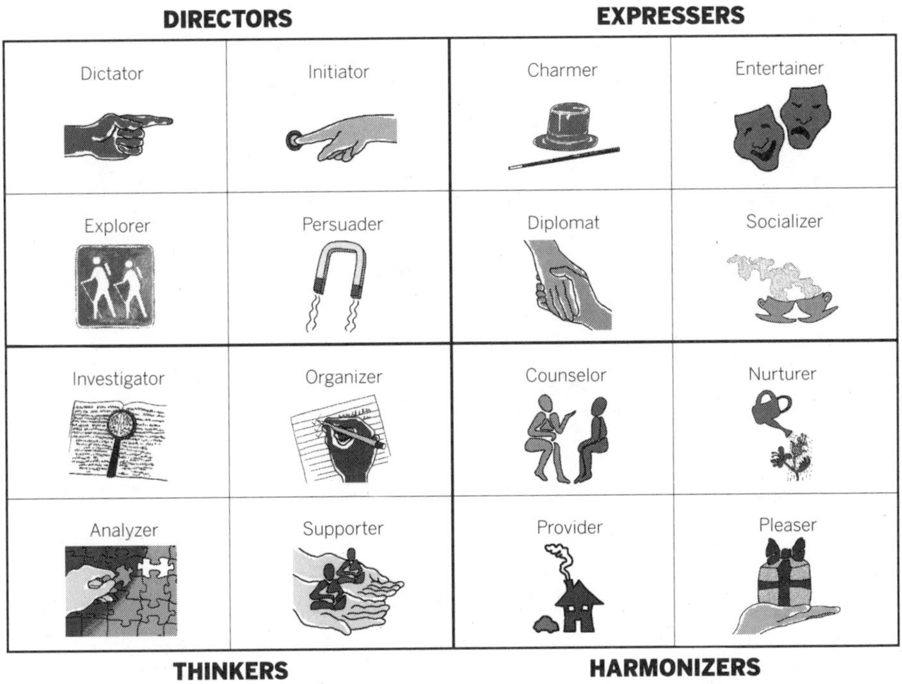

DIRECTORS		EXPRESSERS	
Dictator	Initiator	Charmer	Entertainer
Explorer	Persuader	Diplomat	Socializer
Investigator	Organizer	Counselor	Nurturer
Analyzer	Supporter	Provider	Pleaser
THINKERS		HARMONIZERS	

Styles at the top of the Matrix typically budget less time than required.

is a trademark of Expressers: When talking, they're unaware of the time; when someone else is speaking, they're stealing glances at the clock.

How each communication style manages time affects how people work in groups. By refusing to delegate authority, the Director forces endless details to be brought before her for review. By not planning or executing carefully, the Expresser sets the stage for chaos later on. By adhering rigorously to his process, the Thinker renders it impossible to meet deadlines. And by being unaware of time, the Harmonizer winds up feeling rushed and overwhelmed.

The Matrix, shown again in Chart 12, is a tip-off to how you manage time. Those styles in the center of the Matrix are more apt to balance "planning time" with "doing time." The Diplomat, for example, is likely to conceive a plan and analyze its implications before proceeding. The Initiator, on the other hand, is likely to plunge right in. She'll launch a project with a burst of energy, become frustrated as roadblocks arise, then stop and start again. Even after she takes a few lumps, don't expect the Initiator to change until someone confronts her about her style and helps her understand its shortcomings.

Planning

The different styles also have different ways of planning. Directors like to consider the big picture and overall strategy. They're at their best when distilling a complex situation into a few key goals. But they don't like to be bothered with details—so their plans are often short on actual implementation steps.

Ironically, the Director can get mired down in details. This happens when the Director sees results shaping up differently than she expected. "Am I the only person who's competent around here?" she'll say as she announces that she wants to review each and every decision. Because the Director didn't take the time to plan thoroughly in the first place, management mayhem ensues.

The Expresser has a strong inclination toward strategic planning. He likes to imagine possible scenarios and come up with creative solutions. He would prefer not to analyze the consequences, however. So instead of getting down to actual analysis, he'll leapfrog from idea to idea, from objectives to strategy and back again, hoping to latch onto an idea that meets everyone's needs and thereby excite them into action. If none of his ideas catches fire, he may become frustrated and tune out of the meeting.

The Thinker plans to the last detail, and she makes few errors. But the Thinker's bête noire is believing that she can guarantee success by the process of planning. She overlooks the need to engage in the kind of creative strategic thinking that allows her to identify the best alternative. She may tend to start a project by looking at the logistics and timetable, rather than by gathering a group together to brainstorm.

The Harmonizer will take as little or as much time to plan as he thinks necessary to please everyone around him. Since he wants to please, it's possible for inconsistent or contradictory goals to get incorporated into his plans. Sometimes, these contradictions don't emerge until much later. When they do come to light, the Harmonizer will be genuinely shocked, and either look for help or give up in frustration. All because he allowed himself to get caught between wanting to plan and wanting to please.

Creativity

No one communication style is more creative than another. Each style is creative in its own way. Yet each style can learn a lesson from the others, and in so doing, marshal even greater creative energy.

The Director, for example, creates by doing, by the sheer act of willing something into being. There's no detailed blueprint on paper; sheer willpower makes it happen. But the Director can forget to reflect while he's creating, so his work may be inconsistent or even superficial.

The Expresser is more keenly aware of his feelings than the Director, But the Expresser expends energy talking instead of doing—and so she may not spend enough on actual execution. Critics may say the Expresser needs more perspiration—and a little less inspiration.

Truly creative projects can provoke anxiety for Thinkers and Harmonizers because originality implies conflict with what has gone before. So the Thinker's creative energies tend to be focused on repeating what has already occurred, perhaps in new shapes or patterns. The Thinker likes to engage in precise, detailed work, so his creativity may get channeled into highly intricate art forms.

The Harmonizer prefers to work with people, and so her most creative acts may be collaborative. Putting her on a team is the best way to ensure that her creative energies will emerge. In the arts, Harmonizers gravitate toward those where tradition counts, like ballet or classical music. This sense of tradition is very important to the Harmonizer.

In contrast, the Director and Expresser prefer more risky, avantgarde endeavors. In their minds, tradition is imprisonment. The Thinker falls somewhere in between: Whether following tradition or breaking the mold, he'll be inspired so long as he understands exactly where he's going and why.

Decision Making

Decision making is an art unto itself. Too often we make business decisions—or personal decisions, for that matter—while ignoring how a good decision is made. Complex problem solving is discussed in Chapter II and requires more steps than are outlined here. Basic decision making, however, involves six steps:

Step 1: Develop broad criteria, such as goals and values.
Step 2: Generate possible alternatives.
Step 3: Evaluate three to four best options on the basis of your criteria.
Step 4: Make a choice.
Step 5: Communicate the decision.
Step 6: Implement.

The most common mistakes occur in Steps 1 and 2.

Mistake number one: People spend too little time determining their goals and priorities. Typically, they allow other steps to take place prior to this one. Because they fail to determine their priorities—and fail to communicate these priorities to others—they find themselves trapped by their decisions. Compromise becomes very difficult.

Mistake number two: Once they've determined their goals, people fail to spend enough time generating alternatives. Narrowing the number of options too soon forces people into decisions they later regret.

Within this context, each style has its own manner of making decisions. The Director makes decisions boldly, based on the big picture (but without generating enough options); the Expresser makes decisions based on feeling and intuition (but without sufficient criteria); the Thinker makes decisions cautiously and logically (with a reluctance to come to closure); and the Harmonizer makes decisions that try to please everyone (with an absence of self-based criteria and closure).

Again, the Matrix holds the key in compensating for the weakness of each style. Directors are good at generating bold alternatives. But they need to practice (1) generating more alternatives; (2) evaluating the effects on people more carefully; (3) discussing the alternatives with other people before making the decision; and (4) delegating responsibility and authority in follow-through.

Expressers are capable of imaginatively generating lots of options, and like Directors, they're willing to make tough calls. But they need to practice (1) accepting the need to narrow their goals and values—they can't have it all; (2) giving up the most improbable options so they can focus on reasonable alternatives; (3) bringing a more analytical approach to weighing each alternative; and (4) committing themselves once the decision is made.

Thinkers excel at working through the process of making a decision, especially at examining alternatives. And they are good at execution once the decision is made. But they need to practice (1) setting criteria, particularly when those criteria involve personal values and goals; and (2) coming to closure. Thinkers also need to guard against overcaution when generating alternatives. The best alternatives sometimes lie "outside the box."

Harmonizers are highly considerate of people's feelings and work well in making joint decisions. However, they need to remember that all decisions carry trade-offs and that, to paraphrase Mark Twain, you can't please all the people all the time. Harmonizers needs to practice (1) setting criteria that include personal values and goals; (2) generating alternatives "outside the box"; and (3) coming to closure. Particularly if Harmonizers can brainstorm innovative possibilities, they are assured of becoming better decision makers.

Making Presentations

When making a presentation to a group, it's extremely important to be conscious of your own communication style—and the styles that prevail in the room. This requires analyzing your audience, a job best done ahead of time by talking to someone who knows the audience well. If necessary, you can make a snap analysis by figuring out the style of the key player in the room. Ask a few questions, assess his or her responses, and tailor your presentation accordingly.

If you're aiming your presentation at a Director, show a sense of conviction and single-mindedness of purpose. Remember, Directors go on a "gut" sense; they won't spend a lot of time analyzing your facts and figures. Short and to the point will make a Director feel very comfortable; a detailed discussion about the pros and cons will cause her to lose patience.

When trying to sell something to a Director, remember to focus on two or three important figures and facts, not a dozen. Decipher the underlying trends and make them the centerpiece of your plan. And don't rely on a written leave-behind to sway her; the Director won't take the time to read it!

Directors will respond negatively if you challenge their ability to make a decision. They want plenty of room to make their own decisions. A savvy salesperson will speak up forcefully to a Director, and then leave her alone for a while to make up her mind. Be ready to close the deal on the spot. But if you use a "forced consent close," such as "When would you like to take delivery?" be prepared for a negative reaction. Directors like to be pushed—but not too hard.

Making a presentation to an Expresser is a good excuse for some fun and surprises. Surreptitiously get his picture and use it in your presentation. For example, show him walking along the beach wearing a bathing suit with your logo on it. Paint a visual picture of innovation, of creative energy; put on the most compelling, exciting show you can. The more special effects you add, the more it will trigger a favorable response. Emphasize positive images of people and personal benefits: "Think of how great you'll feel when you drive this car!" A "forced consent choice" close can be an effective technique for an Expresser: "Which would you like to take home today: the dalmatian or the poodle?"

When making a presentation to a Thinker, you should strive to be patient and show the logic behind your conclusions. Don't take short-cuts. Supply the necessary facts and figures to build your case, along with supporting material. "Forty percent of your existing customers have indicated they want this service delivered to their homes each month. If you get 3,000 households at $25 a piece, that translates into nearly $1 million in new sales annually."

When making a presentation to a Thinker, curb your desire to add humor or cute visual gags. Instead, focus on the facts. Prepare yourself to handle any question. Remember, the Thinker sees it as his or her job to pick apart everything and find the flaw. So prepare yourself by considering every conceivable question she could ask. Be sure to leave behind a written summary for her to digest that night. The best way to finalize a sale with a Thinker is by using a question: "Do you have any further questions before we sign the papers?"

When making a presentation to a Harmonizer, emphasize the role of other people—and downplay your own. If you're presenting a project, include the names of everyone who participated. If you're selling, describe the benefits to each person who will be affected. This may require more work on your part, but it's the best way to evoke a positive response. Particularly if you have a more assertive style, go out of your way to show humility and respect. You can turn a sales presentation around by doing some homework and featuring the Harmonizer's people in the show. Showing how a specific product or service will result in "greater harmony" or "stronger relationships" will make a favorable impression on the Harmonizer, too. The most effective close for a Harmonizer is one that doesn't threaten: "I'll give you as much time as you like to make your decision. When should I get back to you?"

Motivating Different Styles

Studies show that people are motivated by many different things. Money ranks in the middle of the list. Rewards of an intangible nature—such as being recognized by the group as a valuable contributor—are usually ranked highest. Awareness of what motivates people, together with the knowledge of how to be an effective communicator, can help you motivate different styles.

For example, when motivating Directors, remember to use an action-oriented approach. Tell them you value them because they make things happen, because they get results. Ask them if they're willing to take on more responsibility. Directors love that word. Tell them the goal and that you want them to figure out how to attain it. Remind them that other people are involved, and that success will depend on how well they involve others. Tell them they'll be rewarded for achieving results.

When motivating Expressers, use an idea-oriented approach. Talk about how the project requires innovative thinking. Tell them how you appreciate their ideas—and that the project will succeed only if infused with fresh thinking. Remind them that you want a clear plan. Reiterate how important they are to this project. (Expressers can handle a little flattery.) Offer financial rewards, but remember that Expressers are motivated by feeling valued as creative, innovative people, not by money.

When motivating Thinkers, focus on their ability to get things done precisely and with attention to detail. Thinkers are motivated by believing they will have time to design a clear, detailed plan; they believe success is achievable if they execute the plan perfectly. Motivate them by talking about the importance of attention to detail. Tell them that what matters isn't that it get done right away, but that it get done right. You can motivate Thinkers by saying the group depends on them designing a clear plan or process. Remind them to check in with you regularly to touch base on their progress. (Unlike Expressers and Directors, Thinkers appreciate having someone looking over their shoulders.)

When motivating Harmonizers, use a friendly, soft-spoken approach. Don't get animated or loud. Establish a comfort zone with small talk before you get down to business. Appeal to their concern and dedication to people. Talk about the importance of the project to the team or company. Let them know they have the full support of other people for this project. Let them know you value their contribution. But don't overdo it. Set the reward system so that everyone on the team gets rewarded if they succeed, not just one or two people. Remind Harmonizers to let you know sooner rather than later if they're getting overwhelmed. (Remember, Harmonizers tend to put off dealing with negative news as long as possible.)

Once the job is done, each style likes to receive praise in different ways. Directors like to be told: "These are just the results we were looking for." Expressers like to hear: "It wouldn't have been the same without your creative input." Thinkers want to hear: "By taking the time to do it right, you really made a big contribution." Harmonizers like to be told: "You've made a terrific contribution to the team."

Negotiating Agreements

Another task people have to perform is negotiating agreements. The negotiation may be informal, like agreeing to the responsibilities in a project, or formal, such as negotiating the terms in a labor contract. Regardless of the degree of formality, each person will have his or her own negotiating style, based on his or her communication style.

Directors view negotiations as a way to achieve specific results. They excel at laying out their position clearly—and at sizing up the other parties' positions. But tough negotiations require patience, analysis, and straight talk; a Director's impatience can undermine that.

If you're negotiating with a Director, remember that he needs to be assured the process is valuable and worth his time—and that he'll get sufficient credit once the deal is done. If you state clearly that you want him to emerge a winner, the Director will stay interested. Directors are pragmatic people, however, and if things aren't going their way during the negotiations, don't be surprised if they walk away. Directors like to employ the "Best Deal First" negotiating strategy. The strategy is: "My time is valuable; therefore, I'm going to lay out my best offer right away. The more time we spend haggling, the more I'll have to take off the table to pay for my time."

Expressers view negotiations and agreements as a way to be creative and attain greater personal fulfillment. They want to leave their personal mark, their creative stamp, on the agreement. Expressers will want to explore all possible ramifications before making a commitment. They'll put new ideas on the table, they'll consider "out-of-the-box" solutions—even after everyone else feels a sense of closure. In negotiating with Expressers, find some way to use and recognize their creativity. If you can incorporate one of their ideas into the plan, they'll be much more likely to commit.

If you're negotiating with an Expresser, be wary of the "apparent deal." Get her to commit in writing to specifics. Make sure the terms of the deal are in writing. Otherwise, you leave the door open for the Expresser to say: "That's not what we agreed to do."

The Thinker views negotiations and agreements as opportunities to get clear about every detail. He or she will play through various scenarios long after the Director or Expresser has lost interest. But the Thinker can be skilled in teasing out details that might otherwise pass unnoticed.

Thinkers have long memories, and if you negotiate in bad faith with a Thinker, it will be very difficult to regain his trust. The Thinker is likely to want to take additional time to think about the agreement, and even want outside parties to review it. To the Thinker, that's a natural step, not a sign of suspicion. Once the deal is done, Thinkers take agreements very seriously. His commitment is a binding personal oath.

Harmonizers view negotiations and agreements as a natural way to get people to work together toward common goals. They will respond positively to the argument: "This is best for us as a team for the following reasons." Because she wants to please people, the Harmonizer may not want to commit to terms on her own; she'll have to confer with others. Once you have the Harmonizer's agreement, look for early signs of waffling and gently inquire whether everything's all right. If not, fix the problem, because once you've raised the issue, she'll think the agreement has been suspended until the problem gets resolved.

Choosing a Business Partner

Most of our working relationships are relatively short-lived. But at some point, we have to make choices about much longer-term relationships—a business partner, for example. The decisions we make about long-term compatibility obviously have much to do with our success—and our happiness. Knowing how the various styles interact can help us make better decisions at these crucial times.

If we communicate best with those who are similar to us in style, then it would seem logical that people who have the same style would be most compatible. However, that's typically not the case. People of the same style often clash. For while compatibility depends on being able to communicate, it also depends on not competing. In other words, compatibility is also a matter of reckoning with the force that drives us to distinguish ourselves from one another.

Two people with the exact same style can work well together for a brief time. In the short term the relationship can be exhilarating. But people need a chance to reestablish their identity, to remind themselves that they have a unique role to play in the relationship.

So this brings us to our first rule in forming long-term relationships:

Rule #1: Choose a partner whose style is different from yours.

Successful relationships result from a balance of styles. Whether yours is a small business, a large corporation, a legal partnership, or an informal alliance, it will be most effective if a broad spectrum of styles is represented.

Look to the Matrix in Chart 13 for guidance. Assertive styles should be balanced with nonassertive styles. Feeling styles should be balanced with analytical styles. Edge-of-the-Matrix (perimeter) styles should find people at the opposite edge. Center styles should find someone who's also in the center. Corner styles should find someone who's on the opposite edge, or at least in the opposite quadrant.

Rule #2: Choose a partner whose style complements yours.

The Matrix reveals some interesting things about compatibility. The Organizer, for example, should choose a Diplomat or a Counselor as a partner. The Socializer should choose an Explorer or an Investigator. The Persuader should choose a Counselor or a Diplomat. The Charmer should choose a Supporter or a Provider.

When used together, these two rules can result in successful partnerships. If this process seems contrived, remember there's more to

CHART 13: USING THE MATRIX TO CHOOSE A PARTNER

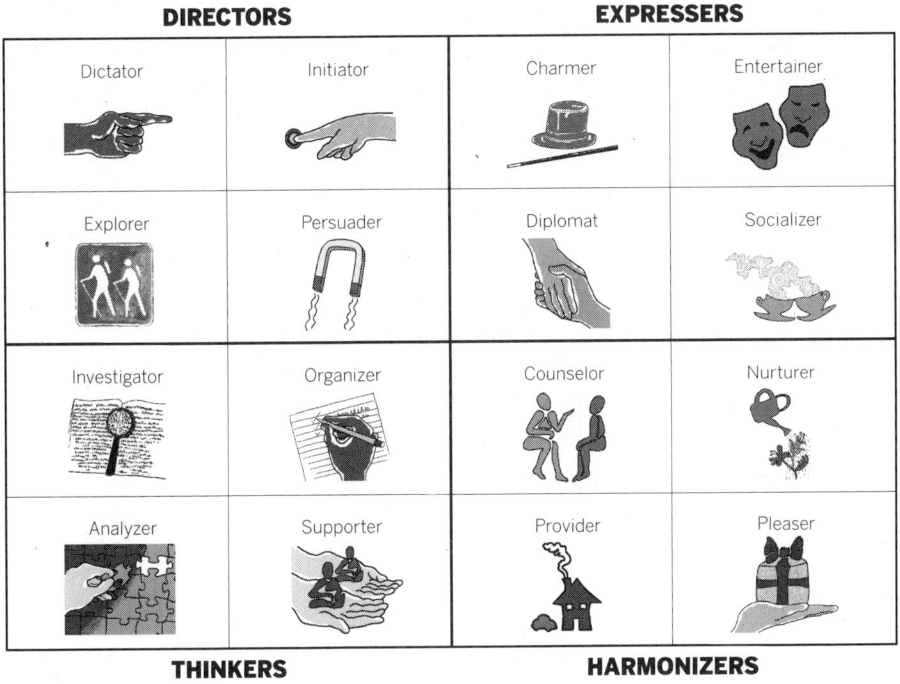

DIRECTORS　　　　　　　　　　　**EXPRESSERS**

Dictator	Initiator	Charmer	Entertainer
Explorer	Persuader	Diplomat	Socializer
Investigator	Organizer	Counselor	Nurturer
Analyzer	Supporter	Provider	Pleaser

THINKERS　　　　　　　　　　　**HARMONIZERS**

choosing a partner than how well you communicate. Sharing similar goals, valuing the same qualities in people, enjoying similar types of activities, possessing complementary skills—these are equally important to evaluate. But understanding the issues you face in communicating—and understanding the need to create a healthy balance of styles—is key to forming a successful long-term partnership.

Conclusion

By now, you can see why understanding the nuances of each style can make you more successful in all sorts of ways. You should practice applying these tools on a regular basis. Keep reminding yourself to look at communication styles as a signpost to behaviors that will influence how people behave in virtually any business situation.

If you're a manager, you already know that managing people can be a challenge. Managerial success depends on understanding how each style operates. Moreover, the burden falls primarily on you, the manager, to modify your style of communicating—at least until you invest the time in training your team in straight talk. Then you can rightfully expect them to share with you the responsibility of working together effectively.

EXERCISE: CHOOSE A COMPLEMENTARY PARTNER

Following the steps below will help you understand how your style of communicating affects various activities you do throughout the day. And it will help you narrow the list when choosing a business partner.

First, fill in your style.

My style:

Next, using the concepts from this chapter, write down words or phrases that describe your approach to the activities indicated.

Time management:

Planning:

Creativity:

Decision making:

Making a presentation:

Then write down three ways you could modify your style that would enable you to be more successful in these activities.

Ways I could modify my style to be more successful:

1.

2.

3.

Finally, write down words or phrases that describe a business partner who would complement you well.

Qualities I seek in a business partner:

1.
....

2.
....

3.
....

Chapter Seven
Implications for
Managing Meetings

Oh, East is East and West is West,
and never the twain shall meet.
—RUDYARD KIPLING, *The Ballad of East and West* (1889)

Is the following scene familiar?

A group of executives is sitting around a conference table. Cups of coffee in front of them, notepads beside them. Casual banter is going on. The leader of the group says: "Okay, let's get started. I don't have much to report today. Things are looking good as far as sales go. Expenses are a bit high, but we think we've got that cornered. So all in all, a pretty good month. Let's hope it continues. Next?"

The baton passes counterclockwise around the room, each team member giving his or her report.

"Production's having a good month, we're awarding two employees with trips to Arizona."

"Engineering had a problem with a boiler in the basement, but we've got it fixed. We've scheduled routine maintenance on the backup generator Friday night. But there aren't likely to be any power interruptions."

"In Systems we're installing new software in the marketing database. Nothing much else going on."

"Sales had two clients return to us this month, we're happy to see them both back in our camp. Should mean a nice upswing in our revenues for the fourth quarter."

People take a few notes. The baton is passed again. Another report. Thirty minutes later, the meeting adjourns.

Has this been productive communication?

Managing Meetings

Is your goal to deal with a tough, multifaceted issue? Or is it to exchange information? Is it a "get to know you" meeting? Or are you looking for creative input? Different goals require different types of meetings, and different styles of communication.

In most organizations, the bulk of conversations take place in the context of a standing meeting. There's the Monday sales meeting, the Tuesday managers' meeting, the Wednesday staff meeting, the Thursday task force meeting, and the Friday planning meeting. The drill varies from company to company, but the amount of time spent on meetings is similar everywhere. It's a variation of Moore's Law (the law of computer chips, which states that processing power increases exponentially every two years): "Meeting time increases exponentially with every doubling in an organization's size."

Ironically, while managers complain that meetings consume too much time, few do much about it. Most managers throw up their hands in resignation. So on and on the meetings go, consuming everything—especially time and money—in their path.

Is there a way to gain control of your meetings? Start by scrutinizing what's really going on. How is the time being used? Is the communication productive? Are people getting what they need? Or is there a better use of the time?

In order to answer these questions, we need to understand the different types of meetings. Some are designed for sharing information. Some are designed to solve problems. Often a meeting designed to accomplish one type of activity winds up trying to achieve a very different end. Communication can break down because it takes place in the wrong forum, in the wrong type of meeting.

Essentially, there are five types of meetings:

Informational: People exchange information.

Problem solving: People try to solve a specific problem.

Brainstorming: People define objectives and generate ideas.

Performance review: People review individual and group performance

Strategic: People wrestle with large issues cutting to the heart of the organization's future, and set goals and priorities.

CHART 14: MATCHING MEETING TYPE TO STYLE

Meeting Type	Preferred By
Informational	Harmonizers
Problem solving	Thinkers
Brainstorming	Expressers
Performance review	Thinkers
Strategic	Directors and Expressers

As you might guess, different styles of communicating work best in each type of meeting. This point has an important corollary: Each style prefers a certain type of meeting. Chart 14 presents a breakdown of which meeting type most appeals to which style or styles. The brainstorming meeting, for example, naturally appeals to the Expresser. Problem-solving meetings typically engage Thinkers. Strategic meetings appeal most to Directors and Expressers. Harmonizers like informational meetings.

If a particular communication style prevails at a meeting, or if one person's style dominates a meeting, it can cause the meeting to shift suddenly. This causes a disconnect in people's minds. A brainstorming meeting called by a Director becomes strategic. An informational meeting called by an Expresser begins generating ideas. People come to a meeting thinking it's one type, only to discover they've somehow stumbled into a different universe.

People's styles can derail a meeting. Directors' meetings can be so short and sweet that you've barely sat down before it's time to go. Expressers' meetings can drift off into what is charitably referred to as "creative time." Thinkers like to follow an agenda, and sometimes they'll stick to it even if a million-dollar idea comes up. And Harmonizers may keep things at such a comfortable pace that people start to snooze.

One manager we know is unable to keep his Expresser style in check. As a result, his meetings drift from point to point. "Gee, I'm not sure where we are on our agenda," he'll say finally. "Can someone help me out?" As you might imagine, his meetings are widely perceived to be unproductive.

Meeting Protocols

Skilled communicators know how to modify their style appropriately from meeting to meeting. They also know that a meeting needs preparation in order to be productive. Preparation can include:

- Giving participants at least two days' advance notice, or as much notice as possible

- Preparing an agenda and distributing it in advance

- Setting the standard that the meeting will begin on time. (One manager shuts the door and locks it five minutes after the meeting starts. However unsubtle, it shows he's serious.)

- Maintaining a time limit for each item on the agenda

- Agreeing to change the agenda only with participants' consent

- Agreeing to communicate what transpires at the meeting

- Assigning a meeting coordinator. This person:

  Sends out the agenda

  Arranges the room

  Starts the meeting on time

  Monitors the clock

  Keeps the minutes

  Pushes the group toward action

  Sees that minutes are distributed within twenty-four hours

  Makes sure the group decides how to share the information from the meeting

Whether an agenda is mandatory or dispensable, and whether minutes should be kept during a meeting or not will vary depending on

CHART 15: PURPOSES AND PROTOCOLS OF EACH
        MEETING TYPE

Meeting Type	Purposes	Protocols
Informational	Exchange information, reach agreements	Agenda optional Minutes optional
Problem solving	Define solutions to problem, reach agreements	Agenda needed Minutes needed
Brainstorming	Define objectives, generate options, reach agreements	Agenda needed Minutes needed
Performance review	Review individual or group performance, reach agreements	Agenda needed Minutes needed
Strategic	Define issues, describe scenarios, set goals, reach agreements	Agenda needed Minutes needed Ground rules needed

what type of meeting is being conducted. Chart 15 shows the purposes and protocols of each meeting type. By following these protocols, in conjunction with understanding the different types of meetings, your organization can use meetings in highly productive ways.

Informational Meetings

Most meetings fit into this category. The meeting described in the beginning of this chapter was ostensibly an informational meeting. These types of meetings follow a very traditional format. Each participant reports events or data. Questions are asked. Notes are taken. No one asks probing questions. They only listen, until it's their turn.

This is the one form of meeting where it's okay to do without minutes or an agenda, as long as people stick to exchanging information. But if agreements are reached, someone should take minutes. Otherwise, people are likely to have different memories of what was said later on.

It should be noted that informational meetings can involve people who know each other well, or people who are getting together for the first time. Regardless, certain habits prevail at informational meetings. People don't pay close attention. They tune out when certain people talk. There are frequent side conversations. In short, informational meetings are not designed for issues to be discussed productively.

Yet important issues do get raised—and decided—at informational meetings. Changes in the benefits program are proposed; a new marketing program is launched. Informational meetings provide safe cover for these types of faits accomplis. By habit, no one asks tough questions. People bring controversial decisions to informational meetings all the time because they would prefer a safe haven to an inquisitive one.

This is what happened in the meeting described at the start of the chapter. At least two major announcements were made with no discussion. The power supply may be cut off when engineering fixes the boiler. And a new software program is being installed in the marketing database.

So beware this fuzzy line. If you sense a decision being made without adequate input or inquiry, call the group's attention to it. Ask: "Is this a decision we should take a look at in a separate meeting?"

Consider another example. The marketing director tells the group: "We've got to revise the fall forecast." The CEO asks whether there's any wiggle room on the expense side. The financial director says that travel budgets "should be reviewed." The CEO nods sagely, tells the finance director to send out a memo, and the meeting moves on to the next topic.

What went wrong here? What began as an exchange of information quickly became an ad hoc problem-solving meeting, with the finance director identifying a problem—travel budgets—and a rushed decision by the CEO. Doubtless, they congratulated themselves after the meeting for their quick thinking, but left unanswered are some important questions. Are there related expenses that will offset the decline in revenues? What impact will the reduction in travel have on sales or other operations? And what's driving the finance director's agenda?

A more prudent CEO would stop the conversation, schedule a separate meeting to discuss what to do about the changed forecast, and set the stage for straight talk.

Problem-Solving Meetings

Problem-solving meetings have a well-defined goal: to gain input on a single problem or issue and to generate an acceptable plan of action. Before the meeting starts, someone has identified the players who need to be present and defined the problem to be tackled.

For example, if the problem is a burst of publicity over a faulty product, different departments will want to contribute. Production, marketing, sales, and finance will all want to be there. Each needs a chance to prepare for the meeting, and to expect that the conversation will occur in a structured, productive way.

Unlike information exchanges, problem-solving meetings need an agenda and minutes. The agenda ensures the active participation of all relevant players; minutes provide a common record of the actions to which everyone has agreed. Minutes also serve as a reminder for everyone to follow up on their specific tasks.

Problem-solving meetings require active input from multiple points of view. Inevitably, if the conversation is a good one, arguments will occur. People will challenge each other's views. Thus, people should be skilled in straight talk. If the topic is particularly volatile, someone with no stake in the outcome should provide a neutral framework for the conversation.

Informational meetings can easily evolve into problem-solving meetings without anyone throwing a switch or even noticing what's happening. Even if the problem is simple—a software glitch—someone should remark on what's going on. "I notice that we're switching from exchanging information to solving a problem. Let's table that discussion until we've figured out who needs to be in the room."

Why distinguish between information exchange and problem solving? In the first place, ten highly compensated managers don't need to drink coffee while two of them debate how to fix a software glitch. Second, unless people are explicitly asked to come prepared to discuss an issue and to bring all relevant data, problem-solving meetings can lose sight of their objective.

Problem solving is an objective unto itself. Even if, for the sake of time, an informational meeting leads directly to a problem-solving meeting, the two should be clearly demarcated. Allow people to leave if they have no reason to stay, and start the meeting by redefining the problem and goal explicitly.

Brainstorming Meetings

Brainstorming and problem solving are related activities—they're both aimed at discovering solutions. But there's a clear difference: Problem-solving meetings address things that have happened; brainstorming meetings address things that will happen, or could happen.

Brainstorming meetings need an agenda and minutes. The agenda should lay out the objective and specific focal points for the conversation. Sometimes the objective is clear; but if the issues are varied and complex, then the meeting requires enough time for framing the issues, gathering creative input, and redefining the objective. Often a brainstorming meeting will end with a clearer definition of the problem—but no solution. That's okay. Eighty percent of the solution is defining the problem.

On the other hand, certain objectives need no clarification at all. "How can we create a blockbuster launch for this new product?" is a good example. The entire meeting can be devoted to creative, out-of-the-box thinking about this question.

Brainstorming meetings require some preparation by the participants. The agenda should go out at least a week in advance; background reading might be distributed to help catalyze creative thinking.

Performance Review Meetings

The purpose of performance review meetings is to analyze past performance with an eye toward improvement in the future. The focus can be group or individual performance. Review meetings can be emotionally charged, because people expect both praise and criticism. It is the job of everyone at the meeting to make sure that praise and criticism are reasonably balanced.

Often the objective of a performance review meeting seems clear— but isn't. For example, the question "Why were sales lower this quarter?" may mask larger and more complex issues that need to be flushed out into the open. "What were the underlying causes? Were they external or internal in nature? When did we know about them? How were they communicated? How did we respond?" Questions like these require a far-ranging discussion, much like a brainstorming meeting.

What do you do when there are very different interpretations of what happened? For example, if someone says: "Our department was not aware of any potential problems with the security system," get people to push back toward the center of the Circle of Assumptions, using a series of inquiries: "Were there any systems to provide an early warning? Did they work?" Avoid questions that place blame on a specific individual too quickly, like: "Whose responsibility was it?" or "Why wasn't someone informed?"

Performance review meetings require an agenda and written minutes. As with brainstorming meetings, the agenda should define the objective and focal points of the conversation; the minutes should reflect for the record any agreements reached. Performance review meetings also thrive when relevant data have been distributed in advance. That way, people can come prepared to test the validity of the data, and to present their own.

Reviews of individual performance are a special type of meeting. Data should be compiled in advance, such as any relevant assessments—including the individual's own assessment of his or her performance. The bulk of the meeting can then be spent comparing and inquiring into these various perspectives until a consensus is reached.

Keeping specific notes of examples of performance, both praiseworthy and not, is the best way to ensure that an individual review meeting is productive. Nothing could be less productive than a boss saying to a subordinate: "I can't think of any specific examples, but I sense you're not as committed to your job as you once were." Unless you can pave the way with concrete data, the road to straight talk is bumpy indeed.

Strategic Meetings

Some meetings are strategic in nature. That is, the goal is to tackle a difficult, multifaceted issue in which the future success of the organization is at stake. Thinking strategically means thinking about the future consequences of our actions as an organization. If the very idea of strategizing intimidates you, remember that no one has all the information necessary to make strategic decisions; it's the interplay of various perspectives that yields the best thinking about the future. Every perspective has value in a strategic conversation.

For that reason, it's critical that strategic meetings utilize every communication style. If the members of the group are heavily tilted toward a particular style, the group itself is likely to display that style—in all its glorious strengths and weaknesses. Strategic meetings need skillful communicators; otherwise, a complex discussion can capsize under the weight of a particular style.

At strategic meetings, the decision whether to use a facilitator is an important one. People need to be able to devote their full attention to the content of the conversation, not to the process itself. By committing up front to using a facilitator, you help ensure a successful outcome. If you're the team leader, you may naturally feel qualified to lead the meeting. But by virtue of your role, you may squelch unconventional thinking. As long as other people are dependent on you for their jobs, they are going to heed your subtle cues. This doesn't mean contrary points of view won't be heard, but those contrary views, in all likelihood, won't prevail at the end of the day. And certainly there will be fewer of them.

Strategic meetings employ every tool described in this book. They also require a set of ground rules. When you need to ensure that straight talk occurs, ground rules are as important for communication as rules of the road are for driving.

Case Study Fear of Engagement

Even when a strategic meeting has been thoroughly planned—agendas distributed, readings prepared, facilitator hired—it can still fail. Often the cause is a fear of actually engaging in a spirited conversation about an important issue.

For example, one strategic retreat we attended for a direct mail company had the following announced agenda:

DAY 1

REPORT ON FUTURE PLANS:
- Customer service
- Fulfillment
- Human resources
- News
- Advertising
- Marketing

DAY 2

MEETING OUR STRATEGIC GOALS:
- Increasing market share
- Improving customer service
- Lowering costs

Each agenda item consisted of a report from a department manager, followed by questions. The customer service manager, for example, talked about the need to install a new phone system. Everyone listened quietly to his analysis of current and projected call rates, looked at the overheads he'd prepared on cost-benefit ratios, and listened to what he said about industry trends. Afterward, people asked some questions about hidden costs, training time, conversion plans, and so forth.

Nothing is wrong with this type of conversation. But as the customer service manager himself said later, it was "an exercise in buy-in—not a strategic conversation." He'd already gotten sign-off from his boss. The new system was coming, regardless of any input that might have arisen at the meeting. All of the questions had been asked and answered by his own staff. Essentially, this was an informational exchange, not a strategic conversation. To his way of thinking, the time could have been better spent.

The agenda and structure of this meeting reflect a fear of engagement. Most managers don't like their ideas being challenged. They prefer to operate at the mode of assertion and advocacy, rather than exploration and inquiry. As a result, opportunities for honest and open communication are often lost.

151

Most organizations engage in some form of strategic planning. Their top executives sit in a room (often at an astronomical hourly rate for their time) and try to engage in significant discussions. They talk about long-term trends, discuss competitive changes, and agree on common goals. Often, however, these strategic meetings become empty exercises because people don't know how or fail to employ the tools of straight talk.

We tell organizations that regular, strategic meetings are critical because of two basic laws of strategy:

Law 1: Successful strategies require that not all opportunities are pursued—only some.

Law 2: Successful strategies require people to consciously overturn the status quo.

These two laws have major implications for the types of communication that lead to powerful new strategies. Reporting on initiatives department by department isn't enough—in fact, it barely scratches the surface. Instead, the agenda needs to be squarely framed as a struggle for scarce resources. Ground rules are needed because people need to engage in a competitive struggle for the company's resources.

Posing certain questions in advance will help ensure that an organization engages in a meaningful strategic communication. Ask participants to address the following questions, and to be ready to share their assumptions, analyses, and arguments.

- If you were a competitor, how would you plan to wipe out our company in five years?

- Of five opportunities you could pursue next year, which four would you reject, and which one would you fund? Why?

- If you ran the company, what would you do differently and why?

We suggest that people engage in a two-part strategic conversation. The first part is homework. Each participant is asked to prepare responses to questions like those above. They circulate their responses to each other—including all relevant data. This happens at least four weeks prior to the actual meeting.

Based on the responses, someone then frames the key issues. He or she identifies the common themes, the opposing viewpoints and arguments, and sets the stage by announcing in advance the two or three issues that will be discussed. Only then is the agenda showing the planned course of the day distributed.

This is a typical agenda:

> **Check-in**
> **Set ground rules**
> **Talk about the first issue as a group**
> **Break into smaller groups; redefine the issue**
> **Groups report back; reach consensus**
> **Group agrees on action plan**
> **Repeat the process with the next item**

It requires diligent planning to lay the groundwork for straight talk about strategy. But it pays off in results, because it ensures that those twelve people sitting in a room are truly thinking—and making decisions—about the organization's future.

The Ground Rules

If everyone were a master communicator—incapable of distorting the facts, clear about his or her own motives, able to accept responsibility to see each perspective clearly—then perhaps ground rules would not be necessary. But no one is a perfect communicator. Even the best communicators fall into traps and pitfalls. The ground rules are the guardrails that guide a strategic conversation safely home.

The following eleven ground rules have proven successful time after time. Each ground rule points to one of the tools or skills embodied in straight talk. The ground rules are introduced here, and because they are so important, they are discussed in depth in Chapter 8.

1. Understand each other's styles.
2. Agree on the meaning of key words.
3. Tackle issues, not people.
4. Permit one speaker at a time (avoid side conversations).
5. Bring issues to the table (avoid "back room" discussions).

6. Keep discussions focused.

7. Explain the reasoning leading to your conclusions.

8. Invite inquiry into your views.

9. Inquire into the reasoning of others.

10. Make "undiscussable" ideas discussable.

11. Identify missing data.

After proposing this list of ground rules, give people time to digest them, to talk about them, and to understand them. Usually this takes thirty to forty-five minutes of discussion. The major point to underscore is this: Ground rules benefit everyone equally. They are a way to ensure a successful outcome. Therefore, assuming everyone wants a successful outcome, everyone should be motivated to abide by them.

At this point, it's natural that someone ask: "Why these ground rules? Why not others?" The answer is: These rules work. You may add to them, if you like. But you cannot subtract from them. These rules are the minimum needed for straight talk.

"What happens if someone breaks a rule?" someone will ask.

Don't be surprised if they do. Human nature being what it is, people will break the rules—even after they agree to abide by them. Usually it's not intentional. From kindergarten on, we're trained to advocate our opinions, not challenge them. We're trained to assert a position until another person yields. We're trained to defend ourselves. Especially at first, people will break the rules all the time. So you need to start slowly, and give each other constant encouragement. The group will learn from your mistakes.

"Who should act as police officer?" someone will ask.

The answer: You all will. Each participant should monitor the quality of the communication. This requires people to "parallel process." People will need to track the content of what's actually being said and, simultaneously, track the quality of the process—what's missing, or not being said. It's like playing a friendly game of softball. Everyone needs to be umpire—even when they're up to bat.

How does this parallel processing work in practice? When the marketing director starts to talk, you've got to be simultaneously listening to her arguments and asking yourself, "Where is she on the Circle of Assumptions? What data is she missing? What's going on in her Inner Script?" Everyone in the room should be acting in the same capacity—acting simultaneously as a steward of and a participant in the conversation.

"What if we're scared to speak up?" someone will ask.

The only way to overcome this fear is to practice. People have to see that the rules work. When you point out that a ground rule is being broken, don't view this as criticizing someone. Instead, view it as helping each other learn a new skill. Keep reminding yourselves: The ground rules benefit everyone. Their purpose is to build understanding, not limit it. None of these rules serve any one person's interests, only the interests of the group.

What happens if a "bad actor" routinely treads all over the rules? Often, all that's necessary is to ask the group whether the ground rules are being adhered to. Calling attention to the behaviors of the group is usually enough to get people to be more sensitive to their behaviors. Another step is for someone to call a quick time-out and invite the person outside to talk about his or her behavior.

Can these ground rules be used in other types of meetings? Of course. But an hourlong meeting doesn't afford the time needed to lay out the ground rules thoroughly. Initially, you'll want to apply them to a meeting of a half day or more. Afterward, you may choose to apply the ground rules to every meeting.

Over time, you'll find that people will make the ground rules a matter of honor. They'll talk about them as being key factors in successful communication. They'll preach their value to the rest of the organization. And, in time, the culture will evolve to a point where the ground rules are seen as an elementary part of every communication—as principles of conduct rather than rules.

At that point, your organization will have truly become a learning organization.

Virtual Meetings

Technology makes it easy to schedule "virtual" meetings. Of the five types of meetings described above, two types—informational and problem solving—can be successful if held in a virtual setting. Why? Because they rely entirely on the exchange of data. They don't require group creativity or interactions. And they are not doomed to failure if one person dominates.

More important, these two types of meetings don't require group consensus. Each person can ask questions, suggest solutions, and listen as his or her colleagues do the same. Ultimately, the group's leader brings closure. There's less focus on process; the end is all that counts.

Occasionally, people try to conduct brainstorming and even strategic meetings via teleconference, videoconference, or e-mail. The rise of telecommunications, coupled with the transformation of organizations into virtual offices, makes it tempting to conduct business using these technologies. While this may be unavoidable for companies whose employees work in different locations, managers should recognize the potential perils:

> **Not all participants will feel their ideas were heard.**
> **People will not feel engaged.**
> **Not all participants will buy into the process.**
> **People will not "own" the outcomes.**
> **Morale may suffer.**

Bottom line, straight talk is impossible in a virtual setting. It can only take place among people who are working together in the same room in real time. Once they experience and appreciate the value of straight talk, people will see why a virtual meeting can serve only limited purposes.

Conclusion

This chapter has illustrated the importance of distinguishing the five types of meetings—and the needs served by each. It has also shown how certain communication styles both prefer and are better suited for certain types of meetings. And it described how people often shift one type of meeting into the type that matches their style of communicating.

All of this underscores the need to be able to identify not only individual styles, but also group styles. The productivity of a meeting is directly related to how well managed it is. Meetings that ramble result from a failure to follow sound protocols and lay down ground rules.

EXERCISE: DEFINE YOUR MEETING STYLES

In the box below, list the meetings you regularly attend. Next to each, identify the type of meeting it is—informational, problem solving, brainstorming, performance review, or strategic. Then identify the protocols followed—that is, whether an agenda is used or minutes taken. Circle any meetings where there's a conflict between the protocols currently in use and the protocols needed for straight talk.

Meeting	Type	Protocols Followed
1.		
2.		
3.		
4.		

Next, list your regularly attended meetings again, then list the communication style that prevails and the appropriate communication style for that type of meeting. Circle any meetings where there's a conflict.

Meeting	Prevailing Style	Appropriate Style
1.		
2.		
3.		
4.		

Chapter Eight
Setting Ground Rules

Too high a price is asked for harmony;
it's beyond our means to pay so much to enter on it.
—FEDOR DOSTOEVSKI, *The Brothers Karamazov* (1880)

Contrary to what Dostoevski wrote, communication between people can be harmonious, even downright civil, even though emotions may be high and differing viewpoints may struggle to prevail. Nor is the price too high. The principle underlying this harmony is straight talk, and eleven ground rules form its foundation.

The previous chapter introduced the ground rules. This chapter is organized around explaining each of them in depth. As you read about each rule, you'll learn how they can lead to communication that is both heated and productive. There is, in fact, no need to distinguish between a conversation filled with passion and one filled with trust.

The Ground Rules

First, here are the eleven ground rules:

1. Understand each other's styles.
2. Agree on the meaning of key words.
3. Tackle issues, not people.
4. Permit one speaker at a time (avoid side conversations).
5. Bring issues to the table (avoid "back room" discussions).
6. Keep discussions focused.
7. Explain the reasoning leading to your conclusions.
8. Invite inquiry into your views.

9. Inquire into the reasoning of others.
10. Make "undiscussable" ideas discussable.
11. Identify missing data.

1. Understand each other's styles.

The first ground rule is to review each other's style of communication. There are two parts to this rule: First, each participant must know his or her style; second, each person has to share his or her style with the group.

When the meeting begins, after the ground rules have been introduced, ask everyone in the room to talk about their style and to include one or two strengths and weaknesses of their style. If appropriate, ask: "What is it about your style that might cause you to react in this meeting in a particular way?" Limit each person's speaking time to three or four minutes; the goal is to give everyone a chance to say something and become known by the group.

Talking about styles of communication is an excellent icebreaker for a meeting. First, it gives every person a chance to get comfortable talking and participating. Second, it will help all the participants feel that they are among equals because everyone is talking openly about their strengths and weaknesses. People with similar styles will have a chance to swap insights. People with different styles will have a chance to get a feeling for the dynamics of the group. Most important, there's no room for pretense when everyone acknowledges that they see the world a little differently.

As each person identifies his or her style, draw a Matrix of Communication Styles on a flip chart and plot each person's position with his or her initials. If any group members don't know their communication style, we suggest they listen closely as the others describe their styles, and then try to identify their own. Ask the group to help them confirm their style of communicating. After you've listed everyone's initials in the Matrix, emphasize the importance of understanding the dynamics of the group.

The example in Chart 16 shows a well-balanced group. Each of the four primary styles is represented by at least two of the nine participants. Given the dynamics of this group, you'd expect that an issue would get a balanced discussion.

CHART 16: A GROUP WITH A BALANCE OF STYLES

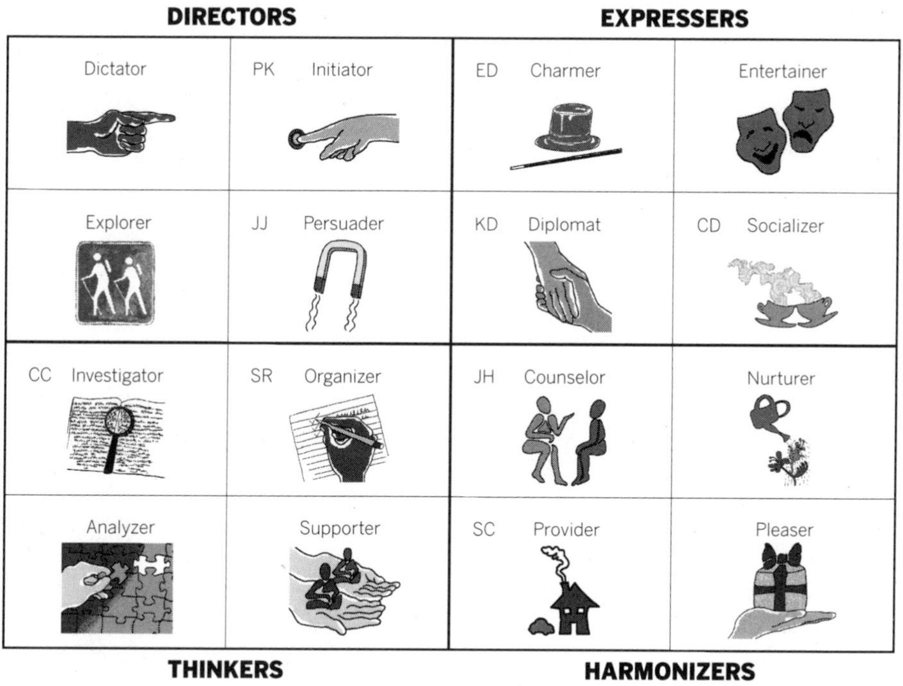

DIRECTORS   **EXPRESSERS**

Dictator	PK Initiator	ED Charmer	Entertainer
Explorer	JJ Persuader	KD Diplomat	CD Socializer
CC Investigator	SR Organizer	JH Counselor	Nurturer
Analyzer	Supporter	SC Provider	Pleaser

THINKERS   **HARMONIZERS**

If the group is tilted toward a particular style or styles of communicating, however, you can expect that style to influence the course of the conversation. An issue may not get the hearing it deserves. The Matrix in Chart 17 shows an imbalanced group. (More details about group and organizational styles can be found in Chapter 10.)

After preparing a Matrix for your group, you should spend five or ten minutes discussing its prevailing styles and possible ways to monitor the group in light of its style. Chart 18 presents some characteristics that may prevail if one style clearly dominates. You might want to make an addendum to the ground rules to compensate for such imbalances.

We want to reiterate why this first ground rule is so important.

First, it allows people to feel that all are on an equal footing—where there are no bosses or subordinates, only different styles working alongside each other.

CHART 17: A GROUP WITH A STRONG PREVAILING STYLE

DIRECTORS		EXPRESSERS	
BK Dictator	GL Initiator EB	Charmer	Entertainer
KM Explorer	RM Persuader MG BK	Diplomat	Socializer
CC Investigator	Organizer	Counselor	Nurturer
Analyzer	Supporter	Provider	Pleaser
THINKERS		HARMONIZERS	

Second, When it comes to tackling tough problems, a key is getting everyone to acknowledge that they see things differently—that their different perspectives are limited. Having people talk about their communication styles is a healthy starting point for straight talk.

Third, it helps identify any prevailing style that could influence the group's dynamic. For example, knowing that the group is tilted toward a Director style will alert everyone to be on guard against jumping to conclusions.

Fourth, checking styles will help people relax with each other. It provides an opportunity for some good-natured ribbing.

"So as a Diplomat, you'll say yes to anything, I suppose."

"You're a Socializer? That explains the *Love Boat* reruns."

Humor is a good ingredient for keeping a conversation healthy and productive. Perhaps we should have a twelfth ground rule: Maintain a sense of humor at all times.

CHART 18: GROUP STYLES AND THEIR POTENTIAL WEAKNESSES

Group Style	Potential Group Weaknesses
Director	Impatient with process; unwilling to ask questions; quick to jump to conclusions; quick to bring topic to closure
Expresser	Easily sidetracked by tangential issues; not able to focus on facts; mistakes impressions for facts
Thinker	Unwilling to bring a topic to closure; too focused on process (may overpolice the ground rules); unwilling to challenge each other's thinking
Harmonizer	Unwilling to offer contrasting viewpoints; unwilling to police the ground rules; may not raise difficult topics

2. Agree on the meaning of key words.

This rule applies to all conversations and all situations. Think about how easily conversations can get offtrack because of loaded terms and labels. Take a phrase like "maximizing productivity" or "thinking strategically." What is, after all, "productivity"? What is "strategic thinking"? Some of the best minds in business have difficulty defining these terms; it's no wonder that organizations stumble over them.

Think of how often communications get derailed in your organization because no one stops to challenge the buzzwords they use. "Commercial television," for instance, seems clear enough. But the television industry spent years debating ways to regulate television content without figuring out first what was meant by "commercial." It still hasn't.

There are no shortcuts to defining key terms. The purpose of this rule is to give people the freedom to challenge words and phrases that seem unclear. Whenever this happens, the conversation should be placed "on pause" until everyone agrees on a definition—or agrees that a word or phrase is too loaded to be used at all. Remember, you can't have straight talk until you agree on what words mean.

3. Tackle issues, not people.

This rule seems obvious. Unfortunately, it's easy to say, hard to do. Much of our behavior is defensive. If someone challenges our views, it is ingrained in us to respond defensively, to challenge the other person's ability to see things clearly. In so doing, we shift the focus from the issue to the person—and in so doing, we break this ground rule.

How can you determine where this boundary lies? You can use the following test: Ask yourself, "Can my statement be interpreted as implying that I see things more clearly, more cogently, more accurately than he does? If so, can I show evidence why, in this particular case, my viewpoint is more accurate and more informed?" If not, assume you've violated the ground rule.

One of my colleagues distills the essence of this ground rule into an epigram: Value learning over your own defending. If you remember that competence in communication is being open to other points of view, assuming your own viewpoint is inherently limited, and displaying genuine curiosity about other people's viewpoints, you'll never get in trouble.

4. Permit one speaker at a time.

The goal of straight talk is to increase understanding among all participants. Side conversations are clearly aimed at something else—at providing a chance for a few people to talk at the expense of the group. Side conversations are distracting; they divide the group's attention, and more often than not, they are a sign of disrespect for the process.

If you are genuinely committed to straight talk, your attention should be 100 percent focused on a single conversation, tracking both its content and its quality. Participants in a discussion need to be scrupulous in policing against side conversations. "Could we have one speaker at a time?" is a good, gentle reminder when people are in violation of this rule.

Nothing gets my dander up more than a person who regularly violates this rule. If someone is a repeat offender, I'll stop the conversation and ask pointedly: "Is there a reason you can't discuss this with the group?"

Shame can be a wonderful remedy.

5. Bring issues to the table.

The next ground rule is: Bring issues to the table (avoid "back room" discussions). The value of this ground rule is twofold: First, it forces people to recognize that some of their best and most honest communication occurs outside the room, where only friendly ears are listening. This may be a more comfortable setting, but it's not going to increase understanding. It is obligatory, given the goal of straight talk, to bring these conversations into the meeting room.

Second, this rule enables people to admit that certain topics are difficult. It enables people to introduce an issue by saying: "This is a back room conversation that I'm bringing up here, because we've agreed to do so. I'm not comfortable doing so, but here goes. . . ." This lets people see the context of the discussion and opens the door to a constructive line of inquiry: "What makes it easier for you to have this discussion outside this room? What repercussions do you fear? What is the source of those fears?"

When we review a conversation based on straight talk, we notice key moments when people become highly energized and engaged. We call them "moments of binding energy"—akin to moments in physics when matter is transformed. These are the moments when the greatest progress is made, when the biggest epiphanies occur.

When someone broaches a delicate topic, it is potentially a moment of binding energy. At that moment, everyone in the room makes an internal decision: whether to proceed, or whether to stop; whether to step off the cliff, or whether to hold back. If there are no ground rules, most people decide to stop. There's no rope or harness. The moment of binding energy doesn't happen.

But if there are ground rules, people will proceed. The framework gives them the courage to probe, to be curious, to step off the cliff. It creates those incredible moments of binding energy.

6. Keep discussions focused.

Of all the ground rules, this sixth one is the most easily violated. What is enough focus? Can't a tangential discussion actually be productive? How do you know when to rein in a conversation? And toward what?

This ground rule is dependent on making sure that everyone understands three things.

First, what is the focus of the current discussion? It may be obvious, but write it down someplace—on a flip chart, on a memo passed out in advance, on the tablecloth. This can be posed as a question: How do we increase market share? How do we increase retention rate? How do we introduce this new product? What is the role of our board in raising capital? (Chapter 9 contains more tips about the process of maintaining a tightly focused discussion.)

Second, what is the relevance of the current conversation to the question? From time to time, especially if someone looks lost or isn't paying attention, place the discussion "on pause" and review the threads of logic. "We began by asking what the role of the board is in fund-raising, and we segued into a discussion of whether we have any precedent for defining the board's role. That led us to a discussion of the original criteria used to select board members when the company was founded."

Third, when will you know when you've arrived? Typically, a discussion ends with a set of agreements and a decision about next steps that everyone signs off on. This stopping point should be articulated up front. It increases the comfort level when people agree that the desired destination is a set of agreements, even though the exact nature of those agreements is still to be discovered.

How do these three elements play out in actual practice. Let's continue the conversation about the role of board members. Let's say it reaches a point where people agree they need more data before they can make a decision. Depending on circumstances, they may stop right there and assign that task to a smaller group, or they may define the new topic as: "Identifying the data we need." If the latter course is chosen, they should write down this new topic, connect it both mentally and on paper (via a dotted line) to the first topic, and then discuss the desired destination—such as a list of data they'd like to accumulate. Then proceed to discuss each person's perspective.

After batting around this new topic, people may agree that the information is too costly or time-consuming to obtain. Let's assume they do. Furthermore, let's assume they decide to role-play several scenarios based on conscious assumptions they make about the data. Notice it's an agreement, marking the end of the previous topic.

Now the conversation has a new focus that needs to be written down (and connected via a dotted line to the earlier topics)—to explore various "what if" scenarios. And, once again, people should agree on the desired destination of the conversation—in this case, to see whether through scenario planning they can agree to make certain assumptions that would render collecting additional data unnecessary.

The beauty of this process is that it enables everyone to track the logical thread of the discussion, even while its focus shifts. People should be able to mark the end of one discussion and the beginning of another. So long as everyone in the room understands this dynamic process, and can communicate to each other how the current topic relates to the original question and to the desired destination, then the focus is maintained. Everyone is playing by the rules.

7. Explain the reasoning leading to your conclusions.

Explain the reasoning leading to your conclusions. This seemingly simple rule is the most important element of straight talk. Adhering to it leads to straight talk. Departing from it can cause communications to break down in a hurry.

If you think about it, we go through most of our daily work not having to explain our reasoning. We reject a claim because the company policy tells us to. We buy a computer because it's in the budget to do so. We solve problems because it's in our job description. We don't normally stop and analyze whether we've made the best decision. Good enough is usually good enough.

This tendency to accept our conclusions on their face—to not challenge our reasoning—is one of the root causes of miscommunication. Because we don't challenge the way we think, we don't develop the muscles that allow us to have productive dialogues. Instead, we engage in a kind of circular logic in which we make an assumption—and then draw a conclusion based on it. Here's an example.

The marketing director tells her staff: "We need a new brochure because the old one is ugly and doesn't work very well. Starting today, we're going to fix that."

Everyone applauds the marketing director's initiative. But her assertion, that the old brochure isn't working because it's ugly, is an assumption. She's concluded that a new brochure will fix the problem. Yet a myriad other factors could explain why the brochure isn't drawing much response. Poor products, poor positioning of the products in the market, poor follow-up with potential leads—these and a hundred other reasons could explain the brochure's lackluster performance. Unfortunately, having made an assumption about the problem, her solution may be flawed from the start.

Yet stop and observe how the group responds to her reasoning. Everyone applauds. Why? Because we respond to action. We love action. It gives us comfort to know a solution is at hand. In essence, she's saying, "Here's a problem; I have the solution; I've saved you the trouble of figuring it out. Follow me."

It's the "easy zone," as one of my colleagues puts it. People prefer the winding path of poor communication to the more rigorous path of straight talk. People prefer the easy zone, even when it goes against their best interests.

8. Invite inquiry into your views.

The next rule is directly related to the Circle of Assumptions: Invite inquiry into your views. The purpose of this rule is to help push ourselves closer toward the center of the circle, toward the data. It lets people know we're open to letting our reasoning be tested and probed. It says, in essence, "I might not see this clearly. I realize there are other ways of looking at it. Can you help me?" You set the stage for effective communication.

Straight talk occurs when people invite inquiry. A genuine display of curiosity creates an environment of constructive communication. It enables people to examine your assumptions. It causes them to look at their own. In so doing, it leads the group toward agreements about data, away from assumptions.

One CEO we admire uses a weekly meeting to get his staff to invite inquiry. The meeting starts at 8 A.M. every Friday. He provides coffee, juice, and muffins. There's only one rule: The first thirty minutes are spent on data. Each manager shares facts. Then, and only then, do they allow themselves to talk about the implications of those facts.

What does this accomplish? It allows the team to focus on what it knows, rather than what it assumes. It forces them to share data. And it allows them to inquire together. As he states: "It causes a ripple effect.

People have begun to focus on what they don't know—but need to know—to do their jobs better."

This CEO's leadership has been crucial to changing the culture of his organization. Known in the past as a stodgy, slow-moving giant, today his company shows surprising agility in getting into new markets ahead of everyone else.

Surprising, that is, except to people skilled in straight talk.

9. Inquire into the reasoning of others.

The flip side of inviting inquiry into your views is captured in this rule: Inquire into the reasoning of others. There's an obvious synergy between these last two rules. People respond to the behavior of those around them. The more you inquire into your own views, the more you encourage other people to feel comfortable when someone probes their assumptions.

How you frame this challenge is vitally important. "How in the world did you reach that conclusion?" isn't genuine inquiry. It really says: "You dummy, how could you possibly think that?"

Under the rules of straight talk, your inquiry must be framed positively. Frame it like this: "I know I'm not capable of seeing everything. I'm interested in understanding your perspective more fully. Can you explain your reasoning?"

If you find the process frustrating, ask for help. "What am I missing here? Can someone help me understand it?" That allows the conversation to shift from you to someone else. And meanwhile, the ground rule remains intact.

10. Make "undiscussable" ideas discussable.

The tenth ground rule encapsulates one of the tools from Chapter 5— Outer Scripts and Inner Scripts. Getting people to divulge their Inner Scripts gets them pointed toward straight talk.

This is one rule that everyone must adhere to—or no one will. For example, one of my colleagues raised a sensitive issue at a retreat of top managers at her former company—when there were no ground rules to protect her.

As she recounts it, the sensitive issue was her boss's behavior. He had a habit of poking fun at other people's ideas and teasing them publicly. My colleague called it the "wet-towel syndrome." She felt the CEO's behavior inhibited people from freely discussing their ideas. The fear of public ridicule was too great.

During a break, my colleague talked to the head of human resources and asked whether he felt the same way about the wet-towel syndrome. He said he did. "If you bring it up, I'll support you," he said.

After the break, the discussion turned to the group's dynamics. My colleague raised her hand. "I have a sensitive point to raise," she said. "Sometimes, we jump on people's ideas and criticize them before they've had a chance to be heard. It's like guys in a locker room snapping wet towels."

The CEO looked around the room. "Anyone else feel the same way?" he said. There was no tone of inquiry in his voice.

No one said a thing.

A month later my colleague was asked to leave the company.

Why is this story relevant to discussing undiscussables? After all, my colleague was fired. What's to encourage other people to take risks like she did?

The point is that when entering risky ground, where feelings can be strong and sensitivities are delicate, straight talk needs to follow. That's why rules are important. My colleague should never have been fired. Someone should have asked if she had any examples to give, any data to convey. But the absence of ground rules allowed the CEO to ride roughshod over her—and her colleagues.

Sometimes, corporate politics can seem like a scene out of the Wild West. And just like in the Wild West, someone's got to lay down the law before reason can prevail. Raising undiscussables can be done successfully only when the ground rules are clear. Otherwise, you can get shot in the back.

People carry on private conversations in their heads regarding undiscussables. "Her idea is crazy." "I'll get fired for sure if I bring that up." We censor ourselves so we won't upset other people. But in so doing, we trap ourselves in a dilemma. On the one hand, we know we need to discuss the issue openly; on the other hand, we don't want to upset other people or expose ourselves to criticism. So we keep mum. We censor our undiscussables. We never have the conversation in public that's occurring in private.

Many times people drop out of a conversation when they feel overwhelmed by this inner dialogue. "That woman! She ran right over my idea. She didn't even listen. I'm so disgusted with this organization, I'd walk away from this job right now if I could."

When people drop out, this derails a conversation. It ceases to be productive. That's why the team leader needs to keep focused on the participants and ask periodically whether they have any undiscussables.

The important thing for you to do, if you're feeling this way, is to recognize that your emotional response has made it impossible for constructive communication. The monkey's on your back to raise the issue and get it out in the open.

If you're a participant in a meeting and feel that other people are reluctant to raise delicate issues, express your feeling. "I have a sense that Jane doesn't feel free to speak her mind. So I'd like to talk about that. What's preventing people in this room from expressing what they feel?" As a participant, you have an obligation to keep the meeting on track any way you can. All you need to say is: "I have an undiscussable. I feel like Jane's ideas were ignored back there, and I need to get that off my chest. Can we back up and reopen that part of the discussion?"

Most important, recognize the assumptions hidden in your undiscussables. You assume that by raising a delicate issue people will feel upset. But they may not. If you test your assumption by bringing it into the open, you're likely to find that people feel relieved to have a chance to talk about it. The resulting discussion may break a logjam that's been preventing the entire group from having a successful dialogue.

11. Identify missing data.

As Chapter 5 explained, one of the most important tools of straight talk is the Chain of Missing Data because it enables people to reach agreement. The final ground rule captures the essence of this tool.

Here's an example of how identifying missing data can create consensus where none apparently existed. Following is a conversation between the marketing manager and the sales manager at a New York shirtmaker.

Marketing manager: Macy's is looking for a new look for fall, and that's what we've got. If Macy's doubled last year's order from us, our numbers would be made. You've got to get your people focused on it.

Sales manager: I've been looking at the overseas market. There's plenty of time for us to sell to Macy's. But meanwhile, our remaining inventory is sitting here. I think we can put two salespeople on the plane and sell it in Hong Kong. But they can't go without fresh catalogs from you. What's the holdup?

Marketing manager: Don't you realize how much you're asking for? My team would have to reprint the entire catalog to give you what you want. We don't have the budget. And we'll lose time. Don't you see how important Macy's is? If we miss that show in Dallas, we're cooked!

Sales manager: You don't seem to understand my business. We have shirts to sell. So our job is to sell them. We don't quit until we're done. And you're supposed to support me!

These two managers should be inviting inquiry, challenging their assumptions, attacking issues—not each other. Unfortunately, that's not the case. But what if they were? What data could help them out of this rut? And where could they go to find it?

It helps to analyze the data missing from a conversation. The starting point is to flag all the assumptions. By creating a Table of Assumptions, as shown in Chart 19, people can see in black and white how each side views an issue.

Next, identify the data needed—and possible sources for it—as shown in Chart 20. As you review this chart, notice how many assumptions can be resolved using the same data—or the same sources of data.

Once you've flagged the missing data, you can consolidate it and then prioritize which data is most important. If the sales manager and marketing manager both went through the exercise, they might come up with the lists shown in Chart 21.

A dispute that caused two managers to lose their tempers now seems to be resolvable. They should put aside their disagreement long enough to allow the steps outlined in the Consolidated Table of Missing Data to bear fruit.

CHART 19: A TABLE OF ASSUMPTIONS

Marketing Manager	Sales Manager
We've got to start selling our fall line now.	We've got to sell our existing spring inventory.
Macy's is looking for a fall line like ours. The time is now.	There's plenty of time to sell to Macy's.
If we doubled last year's sales to Macy's, we'd meet all our sales goals.	We can sell our remaining spring inventory in Hong Kong.
We'd have to reprint the whole catalog.	Our sales people have to get fresh marketing materials.
We don't have the budget to do that.	We could find the money if we made it a priority.

When Ground Rules Aren't Enough

Even if people follow all the ground rules, it's difficult to travel the road to productive conversation if certain people in the room feel they can't trust one another. If that's the case, what can you do?

First, if you're one of those people, check your feelings with someone you can confide in. Express yourself, but make sure you stick to the ground rules of straight talk. "I don't trust Jeff" isn't appropriate. Instead, frame your doubts in the form of a dilemma: "I feel I can't trust Jeff, because I always feel he's putting me down. Yet I want to be part of this communication. I want to check out my feelings with someone else. Can you see a way out of my dilemma?"

If you find that your colleague corroborates your view, then you've got a problem. But at least it's not an untested assumption! Ask your colleague to join you in talking it over with the meeting leader.

If you can't find someone to confide in, then at least alert the meeting leader to the situation. He or she will respect the confidential nature of your concerns. Ask the meeting leader to look for

173

CHART 20: IDENTIFYING MISSING DATA

Assumption	Data Needed	Possible Sources
Macy's is looking for a fall line like ours. The time is now.	Is Macy's looking for a line like we're going to produce? When do we need to contact them?	Meeting with Macy's
If we doubled last year's sales to Macy's, we'd meet all our sales goals.	What were last year's sales to Macy's? What can we reasonably project for this year?	Internal accounting; industry research; meeting with Macy's; internal meeting
We've got to sell our existing spring inventory.	How much marketable inventory do we have?	Internal accounting
We can sell our remaining spring inventory in Hong Kong.	What is the profit projection in Hong Kong? What other options do we have for disposing of that inventory?	Phone calls; industry research; sales call; internal accounting; internal meeting
We'd have to reprint the whole catalog.	What marketing materials are needed to sell the inventory in Hong Kong?	Meeting of sales and marketing
We don't have the budget to do that.	How much would it cost? What's the projected incremental return?	Internal accounting; meeting of key players

CHART 21: CONSOLIDATED TABLE OF MISSING DATA

Missing Data	Possible Sources
Is Macy's looking for a line like we're going to produce ? When do we need to contact them?	Meeting with Macy's
What were last year's sales to Macy's? What can we reasonably project for this year?	Internal accounting; industry research; meeting with Macy's; internal meeting
How much marketable inventory do we have?	Internal accounting
What is the profit projection in Hong Kong?	Phone calls; industry research; sales call; internal accounting
What other options do we have for disposing of that inventory?	Internal meeting
What marketing materials are needed to sell the inventory in Hong Kong?	Meeting of sales and marketing
How much would it cost? What's the projected incremental return?	Internal accounting; meeting of key players

corroborating evidence and to suggest strategies for you to improve the relationship.

And what if there is no meeting leader (or the leader is Jeff)? Go to someone in human resources. This is their bailiwick. Suggest strongly that a facilitator be hired for the meeting. Tell them your desire to follow the principles of straight talk. Express your concerns about your ability to communicate effectively without clear ground rules.

Lack of trust is not uncommon in an organization. People have long memories of injuries done. An organization should be willing to expend considerable resources to heal the wounds. One way is to provide cover for people so they can participate fully in straight talk, which, if successful, can go a long way toward closing gaps in communication.

Conclusion

This chapter laid out the eleven ground rules of straight talk in detail. Each rule works in conjunction with the others. Together, they orient a group's communication toward shared learning and understanding about complex issues.

These ground rules need not be used in every meeting or conversation. But the more they are built into an organization's culture, the more that culture will shift from defending to learning—and the more capable it will be of marshaling its collective knowledge into a powerful strategy.

EXERCISE: IMPROVE THE QUALITY OF MEETINGS

Review the eleven ground rules of straight talk. Then, in the box below, list the meetings you regularly attend. Indicate next to each meeting whether following the ground rules would improve the quality of that meeting.

Would ground rules improve this meeting?

Meetings	Yes	No
1.		
2.		
3.		
4.		

If you indicated that following the ground rules would improve a meeting, list below the names of people whose sign-off would be needed to put the ground rules into effect. What objections might they raise? How would you counter those objections?

Names	Possible Objections	Counterarguments
1.		
2.		
3.		
4.		

Chapter Nine
Resolving Conflicts

It is most true—our style betrays us.
—ROBERT BURTON, *Anatomy of Melancholy* (1621)

People get into conflicts all the time. Why?

As we've seen, people naturally gravitate to the outer rings of the Circle of Assumptions. This is especially the case when they're under duress or feeling pressured. As defenses go up, straight talk goes down. So in a typical organization facing typical pressures, straight talk is more difficult. People will attack others rather than challenge their own thinking. Under pressure, people move away from the data—and into battle mode.

In our research, we've found an epidemic of unresolved conflict inside modern organizations. Much of it can be traced back to unresolved conflict caused by poor communication. Straight talk can erase much of this unresolved conflict, but it takes time—and commitment across the organization—to change people's patterns of communicating.

You'd think organizations would realize they have much to gain from resolving their conflicts, from understanding each other's points of view. But people take their cues from those around them—from the world of politics, for example. When is the last time CNN broadcast an exchange of artful inquiry on the Senate floor? Or the last time voters recalled an elected representative for unproductive communication? If our public debates set the tone for our private discourse, then it's no wonder that our organizations are riddled with conflict.

In this chapter, we'll explore the types of communication conflicts that can arise in an organization—and how to deal with them. Many of these conflicts have been touched on in earlier chapters. As we review each type, we'll look at techniques that straight talk provides for resolving them. In the process, we'll set the stage for a different kind of discourse.

As you develop these skills, start to train your ear to recognize the types of unproductive communication that occur in your organization. Remember that, although unskilled communicators make for entertaining politics and good television, if people model themselves after what they see in the media, they cheat themselves of the ability to resolve complex questions. Political debate is not a good model for straight talk.

Conflict over Ground Rules

Some conflicts are healthy, of course. A brainstorming meeting is more successful when two opposing camps emerge. A sales manager should be able to challenge a research manager. As long as the conversation stays focused on the facts and issues, a conflict is clearly okay.

One form of conflict arises because people have different notions of what is and what is not "healthy." Some people think public shouting matches are acceptable. Others disagree. Neither is necessarily right or wrong. But an organization encourages conflict by failing to articulate clear standards.

Take the ground rule to "tackle issues, not people." Is it okay for two colleagues to challenge each other's views in the privacy of their offices? How about in front of other employees? Is it okay for one colleague to call another "unreasonable"? Is it acceptable to say a meeting "hasn't been very productive"?

What's out of bounds? Any person who stoops to name-calling, to personal attack, or to veiled threats is out of bounds. Racial, ethnic, or religious slurs and sexual harassment are clearly unacceptable. So are threats or acts of bodily injury, or threats or acts of sabotage.

Organizations should take a particularly firm stand when someone communicates in a hostile tone of voice—when his or her behavior clearly aims at harming another person. We encourage managers to adopt a "two-strikes" policy on hostile behavior. If people speak in a hostile way, they have only one chance to improve. The second time it occurs, they're out. There is no third strike.

Each organization should, of course, define its own standards of unacceptable behavior. Whether your company adopts a more lenient or less lenient approach is less important than the fact that a clear policy is communicated throughout the organization.

Once an organization establishes that certain types of conflict are, in fact, healthy and acceptable, it can monitor itself and sanction people who violate the standards. Those three activities—defining, monitoring, and sanctioning—give the organization its moral rudder.

Conflict over Style

Not surprisingly, each style is prone to specific types of conflict. As you become skilled in straight talk, conflict over style is one of the easiest types to diagnose. Every discussion about what is or is not "healthy conflict" will be influenced by the styles of communication that prevail in the room.

At the end of this chapter, we'll review how each style deals with conflict. For now, consider the following story.

A small management company is owned by two partners. Jerry is an Investigator, Bill is a Charmer. Jerry likes to make sure he understands everything that's going on. Unless a project is going according to plan, he assumes it's not being handled well. Bill, on the other hand, likes to try out new ways of doing things—even if they're untested. He's more willing to "wing it," as Jerry puts it.

Adding to the potential for conflict between them is the fact that they work out of different offices in different cities. Their lack of face-to-face time means that small conflicts can get magnified over time.

One of their projects—installing a new management information system for an accounting firm—nearly capsized because of their communication styles. On this project, Jerry was the leader, but Bill was on-site coordinator. At the time the blowup took place, their roles were changing. Bill was taking on greater leadership for the project, while Jerry was moving into an advisory role.

The day of the blowup, Bill flew to Jerry's office to review the budget for the remainder of the project. Bill wanted Jerry to agree to a key change: They were spending too much time in planning meetings; there weren't enough dollars in the budget. Either the planning sessions would have to be reduced to one a month—or they'd have to take a cut in pay.

"I think we should cut the number of planning sessions," Bill said as they started the conversation in Jerry's office. "We can't justify the expense."

Jerry looked over the budget and said: "I don't see a budget here for internal communication with the client. I've said before, without good communication, this project is bound to fail."

Bill pointed out that a budget for communication was included, but Jerry pounced. "This is precisely the reason we need these planning meetings. You've overlooked one of the key factors of success in this project."

The conversation quickly deteriorated. Jerry scrutinized each line of the budget. Bill argued that Jerry was missing the point. They were down to the wire, and there simply wasn't enough money to maintain the status quo.

"Then we'll go back to the client and ask for more," said Jerry.

Bill was exasperated but didn't want to lose his temper. Jerry looked at him and said: "What's that look on your face all about? Do you feel differently?"

"I think you know that's impossible," Bill said. "The client would laugh us out of the room. Why are you being so unreasonable?"

"Me?" said Jerry incredulously. "You're the one being unreasonable. How can you expect me to fulfill my role in this project if you can't even find money in your budget for us to meet?"

"We're meeting right now," said Bill, "but it's not proving very productive. I'll talk to you in the morning."

Bill stowed his laptop. Jerry exited for another meeting. Bill spent fifteen minutes talking to another colleague, and then headed for the door.

Jerry saw him leave and waved good-bye. "Drop in anytime, Bill, anytime you're looking for a fight."

Bill's sense of humor was shot. "Screw you," he said.

That afternoon Bill called me to talk about what had happened. He said he realized that he and Jerry had different styles of communicating. "But in the heat of the moment, that knowledge doesn't seem to help. He reverts to his style, and I revert to mine."

We talked about the need to acknowledge those differences openly at first, so that the conversation could begin with a clear recognition of their individual preferences—and limitations. We talked about the need for ground rules tailored to their different styles. Most important, I told him, was the need to accept that under pressure, they were sure to get into conflicts. So they needed to lay out the rules of engagement, the rules for "healthy conflicts."

As a result, we established the first of several ground rules for Bill and Jerry:

1. Prior to any sensitive discussion, we'll remind ourselves of our styles of communicating.
2. Anytime we attack each other, it's a violation of the ground rules.
3. Anytime a ground rule is violated, it's our responsibility to talk about it.

Conflict over Purpose

Another type of conflict is embedded in the story about Bill and Jerry. It stems from the failure to define the purpose of a conversation. When this happens, two people can have two very different expectations. The difference in expectations sits like a trap, waiting to spring at a moment's notice.

In this case, Bill's purpose was resolving the problem of the budget. Jerry's purpose was controlling the process. From Bill's perspective, he'd laid out his goal at the outset. But Jerry thought there was a different goal: making sure the project was on track.

Would the conversation have been more productive if they had defined their expectations up front?

"Maybe," said Bill. "We would have felt more comfortable. We would have both felt that our specific issues were going to be addressed."

As a result, we established another ground rule for Bill and Jerry:

4. We'll agree on an agenda before we start addressing issues.

Conflict over Assumptions

If two people fail to see the assumptions they've made, it's easy for conflict to arise. When Jerry suggests going back to the client for more money, Bill thinks he's crazy. He assumes there are no further resources available. Bill's untested assumption allows the level of conflict between them to escalate.

By inquiring into each other's viewpoints and exposing the assumptions they've made, this particular conflict will disappear. Jerry and Bill could have (1) agreed to explore Jerry's assumption, or (2) agreed to assume there was no more money available. In either case, the conscious focus on assumptions would allow the communication to shift to the possible consequences of that assumption, rather than to who was right.

This resulted in a final ground rule for Bill and Jerry:

5. We'll make sure we balance our assertions with thorough inquiry into our assumptions.

Conflict Resulting from Ambiguity

Another type of conflict arises because questions or issues have deliberately been left ambiguous. The rationale is that resolving the issue would result in more conflict than not resolving it.

Here's an example. Harry is head of programming for a television network in New York City. The network and its local affiliates have warred for years over scheduling. The network wants to retain the power to dictate when programs air; the local stations want to keep that power for themselves.

Harry argues that the stations would not benefit from a clear resolution of this conflict. "We're better off tolerating ambiguity than having a strict policy that hurts some markets more than others," he says. As a result, the standard varies from station to station. Some stations control all their scheduling; some don't. It's not fair. But the cure—rigid controls and broader administrative rule—is worse than the disease, according to Harry.

Harry's policy succeeds because most station executives trust him. The problem, of course, is that Harry won't be around forever. In fact, Harry is likely to leave a legacy of mistrust deeper than he can conceive. Because without agreements and clear understandings that supersede any one person, an organization can topple into chaos.

We haven't won the argument about ambiguity with Harry. But it raises an important point: Some conflicts arise because decisions and policies are allowed to be deliberately ambiguous. Why does one employee get suspended for smoking pot, another fired? Why does one salesperson make a base salary plus commission, while another is paid commission only? Why does one department executive get a company car, another not?

CHART 22: RESPONSES TO CONFLICT

Style	Approach	Positive Response	Negative Response
Director	Not averse to conflict; often the trigger	Responds initially by holding ground; if presented with evidence, will negotiate	Undermines other people; attacks their authority
Expresser	Not averse to conflict; sometimes the trigger	Responds by looking at big picture and searching for solutions	Criticizes the behavior and attitudes of other people
Thinker	Avoids conflict; normally not the trigger	Responds by analyzing causes and looking for compromises	Resentful; slows down productivity; may withdraw
Harmonizer	Avoids conflict; rarely the trigger	Responds by inquiring after others and seeking safety in the group	Withdrawal; seeks relief by escape, getting sick

Conflicts resulting from ambiguity inevitably give rise to deeper, more damaging conflicts. How to resolve this? Challenge the assumption that ambiguity is preferable. Compile a list of areas where policies are unclear or vague. Then have a discussion about it. Who knows? You might find yourself revising your assumptions.

How Each Style Manages Conflict

Each communication style tries to manage conflict in different ways. The summary in Chart 22 shows how each style approaches conflict and responds to it, in both positive and negative ways.

The "trigger" that sparks people to react negatively varies, depending on a person's communication style. For example, Directors are triggered by the perception that the span of their authority has been reduced. For Expressers, it's feeling that their ideas aren't valued. For Thinkers, it's thinking that procedures aren't being followed. For Harmonizers, it's thinking that other people's feelings aren't being considered.

These triggers are style specific. Questions of authority, for example, will not trigger a Thinker. Likewise, sensing that too little attention has been paid to other people's feelings won't trigger a Director.

Recognizing a person's conflict triggers can be useful in steering a productive conversation. Sensing that a Director hasn't participated fully in the discussion, you would ask her directly whether there are questions she'd like to raise. Sensing that a Harmonizer has tuned out of the conversation, you would ask whether there are any concerns about how the group is working together—and look in the Harmonizer's direction.

In instances in which conflict arises, you have three strategies to choose from. The strategy you choose depends on how you read the room.

Injecting Inquiry

The initial and correct response when a conflict occurs in a group is to listen, acknowledge the various points of view, and then inject inquiry to bring the conversation back toward the center of the Circle of Assumptions, back toward the data.

At the same time, make sure that people are focused on the same purpose. Is the goal of the conversation clear? Are other agenda items getting in the way? If so, inquire whether there are any undiscussables.

If the pattern continues, consider talking to the people involved during a break outside the room. Ask them whether they have any issues that prevent them from participating in the conversation in a constructive manner.

Highlighting

If the conflict surfaces again, your second option is to use the conflict to highlight the opposing points of view. You can say something like: "I notice that Dick and Sylvia are arguing with each other about this topic. Has anyone been influenced by their arguments? If not, why not?"

Then lead the conversation to a discussion of the issue, using Dick and Sylvia's competing perspectives to push for a richer appreciation of the underlying data missing from the conversation. This has a second purpose, too: to help Dick and Sylvia become aware of their pattern, and possibly avoid it in the future.

Highlighting poses some risks: It does put people on the spot and make them accountable for their actions. You'll have to decide whether Dick and Sylvia can handle the implied criticism, and also whether the group trusts you to be acting in its best interests. Assuming both things are true, highlighting is a useful tool. If the same pattern continues, however, don't use the group's time to discuss it again. Take Dick and Sylvia aside and find out what's going on.

Focusing

A more risky intervention, but one that is warranted when a group gets bogged down by a recurring conflict, is for someone to focus on the dynamics of the conflict so that it can be discussed directly.

For example, if two people seem to be replaying the same dispute again and again—to the detriment of the group's progress toward a goal—someone needs to say: "I notice that Dick and Sylvia are having the same conversation again and again, and they're disrupting the flow of our conversation. Why do you think this is happening?"

Now you've shifted the focus to their behavior and have asked for feedback on its causes. Typically, you'll get few responses at first. Then, after listening to the silence, you can pose the question another way: "What information could be useful to Dick or Sylvia in this situation?" This framing of the question will likely generate several comments.

Depending on the mood of the group, you can pursue one of two options: (1) move the conversation back to its original focus, having allowed the group to give feedback to Dick and Sylvia, or (2) ask Dick and Sylvia to discuss openly the reasons for their behavior, and then invite comment from the rest of the participants.

This intervention puts the conversation "on pause" while you focus on personal feelings. People need to feel that they can be open about their feelings, and that requires a certain chemistry in the room. One should thoroughly understand the dynamics of the group before "focus-ing." Even then, you've got to be prepared for someone to say: "I'm not comfortable talking about this."

In which case, having opened the door to conflict resolution, you could respond with: "Can you tell us why?"

Case Study A Healthy Dialogue

Following is a transcript from the dialogue that took place after "focusing" on the conflict between Dick and Sylvia.

Dick: I'm continually bothered by Sylvia's way of assuming that she knows what's best for us. She seems to think she can invent a new way of selling our products, and that the rest of us will defer to her. Frankly, I've got a lot more experience than she does, and she doesn't appear to respect that.

Sylvia: Well, I'm bothered by Dick's way of assuming that he knows best. He's constantly reminding us to do it by the book, when there's no book—at least not in this case. Frankly, our cre-ativity is what keeps us competitive. I think his approach is funda-mentally flawed.

Group spokesperson: So, Dick, you think Sylvia takes too many risks, while Sylvia, you think Dick is too cautious. Is that right? What do other people think?

(Note that the spokesperson has resisted the urge to draw the obvious conclusion: That Sylvia and Dick are experiencing a con-flict in style. He's instead recognized that his role is to encourage other people to talk.)

Babs (a subordinate): I see Sylvia and Dick as rivals for the direc-tion of this company. They both want to lead it. And they're both natural leaders. However, for now anyway, Dick is the leader. So Sylvia should ultimately give way.

Meg (another subordinate): I don't see it that way. Sylvia doesn't need to defer. But she does need to make her arguments in a more reasoned way. I'd like to see them ask each other more questions. I'd like them to explain their reasoning. No offense, Sylvia. (Laughter in the room.)

Babs: Yes, what Meg says is true, and I'd also like to see them give credit where credit's due. Too often, Dick and Sylvia are warring with each other, so we don't get a sense that they respect each other—or even like each other. That puts all of us on edge, because they're such strong personalities. I never know whether this is a friendly joust or a duel to the death. I'd like them to back off for a while and appreciate each other's contributions.

Spokesperson: How do you think they could do that?

Babs: Well, Sylvia could say things like: "Dick's approach is sound and is perhaps the way we should go on this." And Dick could say: "Sylvia has once again shown a flash of creative genius." That's what I'm talking about. Appreciation. Acknowledging their unique talents.

Spokesperson: Does everyone agree with what she said?

Dick: Sounds good to me.

Sylvia: Me, too. I think Dick and I forget to acknowledge each other's contributions, especially in front of others. While we may be okay with our fights, other people may not be and it may make them feel very uncomfortable. That's not smart. So we should recognize that the cause of the discomfort is us.

Spokesperson: Okay. So we've defined the problem, at least in part, and defined a solution. Do you want to keep talking about it some more, or shall we go back to the topic?

Dick: I think this has been very valuable. I'm glad to get the feedback.

Sylvia: I agree. I want people to know that I don't want Dick's job. He's the leader. He's invaluable in that role. And if I'm the fly in his ointment, well, then, I'll try to make myself a bit sweeter. (Laughter.)

Spokesperson: Okay. So we'll go back to the topic? Is this what the group wants?

Babs: I think we'd like them to back off each other a bit, but not from the conversation. That's the distinction in my mind.

This transcript is a good example of the benefits of "focusing." The sources of the conflict get clarified (in this case, the fact that Dick and Sylvia had erroneously assumed that other people were comfortable with them airing their conflicts in public); the parties involved tend to appreciate the chance to give feedback; and the conversation can proceed with heightened energy and enthusiasm.

But not always. Once, we were taking part in a conversation in which one manager, named Glen, kept saying that regardless of what decisions were made at the meeting, he alone was in charge of running his department. We stopped the discussion to focus on his defensive reaction. After ten minutes of talking, Glen got up, said "Excuse me, but I have things to do," and left the room.

We took a break, half expecting Glen to be outside the room waiting. But he wasn't. Ten minutes later, no Glen. A half hour later, still no Glen. People were anxious about his whereabouts, so we adjourned in order for people to check up on him.

But Glen had not gone back to his office. Nor, apparently, had he gone home, since calls there were unanswered. Someone decided to notify the police.

That evening, we heard from one of Glen's colleagues. Glen had gone driving. He said he needed time to think. Later, Glen told us that our intervention during the meeting was the best thing that had happened to him in twenty years. He said it made him see how people perceived him. It was the same way he perceived his own father. And he vowed to break the pattern.

Moral of the story: Focusing on negative behaviors to resolve a conflict is difficult and risky. But it can be rewarding for all.

Cycles of Conflict

When in conflict, different styles often react in dramatically different ways. They might show anger, aloofness, depression, or neediness. They might confront the conflict, or avoid it. Moreover, these different reactions might all be in response to the same communication conflict. This can obscure the source of the conflict and make it difficult to diagnose. By separating the responses (which vary) from the underlying conflict (which is the same), an individual or group can recognize the fundamental conflict, and then attempt to break the cycle.

Psychologists talk about cycles of conflict for individuals. Groups and organizations pass through various stages when they are in conflict, too. Typically, the cycle includes (1) expectations, (2) letdown, (3) anger, (4) resentment, and (5) avoidance.

Not every individual or group passes through all five stages. Some will pass immediately from expectation to avoidance. But if the group can talk about what stage it's in, it can begin to break the cycle.

Expectations

Given the many ways conflict can manifest itself, from angry words to international hostilities, you'd imagine that the causes of conflict would vary as dramatically. But in fact, conflict typically begins with assumptions and expectations. You expect the presentation to be finished by 6 P.M. She expects you to be home for dinner. Nation X expects nation Z to respect basic human rights.

So the first stage of conflict is typically a feeling that expectations are not in sync, not aligned. Think of the front wheels of your car. If they're not pointed in the same direction, you're in for a bumpy ride. Expectations are exactly the same.

Setting expectations is unavoidable. We base our lives on expectations of others. "We need your manuscript by next week." "I need you to pay your bill." The cycle of conflict always begins with expectations.

But not all expectations result in conflict. Why? Because sometimes the expectations are communicated clearly, all parties agree, and all parties hold up their side of the bargain. It's only when the reality fails to meet expectations, only when they are out of alignment, that conflict occurs.

There are two keys to keeping expectations aligned. The first is communicating them clearly. This requires you to be conscious of your expectations. All of them. And it also requires you to state them clearly, discuss them, and revisit them frequently to be sure no adjustments are needed.

The second is a willingness to make minor adjustments in your expectations. Easy to say, hard to do. Showing flexibility can be perceived as a sign of weakness. But as a long-standing wisdom attests, try to be "the bending reed which does not break."

Why doesn't this adjustment of our expectations happen more regularly? The fear of appearing vulnerable, the fear of challenging our thinking, is certainly one reason. It's easier to keep our expectations firmly fixed than to express them and negotiate an acceptable revision. Easier—and far more destructive.

One of our clients, a marketing v.p. for a food-store chain, asked his administrative assistant to take a leave from her day-to-day job in order to design a customer benefits program. He made no promises, but hinted that if she did a good job there might be a promotion in it for her.

She worked fourteen-hour days for three months on the project. Many times she was tempted to ask for help. But she didn't, expecting that her boss would reward her with a promotion.

When she completed the project, it was rolled out to much fanfare. The CEO heaped praise on her. She got a nice bonus check. But the marketing v.p. told her there was no money for a new position. Budgets had been cut back. Greatly disappointed, she returned to her old duties. Two months later, when a job offer came from another company, she jumped ship. And in her exit interview, she spoke scathingly of her boss. He'd made false promises, he'd created unbearable working conditions, he'd not been straight with her.

Whose fault was this? The boss's, clearly. He needed to be clear about his expectations. But she, too, was at fault. She also needed to be straight about her expectations. She magnified a hint into a promise. He might have been able to align her expectations with reality had she been clear about them.

What prevents us from being clear about our expectations? People don't want to risk appearing too self-interested. They'd prefer to keep their goals muddy and vague, rather than let their motivations show. This is one of the quixotic laws of human nature, at least in our culture. We are inherently self-interested, yet inherently loathe to letting our self-interest out in the open.

In this paradox lies one of the communication keys to helping people avoid conflict. People need to be told that there's nothing wrong with expressing their self-interest. They should feel free to let their desires be known. Everyone is motivated from self-interest, and that's perfectly acceptable. But it's important for the group that you make your self-interest clear. That way everyone knows what you want. And that way, those around you can work on reaching agreements that allow everyone to maximize their gain.

Another cause of poorly aligned expectations is the fear of letting people down, of being incompetent. "If changes had to be made in the schedule, why didn't you communicate them?" "If the loan couldn't be repaid, why didn't you let us know ahead of time?" The root cause of this behavior is obviously fear—fear of getting caught, fear of punishment, fear of being vulnerable.

So what should you do? Communicate all the time. Close the gaps between expectations and reality before they get too large. Give interim updates and make midcourse adjustments. Raise the level of accountability throughout the organization by raising your own. By letting people know that you can admit mistakes, you allow them to admit mistakes, too. Fallibility and humility are powerful tools. Communicating them makes the difference.

Letdown

When expectations are not met, you first feel let down. The period of letdown is usually brief. People often move to an aggressive emotional response rather quickly—and end up escalating the conflict. But there's much to be gained by letting the conflict stay in the letdown stage, and not allowing it to grow into anything more.

The letdown stage is not so emotionally charged. You can still have a rational discussion. You can say: "I feel let down, and I want to talk about it." It's far easier for people to hear that you feel let down than that you feel angry or resentful. If you keep it right here, you've laid the groundwork for a productive resolution to the conflict.

As you talk about feeling let down, the obvious response is to figure out what could have been done differently. It's human nature to point fingers at other people, but the first player to examine is yourself. How did you contribute to the misalignment of expectations? What was your role in the communication breakdown? By focusing there first, you enable other people to admit responsibility, which they will do if they are competent communicators.

Most of the time, you won't have communicated to anyone—yourself included—how much you'd invested in a particular outcome. Was it reasonable to expect a promotion because you took on the extra work? After all, everyone else in your company is working harder, too. So be more explicit about your hopes. Consult with others to make sure everyone is in line with reality. And resolve to make your anticipated rewards explicit to those who need to know.

Anger

The next three stages of the conflict cycle are all emotional responses. We know what anger feels and looks like. The question is, how can straight talk help when someone has hit this point in the cycle?

There are a couple of techniques. The first is to direct the anger, using the ground rules you've established. Let your anger stay focused on the perceived cause. If you're angry at someone, go somewhere private with that person and have it out. Don't let it spill over onto other people. Otherwise, you lay yourself open to the charge of being irresponsible and immature.

Second, express your anger in the form of a dilemma. Express it in the following terms: "I feel very angry. And I feel caught in a dilemma, because while I don't like being angry with you, I feel it, and I need to express it before we can talk reasonably about it. So just let me vent."

This allows the other person to appreciate that you are trying to be considerate, which may allow the conversation to take a far less emotionally charged course.

Resentment

Resentment is the feeling left in anger's wake. In fact, its Latin root means "to feel again."

Yet resentment is less obvious to other people than anger—and sometimes less obvious to yourself. Some psychologists argue that resentment is just a mask for anger—anger that you're afraid to show for fear of repercussions. This is why spouses resent each other, children resent their parents, students resent their teachers, employees resent their bosses, and on and on. They're afraid to let their anger out in the open. Resentment is safe because it's more private. People allow themselves to feel resentful instead of angry because it's a way of maintaining control.

The irony, of course, is that resentment is plainly obvious. The tone of indignation crackles in your voice and reverberates in your body language. Most people sense resentment very quickly and are immediately attuned to it. Their response? "Watch out. This person is a live fuse waiting to explode."

Escaping this stage of the conflict cycle requires finding a way to admit that you are feeling resentful. The same tricks work. First, direct your resentment to the person who caused it. Second, express it as a dilemma to show that you trying to be considerate of other people's feelings. "My dilemma is that I feel resentful, yet I want to try to preserve our relationship. Would you give me some time to explain?"

Avoidance

As anger and resentment fade, the cycle of conflict leads to avoidance. In this stage, your lack of communication can take bizarre forms. You chart a course to your office via the back stairs to avoid running into your boss. You close the door and hide under your desk to avoid a colleague. You call in sick to avoid meeting an old customer.

Through avoidance, you try to keep your feelings under control. Ironically, this creates a self-perpetuating cycle. The more you avoid communicating, the more strain you place on your relationships, which only increases the conflict and leads to more avoidance. This stage in the cycle can lead to classic symptoms of paranoia. You imagine negative scenarios, and then go to extreme lengths to avoid confirming whether they are true or not.

To break the cycle, find an ally. Bring the problem out into the open. Seek out someone who can act as mediator: a trusted colleague, perhaps. Get him or her to help you analyze what created the initial breach. Ask for help in understanding the way you're framing the situation. Then ask the mediator to role-play with you various scenarios for reaching a reconciliation.

Again, expressing your fallibility in the form of a dilemma will help get you out of the labyrinth: "I have a dilemma. On the one hand, I'm ashamed to admit what I feel; on the other, unless I do, we won't get anywhere. So let me tell you what I've been feeling."

Managing Conflict

Straight talk is more likely to occur in environments that are free of unhealthy conflict. But what about stress? Should organizations try to reduce stress?

Conflict and stress are interrelated. But they are different. It is generally accepted that conflict is measured by the level and intensity of the disagreement, whereas stress is defined in physiological terms such as blood pressure and heart rate. Many people learn how to deal with conflict constructively, allowing the stress to be discharged. Others do not, so the stress slowly builds up.

The point is this: Just because an organization experiences a lot of conflict doesn't mean it has to feel a lot of stress. Straight talk, as we've seen, can actually encourage disagreements. It invites people to lay out their competing perspectives. But by allowing the conflict to be played out in a constructive manner, stress is vastly reduced.

This section is designed to help you refine your style of managing conflict. It's organized around each of the four basic styles.

You can use this section in two ways: You can read about your style and how you could manage conflict better, or you can read about all the styles. The latter approach is especially useful if you want to hone your management skills. Whichever method you choose, try to apply cases from your own experience and envision how you could use conflict management tools to improve those outcomes.

The Director

When experiencing conflict, Directors will speak in very abrupt, direct, seemingly insensitive ways. They'll use the fewest words possible to get their point across. If you're a Director, learn to identify the signs. Don't let yourself close down. Allow the people around you to understand why you're angry.

If you're in conflict with a Director, don't apologize. Tell her in a very clear, assertive tone of voice: "I don't understand what's got you so upset. Could you please explain it in more detail?" If you have bad news to tell a Director, tell her right up front. Directors want to be the first one to know everything. Also, by emphasizing the negative nature of what you're about to say, you might elicit a positive response.

Let a Director speak first. Then you can respond. But don't expect honesty or candor in stressful situations—the Director is skilled in getting what she wants and may paint a distorted scenario to do so. If you think a Director isn't being honest about her feelings or her agenda, tell her: "What I want is a good relationship with you. That won't happen unless you want it, too, and you're willing to tell me what you really think."

Sometimes, if the conversation gets stuck, it may be best to call for a cooling-off period. Make an appointment to get together the next day. Don't let his or her anger dismay you. Try to understand the underlying conflict, and say: "I think I understand what got you upset. Let's get together and talk about it."

EXPRESSERS IN CONFLICT WITH DIRECTORS

If you're an Expresser, you have three challenges in dealing with a Director. First, you like to think aloud, which only confuses the Director. You need to train yourself to listen carefully—and then respond after you've had a chance to analyze the situation.

Second, you should rein in your emotions as much as possible. If you know there's going to be a confrontation, pick a time when you feel in control. Directors want tough-minded analysis and action. Show them the numbers. Prepare two or three alternatives. Negotiate from a position of knowing what's most important to you. This is hard for Expressers. But force yourself to make choices.

Finally, Expressers tend to focus on people, the Director on tasks and projects. To resolve a conflict with a Director, get on the same wavelength. Don't say: "I'm teed off that our sales staff doesn't seem to be using our new software." Say: "In the context of our overall strategy, our sales team's failure to adopt our sales management software is a serious problem." Then offer two or three solutions.

THINKERS IN CONFLICT WITH DIRECTORS

If you're a Thinker, you share with Directors the quality of following your head, not your heart. But dealing with a Director in a stressful situation is challenging for you. First, curb your tendency to dissect things. Instead, get right to the point, state what ought to be done, and negotiate an agreement. It's a good idea to follow up with a memo.

Bad news is bad news, so don't wait to deliver it until there's a better time. The right time for the Director is right away. Your matter-of-fact style will help the Director think you've got everything under control.

HARMONIZERS IN CONFLICT WITH DIRECTORS

For a Harmonizer, dealing with a Director can be stressful under any circumstances. Remember to prepare what you're going to say, keep it short, and be assertive. Don't gloss over the facts or try to hide anything. State the worst news first. Above all, don't try to shift blame elsewhere. The Director cares less about whose fault it is and more about whether you can fix the problem.

In negotiations, follow the same rule: short and emphatic. Pound the desk a couple of times. State your point of view. Don't let yourself be ambushed by someone trying to look good by making you look bad. Make sure you've got adequate information to support your case.

It's tempting for you to shelve bad news or pretend it's going to get better. Don't succumb. The Director wants to know, needs to know, and will help you put it into perspective as long as she's assured you have her best interests at heart.

The Expresser

Under conflict, Expressers let their feelings show. They get angry. Sometimes they withdraw. At other times, they immerse themselves in activity. Often they put on a false face of good cheer. Whatever the escape mechanism, the emotional toll is high for the Expresser. And it often manifests itself in surprising ways.

When a conflict arises with an Expresser, try to help him face the situation squarely. Otherwise he may fool himself into thinking things aren't so bad. Once I was in the office of the CEO of a broadcasting company when he learned his major competitor had gone bankrupt. "Our major competitor just went bankrupt," this Expresser said. "We'll buy his inventory and double our market share in a month!" But six months later, his company was the one facing bankruptcy. By seeing only the "good news," he failed to see the chain reaction of bankruptcies under way in his industry.

Be wary of what an Expresser says when he's in a conflict. He may say: "We can't go on like this. We're going to have to slash the budget." But the Expresser may be thinking out loud. Ask him to analyze and clarify everything he says. Give him a chance to change his thinking, and he very well may.

Expressers don't mind a confrontation as long as they perceive that an underlying sense of trust exists. So take time to reiterate your mutual desire to arrive at a fair conclusion. If there is a lack of trust, the Expresser will interpret the conflict personally and seek revenge. From personal and professional experience we've learned: Beware the vengeful Expresser!

DIRECTORS IN CONFLICT WITH EXPRESSERS

In a stressful situation, Directors need to let Expressers vent their feelings. Don't walk away; let the Expresser talk it through. Then help the

Expresser organize his thoughts. Use your big-picture skills to round out the Expresser's view of the situation. Help him review the long-term consequences. Remember, the Expresser wants to trust you, so be patient. He's not going to make a decision right away.

In negotiating with an Expresser, Directors should remember to be careful about assuming that the Expresser has determined his priorities. The Expresser may appear to know what's most important to him, when in fact he's still trying to assess the situation.

The Director's instinct is to deliver bad news right away. Make sure you show sensitivity when you do. When you've got bad news to tell an Expresser, tell it in human terms: "I feel really bad about this, but here's what happened."

THINKERS IN CONFLICT WITH EXPRESSERS

Thinkers are well equipped to handle conflict with Expressers. As the Expresser vents his feelings, the Thinker can listen attentively and consider the appropriate steps. Once the Expresser calms down, he'll value the Thinker's thoughtful approach and negotiating style.

Thinkers should beware falling into the trap of trying to come up with creative solutions for the Expresser. Most of the time, the Expresser will have considered hundreds of options, but none of them in great depth. Instead, play the role of sage counselor, reviewing the best alternatives and pointing out the pros and cons of each.

HARMONIZERS IN CONFLICT WITH EXPRESSERS

Harmonizers should feel intuitively comfortable with Expressers—no matter what the conflict—because both of them care about people's feelings. Harmonizers should capitalize on that trust by helping the Expresser understand how each person involved is affected. As a Harmonizer, you can defuse a stressful situation by emphasizing how much the Expresser wants to find a solution. Then you can show the Expresser which solutions will minimize damage to others—and in the process negotiate a favorable outcome for yourself.

If a Harmonizer is a bearer of bad news, you should take pains to couch it in human terms and underscore how much it affects you personally; this will probably come naturally. The Expresser will usually respond very positively.

 The Thinker

In conflict, Thinkers tend not to communicate their feelings, making it hard to read their mood. They'd rather retreat than risk an angry outburst. This pattern makes it hard for other people to communicate with them. It can also cause people to underestimate the level of conflict the Thinker is truly experiencing.

Conflicts with Thinkers almost always arise over disagreements about the right way to get things done. This is when the Thinker can display a stubborn streak. Don't expect the Thinker to get roused up or change her mind just because you disagree. From her perspective, she's right, you're wrong. This black-and-white view of the world is a trademark of the Thinker.

In practice, this means choosing one of two strategies in dealing with a Thinker when a conflict occurs: (1) be extremely thorough in thinking through with her the desired outcome and the process to achieve it; or (2) admit that you don't know how to resolve the situation and that you need her help. Both strategies require a large investment of time to pay off.

When a conflict does occur, the Thinker will expect you to focus on fixing it. She'll want you to appreciate how much time she has invested and replay the entire situation. To the Thinker, this is a necessary step toward ending the conflict. Once you've agreed to resolve your differences, the Thinker will want to agree on exactly what occurred, draw up an action plan, and decide on the exact outcomes desired. She'll appreciate language such as: "I'll let you know in writing by this time tomorrow exactly how this plan will be implemented and by whom."

If the conflict with a Thinker is over her performance, make sure you've kept detailed records of every infraction. Otherwise, you'll be overwhelmed by the Thinker's prodigious recollection of events. Don't say: "Our production cycle was delayed because you were late with our budget." Instead say: "Your failure to approve our budget caused us to fail to meet production deadlines on March 10 and April 3 and cost the company $20,000 in potential sales."

Trust and loyalty are very important to the Thinker. She trusts that other people will stand up for their decisions and shoulder the responsibility for their mistakes—regardless of the results. If someone tries to pass the buck, the Thinker will see it as a major breach of ethics. However, the Thinker isn't likely to force a showdown. Instead, she will let things simmer and stew until someone else forces the issue.

In the worst case, the Thinker will challenge you behind your back. She'll see you as an obstacle to things getting done as they should. She'll say nothing about her feelings to you directly. But she'll do what she can to ensure that you're safely moved out of the way.

DIRECTORS IN CONFLICT WITH THINKERS

The Director wants things done right away, and the Thinker wants things done right. So a major source of conflict for these two is over time management. Typically, the Director will say: "Finish this by Friday." When the Thinker protests, the Director will listen with only half an ear. The Thinker will be reluctant to ask more questions because of the Director's obvious lack of patience.

Once a conflict arises, Directors need to be careful in handling it. Both of you can be very stubborn—and you don't want to cross the line to unacceptable conflict. Set aside time at the end of the day or on a weekend when the two of you can dissect what went wrong—and reach clear agreements on the steps you're going to take. Failure to invest time in understanding what went wrong will leave the Thinker with the clear impression that you don't really care about the process—or the outcome—and cannot be trusted in the future.

The same rules apply to a Director delivering bad news to a Thinker. You'll need to explain exactly what happened and analyze all possible outcomes. Calculate in advance the time you expect this to take. Then double it. That's what it will really take.

EXPRESSERS IN CONFLICT WITH THINKERS

For Expressers, a major source of conflict with Thinkers is being imprecise in articulating goals. Expressers often portray goals in broad, general terms: "We need more information about the market for natural toothpaste." Or: "We need to set aside money for contingencies." The Thinker will think of a few preliminary questions and the Expresser will respond—but not with the degree of precision that the Thinker prefers. Typically, then, the Expresser will ask the Thinker to figure out a solution and report back.

When a conflict occurs, Expressers need to ask questions and find out exactly what went wrong. Again, this is going to require an investment of energy and concentration that the Expresser will find taxing.

But in order to maintain trust with a Thinker, the Expresser must show respect for her work. Only then can you negotiate an agreement on what to do next.

When delivering bad news, Expressers should take time to organize their thoughts. Give the Thinker ample warning that you need to discuss something important. Find out when it will fit into her schedule. Then make sure you've cleared the deck so you can take the meeting.

HARMONIZERS IN CONFLICT WITH THINKERS

Harmonizers typically get along well with Thinkers. So a conflict is unlikely to occur. When it does, it may be repressed, because neither Harmonizers nor Thinkers like open confrontation. Signs of repressed conflict could be avoidance, depression, or even forced jocularity.

One technique that a Harmonizer client used was to "check in" every week or so with his staff. After some initial chitchat, the Harmonizer would say: "Our relationship means a lot to me and I want to keep it positive. Is there anything I've done this week that we should clear up? Any misunderstandings?" Having laid such positive groundwork, it was easy to follow up with an agreement to mend any problems.

As a bearer of bad news, the Harmonizer should inform the Thinker in careful detail about every contributing factor. Thinkers like to be told events in chronological order, so instead of starting with the most significant point, as you would with a Director, start at the beginning. Leave nothing out.

The Harmonizer

Under conflict, Harmonizers try to escape. So the first rule in managing conflict with a Harmonizer is that it is often difficult to detect when a conflict exists. Harmonizers will rarely show outward signs of anger or temper. Instead, they will show their displeasure in subtle ways. This can range from no eye contact to outright physical avoidance.

If you suspect that conflict does exist, the best strategy is to find time away from the normal course of business for the two of you to talk. Start by inquiring about friends, family, and personal developments. Then raise the issue in nonthreatening language: "I have the feeling there's something not quite right in our relationship. It's very important to me that we have a good relationship. Would you mind discussing it with me?"

Once the Harmonizer admits that a conflict does exist, you can follow up with: "Would you mind describing to me exactly what's bothering you?"

The Harmonizer often experiences conflict over his perceived role in the group. If the Harmonizer feels slighted, undervalued, or disrespected, there's only one appropriate response—honesty. But honesty can take many forms, and in dealing with Harmonizers, one should make a point of emphasizing their value before offering any criticism.

In negotiations with Harmonizers, be prepared to deal with the argument of tradition and orthodoxy. "This is the way we've always done it, and it's always served us well." The Harmonizer needs to be shown how people will be affected negatively unless a new agreement is reached.

If the conflict is over the Harmonizer's performance, you should be prepared for a lengthy litany of the many unrecognized contributions the Harmonizer makes. And he will be right! In many cases, the Harmonizer works diligently behind the scenes to ensure team harmony and productivity. So make sure you've done your homework and know exactly how to define the performance issue.

DIRECTORS IN CONFLICT WITH HARMONIZERS

Directors need to temper their desire to be blunt and direct when dealing with Harmonizers in stressful situations. Understanding the root of the conflict is the only sure way to repair a rift in the relationship. Unlike the Thinker, who might only require a change in process or policy, the Harmonizer needs to believe that your feelings about his value have not changed. This will not be easy, for once the Harmonizer has pinned the label of "insensitive" or "disrespectful" on you, it will require a major investment of your time to convince him it's unwarranted.

If you have bad news, underline your sensitivity to the situation. Make sure you choose a moment when the Harmonizer has plenty of privacy in which to react and plenty of time to discuss his feelings about what ought to be done.

EXPRESSERS IN CONFLICT WITH HARMONIZERS

Expressers enjoy free-flowing conversations filled with imaginative ideas and have a high tolerance for ambiguity. The Harmonizer likes order, structure, and predictability. Put these two together, and you have a recipe for conflict.

If you are an Expresser, you may think you're being quite clear when you say: "We need to totally rethink the way we're handling this client. Put the team together and give me your best thoughts at the sales meeting tomorrow." The Harmonizer goes off thinking he understands the problem. But he doesn't. You have failed to define the issues or the goals.

When the conflict occurs, the Expresser needs to handle the situation gingerly. You need to recognize that your preference for loose talking and ambiguity doesn't serve this situation well. You need to take responsibility for your lack of clarity. You should point out exactly where the misunderstanding occurred, and state your resolve to change your style of communicating. And then the two of you should decide how to handle the client.

In presenting bad news to a Harmonizer, use the opportunity to demonstrate your concern for everyone involved. If you have a solution, show how it minimizes damage to other people.

THINKERS IN CONFLICT WITH HARMONIZERS

Thinkers get into conflicts with Harmonizers over process. For example, a Thinker may view a Harmonizer as lacking the necessary precision and attention to detail. "If you had followed instructions, this wouldn't have happened," the Thinker will be tempted to say.

But this type of direct criticism will likely cause further erosion in the relationship and not be effective in rectifying the behavior. Instead, Thinkers should strive to demonstrate their concern for the Harmonizer, take time to engage in small talk, and stress the importance of their relationship. Having laid a foundation of trust, the Thinker can then focus on the problem. But ask a question rather than state the criticism directly: "Have you figured out what went wrong with the batch process on module number seven?"

The same technique applies when the Thinker is the bearer of bad news to the Harmonizer. Make sure you demonstrate your sensitivity to how each individual will be affected.

Conclusion

If these tips strike you as being manipulative, you're right—they are. But that's the point. By learning how to modify your behavior in stressful situations, you show your desire to strive for a productive solution, rather than fan the fire. By using straight talk, you can cut short the otherwise exhausting cycles of expectation and anger, anticipation and letdown, and avoidance and resentment.

More important, conflicts need not continue beyond the useful point of underscoring differences in our styles, our opinions, our values, or our goals. It's when we repress the differences out of fear of the repercussions that conflict begins. If everyone understands each other's position, it's far easier to go down the road to a productive conversation and reach effective agreements.

EXERCISE: RESOLVE A LONG-STANDING CONFLICT

Write down the names of three or four colleagues or friends with whom you regularly experience conflict. Then write down their styles (or your assessment of their styles). Next, write down what you feel is the source of your conflict with each of them.

Person's Name	Person's Style	Source of the Conflict
1.		
2.		
3.		
4.		

What would you say to each person to enable you to acknowledge your conflict and move on? Remember to try to express this as a dilemma.

1.	
2.	
3.	
4.	

Chapter Ten
Understanding Organizational Cultures

The great law of culture is:
Let each become all
that he is capable of being.
—THOMAS CARLYLE (1795–1881)

Charles, a stocky man in his early sixties, began his career as an investment banker on Wall Street. After earning enough money to retire when he was fifty, Charles decided to try something new. So he founded a book publishing company.

Charles had a string of successes with computer books. His specialty was books that revealed the secrets to solving computer games. He also published an Internet directory that sold well. But a bold new idea called Digital Classroom began siphoning away much of his time—and working capital.

Charles hired us to diagnose the problems in his business. We asked for his diagnosis first. He said: "My top people are not very good at planning and executing. They have lots of good ideas. But we seem to have a hell of a time getting things done. Everyone takes off in different directions."

We suggested that his organization might benefit from understanding its style of communicating and how that style affected the organizational culture—both in good ways and bad. "If your diagnosis is correct," we told Charles, "then our audit should reveal why."

We interviewed the senior managers and found them to be smart, reasonable people, with a typical workload and comparable pressures to those seen in other companies. But when we gave them the Communication Styles Profile, we discovered an interesting thing. Nine of the twelve were Directors. Only three people had other styles.

We worked with them for two days, helping them understand their styles of communicating and how those styles affect the way they work together. This is an excerpt from our follow-up report to Charles:

> In summary, your company is prone to rushing into things without spending sufficient time analyzing the problems and planning. The senior management team is weighted toward a style of communicating that favors this approach. This has a direct impact on the team's performance—and your organization's.
>
> We've helped your senior managers understand the consequences of their styles. They now have the necessary skills to bring a more balanced approach to their work together. This will tend, over time, to reduce much of the conflict they experience. Our experience shows that this will also improve the overall performance of your company. We recommend a follow-up survey in twelve months.

After we submitted our report, Charles took me aside and asked whether I really believed in this stuff. I told him this type of analysis had proven valuable in organizations of all types. We were convinced his culture would change once its managers recognized their communication tendencies and weaknesses—and worked to counter them. This, we said, was the best way to leverage long-term improvement.

Then I added a footnote. I said that this cultural change would only occur if Charles recognized his role, too. Whether by choice or accident, the people he'd hired to run his company were mirror images of himself. The culture wouldn't change unless—or until—Charles recognized his role and changed his hiring criteria.

Charles's response summed up the underlying problem:

"I don't need to change," he said. "I own the company."

Organizational Cultures

This chapter dives into one of the more interesting uses of the communication tools described in this book: learning how to identify the style or culture of an entire organization.

As you read the following descriptions of each organizational culture, consider your own organization. What type of culture is it? How do you contribute in both positive and negative ways? What type of culture should you be aiming for?

 Director Cultures

Director cultures can be very successful if everyone is focused on a single goal. One Silicon Valley start-up with a Director culture had a hugely successful initial public offering because everyone in the organization was focused on maximizing sales of their new Internet platform—and everyone was a self-starter. Later, after a new CEO was brought in, the company shifted toward a Thinker culture—a more appropriate balance for a maturing company.

On the downside, Director cultures often suffer from having conflicting goals. Too many Directors result in internal power struggles. Because Directors are accustomed to dealing with conflict—in fact, thrive on it—the organization may lack the vision to recognize this problem. Thus begins a downward spiral.

Entrepreneurial companies often suffer the ill effects of the Director culture. Hard-charging founder-CEOs typically hire other "go-getter" types to help them achieve their ambitious goals. As companies come under increasing pressure to meet these goals, each Director articulates his or her own "bottom line" for how to achieve them. Because Directors typically invest little time in communicating, the core team becomes confused and divided. They blame each other for what's going on—yet ignore the fundamental cause of the conflict.

As the company grows beyond the core founders, the Director culture can develop a severe case of communication constipation. The terse, "don't-talk-about-it, just-get-it-done" style of the Director results in poorly run meetings and a lack of coordinated follow-through. In such an environment, middle management becomes quickly alienated, further compromising the organization's effectiveness.

We've worked with many Director cultures, and we're always struck by how blind they are to their failings. One of our client companies was led by a man of undisputed brilliance. But the company was literally at odds with itself. He'd articulate conflicting goals; staff were left to try to interpret the "goal du jour." The company became a dangerous breeding ground for power games. Senior management found itself victimized by end runs by the CEO. Middle managers vented their resentment to their staffs. Far more time—and money—was spent patching up superficial problems than either addressing the underlying issues or meeting customer needs.

When we were hired, we surveyed the management team and then spent a day reviewing the results with them. We diagrammed the vicious cycle of behavior that was tearing them apart. We talked about the need to develop a more balanced management style. We introduced them to the tools for achieving consensus and for having productive meetings. Ultimately, none of them worked, because Noah, the CEO, didn't believe in them.

"We've got too much to get done. We can't spend so much time in meetings," he'd declare. We tried to make him understand that before there could be fewer meetings, there needed to be agreements about change, and this required meetings.

Ultimately, this was a success story. One of our partners got the brilliant idea that Noah needed a new toy. We persuaded Noah to start a used car shopping service on the Internet to divert his attention. With his mind focused on the new venture, and the core business led by a more consensus-oriented CEO, the company started to thrive.

Typically, Director cultures can be modified by the introduction of a team-based organizational structure. Especially if all team members are made equal (rotating team leaders is a good way to accomplish this) and allowed full access to information, a Director culture can quickly become more consensus based.

Expresser Cultures

Expresser cultures typically have lots of creative energy and ideas, but find it difficult to focus or set priorities. One of our clients, a software company, suffered from this problem. At a morning sales meeting, the CEO would suddenly get an idea for a new software product, the marketing director would start describing the ad campaign, the sales manager would talk about potential customers, and everyone would get carried away by the possibility of reaching this new market. The brainstorming, as you might imagine, was terrific; but the company was having a tough time meeting its goals.

When we pointed out this pattern to members of the management team, they said this was how most of their meetings went. "We like to keep it loose. That way, we all have fun and get to participate."

While this sounds great, particularly for creative people, the lack of discipline can destroy an organization. Without priorities or analysis, a company can be too easily swayed by an idea that feels right, but whose timing may be wrong for the market.

Expresser cultures are often good at creative marketing, but weak at the detailed analysis or big-picture understanding needed for success. They can come up with a bold idea—after lots of brainstorming, of course—but then fail to delve sufficiently into the details or test for possible negative consequences. For example, one clothing company agreed on a strategy of going after younger customers by showing teenagers dressed in business suits holding meetings and making deals. However, many older customers felt alienated by the new marketing campaign and stopped buying their products.

At a time of crisis, Expresser cultures are often left flailing. Unaccustomed to the kind of dispassionate decision making necessary when all the world is losing its head, the organization can consume crucial hours trying to decide how to respond. Clear, focused, self-challenging discourse eludes them. Meanwhile market events, along with unfavorable publicity, overwhelm them.

Expresser cultures often have poorly defined lines of authority. The CEO will skip a layer of management and work directly with departmental staff. An impromptu brainstorming session may begin without sufficient input or buy-in from key members of the enterprise. New employees may start work without a clear definition of their jobs, or a clear picture of the lines of authority.

The solution, of course, is to recognize the Expresser pattern and counter it by being more deliberate and detailed. Expresser cultures need to constantly ask themselves: Have we set clear priorities and deadlines? Do we have clear lines of authority? Have we considered the impact of this decision on our other goals? Is everyone who needs to know in the loop? Do we know who's responsible for follow-up? And most important, are we all agreed on who's doing what and by when?

Thinker Cultures

Thinker cultures typically excel in planning, communication, and follow-through. Since these are important elements of an organization's success, Thinker cultures are often success stories.

On the downside, a Thinker culture can suffer from "analysis paralysis"—especially where significant risk is involved. All change entails risk, and the Thinker culture may not respond quickly enough to change—with the result that change has to be forced on it.

Because of their absorption in planning, communication, and follow-through, all of which are consensus-based activities, Thinker cultures often lack an overarching vision or goal. One Thinker culture labored for two years to articulate a strategic vision (the norm is three to six months). Thinker cultures are notorious for blending conflicting goals into their mission statements. This pattern can only be broken by someone saying clearly: "This is our priority. Everything else is secondary. Now, what can we stop doing?"

Thinker cultures typically avoid facing conflict, even if the needs of the business require it. People are reluctant to challenge traditional behavior, to question assumptions, to rock the boat. Given the principles of straight talk, the dangers of conflict avoidance are obvious.

Given these patterns, it's easy to see that a Thinker culture can lapse into bureaucracy. To counter this, Thinker cultures need a strong dose of innovation and risk taking. One way is through regular "workout meetings," where people gather in one place and make on-the-spot changes.[1] Another is for someone, usually the boss or team leader, to insist on deadlines for action. As an incentive, the group can be rewarded for initiating a minimum number of changes within a certain time period.

Harmonizer Cultures

Harmonizer cultures are relatively rare in small companies, because Harmonizers typically don't gravitate toward risky work, or to organizations where power is vested in one person. Harmonizer cultures are more prevalent in large corporations, in governmental organizations, and in not-for-profits.

---

1. Workout meetings were made famous at General Electric. All managers and staff meet in a large room. Each person lists one change he or she would like to implement, and then writes down who needs to approve the change. Each person then goes around the room to get the necessary sign-off on the spot. Only three outcomes are allowed: Change is immediately approved; change is not approved (with exact reasons listed); or change is to be studied, to be reported back on in thirty or sixty days, with the burden of proof on those denying the change to show why it should not be implemented.

Harmonizer cultures are team oriented. They invest resources in personal recognition programs, company picnics, coffee klatches, support groups, personal leave days, and "dress-down" days. People feel involved, know what's going on, and have a sense that they are genuinely appreciated for their contributions. Harmonizer cultures are happy, healthy environments where people come first.

The downside of Harmonizer cultures is that they tend to get bogged down by conformity. Everyone's so eager to please that no one's willing to buck the tide or take a controversial stand.

One of our clients, a not-for-profit arts organization, had a tradition that each employee should be taken to lunch by a manager once a quarter. For a manager with fifteen employees, this meant nearly 25 percent of his noon hours each quarter were taken up with employee lunches. While this was a nice idea, it left too little time for meeting with donors, negotiating with artists, or for other needs. Yet when we suggested dropping the program, there was resistance by employees who complained that the old "family feeling of the company" was being eliminated, and that new management was pointing the company toward ruin.

How can you balance a Harmonizer culture? One solution is to invite dissent whenever possible. At each meeting, for example, appoint one person to actively challenge the prevailing sentiment. Make it that person's temporary job to pose challenging questions, such as: "On what facts do you base your conclusions?" "What additional data would make people change their minds?" "How could our competitors hurt us most?"

In the process of responding to those questions, a Harmonizer culture is forced into discussion that centers on underlying issues, explores assumptions, and brainstorms alternative solutions. One management team we worked with had a rewards program that specifically called for celebrating people who went "against the grain." The prize was a loaf of special homemade bread made by the president. Given its Harmonizer culture, that was a brilliant form of recognition.

Diagnosing an Organization's Culture

How can you determine an organization's style? If it's a relatively small organization, start with the CEO. Nine times out of ten, his or her style will dictate the style of the organization.

CHART 23: CULTURES OF THE FOUR STYLES

Director Culture	Expresser Culture
Goal oriented	Idea oriented
Emphasis on bottom line	Emphasis on people
Makes quick decisions	Entertaining, fun
Always on the go	Willing to take risks
Willing to take risks	Many meetings
Abrupt, not communicative	Lack of clear priorities
Lack of meeting time	Difficulty with follow-through
Thinker Culture	**Harmonizer Culture**
Fact and process oriented	Relationship oriented
Emphasis on precision	Emphasis on team
Stresses academic credentials	Avoids conflict, change
Lots of quality control	Makes decisions slowly
Unwilling to take risks	Not clear about purpose, goals
Tendency toward missing deadlines	Tendency toward bureaucracy

For a larger organization—say, with more than one hundred employees—the division heads or senior management team will determine the culture. If they tilt toward a particular style, then the organization will mirror that. A lack of balance in senior management will affect the styles of hundreds, even thousands, of subordinates, and cause the organization to behave in predictable ways.

Chart 23 shows the predictable tendencies of each different type of culture. See if you can diagnose the organizational culture in the following example.

A magazine company had five publications geared toward sports-oriented readers, including a skateboarding magazine, a surfing magazine, and an in-line skating magazine. According to the founder and co-owner, the company had many problems. Materials weren't getting to the printer on time. Relationships between departments were a mess. He wanted us to see what we could make of it.

When we arrived, our first impression was of a very hip, very fast-paced environment. Most of the work took place in a large open area called the "pit." There was a separate room for people to unwind with pinball machines and video games. People could work whatever hours they chose.

We talked to the publisher, a woman in her early thirties, who downplayed the problems. She told me their operation was typical of magazines with a high rate of growth. She admitted feeling frustrated by the planning issues. She also said that most of their managers had come to work for the company right out of college, and the highest achievers had been promoted to management positions. "We place a high value on loyalty to the company," she said.

We gave the top managers the Communication Styles Profile, plus another diagnostic survey. From our interviews we learned that the organization encouraged spontaneous, informal hallway meetings in which people made decisions. But the people who needed to be a part of the decisions were sometimes left out—and not informed after-ward—although this was nothing deliberate on anyone's part.

"It was the way the culture evolved," one person wrote.

Okay. Let's stop here. What kind of culture is it? Once you've made your guess, read on.

The Communication Styles Profiles showed that, of the ten senior managers, six were Expressers, two were Thinkers, and two were Har-monizers. None was a Director. After showing them a Matrix with their prevailing styles highlighted, we asked them what they made of it.

"I'd say we like to meet too much," said one.

"I'd say we have a problem with follow-through," said another.

"I'd say we show all the symptoms of a classic Expresser culture," said a third.

"I'd suggest we all resign and start over," said someone else.

Achieving a Balanced Culture

Knowing how to achieve a balance of styles is a sign of mature manage-ment. But the reverse occurs more frequently. The boss selects subordi-nates who are similar in style to his or her own; key managers reinforce behaviors they're comfortable with, rather than those that might pro-vide the necessary balance.

The Rule of the Center is as true for organizations as it is for indi-viduals, but organizations can't shift styles as easily as individuals can. When an organization is out of balance, it has three main options:

(1) Add senior-level people with styles that balance the prevailing style, (2) create systems that correct the imbalance by rewarding specific behaviors, or (3) accept the status quo.

CEOs and presidents of organizations in particular need to recognize their role in shaping a culture. When a boss is aware of his or her style, a conscientious effort to motivate behaviors within the organization that balance that style can be made. Typically, these behaviors can be induced by creating specific systems and processes within the organization.

For example, in a Director culture, you can make sure that enough meetings are scheduled to keep people informed and involved. In a Harmonizer culture, you can create an executive team and empower it to make critical decisions. In an Expresser culture, you can insist that people form tight agreements about what needs to be done when. And in a Thinker culture, you can reward people for innovative thinking.

Chart 24 presents a checklist of possible actions that can be taken to address the weaknesses that crop up in each type of culture.

In the case of the magazine company, we asked the senior managers to envision specific changes that could create a more balanced communication style throughout the culture. "Let's change your behaviors," we suggested, "by changing your systems."

The publisher suggested they map out every step in the process of producing the magazines to identify the crucial decision points. Once they did that, she argued, they could schedule the appropriate meetings to get the work done efficiently. Her idea was accepted.

Four task forces were formed to create this process map. None of them actually finished the task—not surprising, given the culture. Instead, within two weeks they decided they knew where the problem lay. All they needed was one single "megaplanning meeting" each week. Everyone would come. Every decision would get made. Democracy would rule.

As you might imagine, this didn't work either. There were too many items on the agenda. Too many people were involved. So the publisher decided to break the staff into teams. There would be a content team, a design team, and a production team. Each team would have a team leader. These three teams with a total of eighteen people would make the major decisions.

But teams weren't the answer either. The next issue of the magazine was seven days late. That prompted the founder, the man who

CHART 24: STRENGTHENING ORGANIZATIONAL CULTURES

Director Culture	Expresser Culture
Hold regular Q&A meetings with all staff. ognize the importance of people. Push decision making down the hierarchy through increased information sharing. Make it a rule to decide at each meeting who needs information. Hire people with strong people skills in key jobs.	Create a system for tight agreements on next steps and Rec- follow-through. Eliminate unnecessary meetings. Induce people to write tight, concise reports. Emphasize financial analysis in all reports and plans. Hire people with strong analytical skills in key jobs.
Thinker Culture	**Harmonizer Culture**
Hold regular strategic reviews to focus on the big picture. Create a rewards program for innovation. Use "workout meetings" to eliminate bureaucracy. Reward risk taking in new projects. Hire people with strong people skills in key jobs.	Form an executive team to make fast decisions. Streamline decision making wherever possible. Use "workout meetings" to eliminate bureaucracy. Motivate project teams to take risks. Hire people with strong analytical skills in key jobs.

originally hired us, to ask why we hadn't been more effective. We told him we couldn't force change to happen.

"What's the problem?" he asked.

"The problem is the culture. Until the culture changes, the weaknesses will remain."

"Can we change the culture?"

"Perhaps. But where do you think the culture comes from?"

"Where?"

"From the top. From your publisher. It starts with her."

The following week, the founder took her aside and talked to her. She admitted the need to create a more balanced culture. Within a week, she and the founder had decided to hire a new publisher. She'd devote her energies to new projects.

A year later, when we conducted a second organizational survey, the results showed a new culture was taking hold. The new publisher, an Investigator, had scrapped the work teams. She had carved two meeting rooms out of "the pit" and scheduled three standing meetings each week.

The process map had also been completed. It showed that production deadlines were too tight to handle the inevitable last minute screwups. A staggered production schedule was established; each section had to go to press by a specific deadline. Managers who missed their deadlines lost ten points toward a monthly bonus (out of a hundred points total)—regardless of whose fault it was.

In short, she put in systems and processes. She leavened the Expresser culture with a bit of Thinker and Director mentality.

The reaction? People groused and grumbled. But the overall sentiment was summed up in one manager's comment: "We aren't running around as much from meeting to meeting as we used to, and it's not as much fun. But we know what we're doing. And we're getting the job done."

Culture and Conflict

All four cultures share a common element: They each give rise to unresolved conflicts. This occurs because cultures create, by their very nature, conventional ways of thinking. "All that matters is the bottom line." Or: "No idea is a bad idea." Or: "Take care of the details, and the rest will take care of itself." Or: "Be a team player." These are all typical buzz phrases that pass for conventional wisdom in each type of culture. (By now, you should know which goes with which!)

As you might expect, cultures work overtime to stifle people who challenge conventional wisdom. In subtle and not-so-subtle ways, people who honestly disagree with a prevailing view will feel unable to air their opinions. They'll feel muzzled, unable to register their view. If they do air their opinion, they're accused of "going against our core values" or "undermining the things we stand for." Few people can withstand such a withering attack—especially when it comes from one's own culture.

Thus culture and conflict go together. Culture—no matter what type it is—inevitably gives rise to unresolved conflicts. Where you find a strong culture, you'll find that the conflicts are all that much more serious.

The only culture in which this does not occur is one based on the principles espoused in this book, on straight talk. Only by continuously acknowledging the value of different perspectives, only by constantly testing everyone's basic assumptions about what is and is not "good for the organization," can an organization rid itself of the tendency to create conflict within itself.

It's the role of the senior executive, therefore, to be particularly supportive of countervailing sentiments and ideas. By looking beneath the content of the idea and examining its source, the senior executive will see that his or her very resistance to the idea is what makes it valuable to the organization's well-being.

Case Study A Software Company Reboots

We were asked by the president of a small software company to help his people "get focused," as he put it. The company specialized in customized accounting packages for small businesses. Competition was heating up, and the president was having problems getting his management team to agree on how to respond.

As a first step, we asked the four-member management team to take the Communication Styles Profile. Clark was the president; Liz was the chief operating officer; Bill was the director of marketing; and Ann was the chief financial officer. The results, shown in the Matrix in Chart 25, were not surprising, given the problem of lack of focus: Three of the four were Thinkers or Harmonizers.

We met with the team for a two-day retreat at Lake Tahoe. We spent the first day talking about their different communication styles, and then about cultural styles. In the middle of the afternoon, they had an epiphany: The reason they had such a hard time setting goals wasn't because their business was difficult to manage, but because of the culture they'd created. Yes, they agreed, it was nice to have a harmonious workplace. Yes, they were excellent at handling details. But they weren't good at making decisions. And it was hurting the company.

"We have met the enemy," said Clark, quoting a line from the comic strip Pogo, "and it is us."

CHART 25: STYLES OF THE MANAGEMENT TEAM

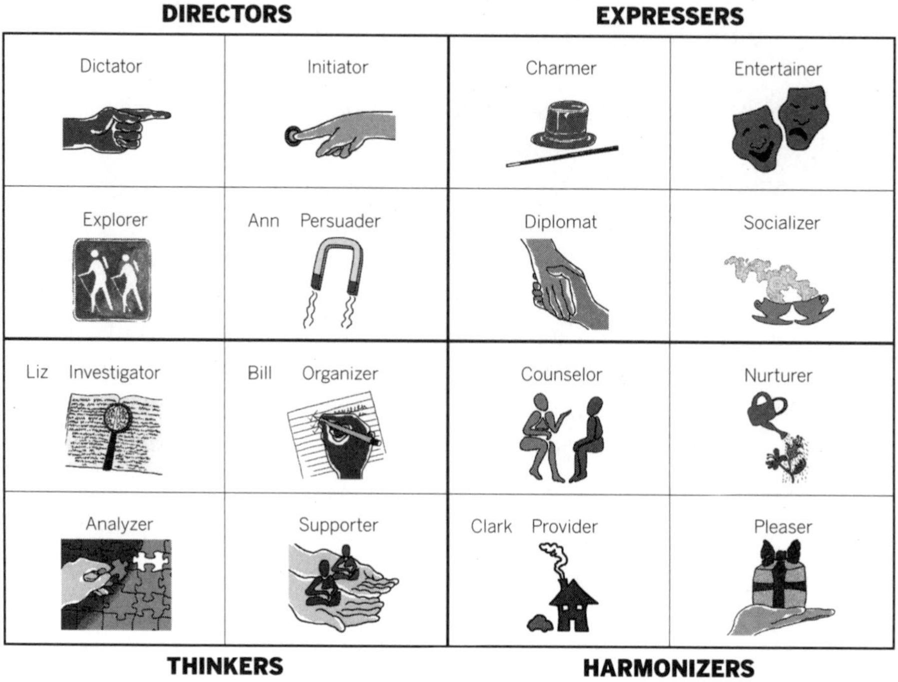

DIRECTORS   **EXPRESSERS**

Dictator	Initiator	Charmer	Entertainer
Explorer	Ann Persuader	Diplomat	Socializer
Liz Investigator	Bill Organizer	Counselor	Nurturer
Analyzer	Supporter	Clark Provider	Pleaser

THINKERS   **HARMONIZERS**

That evening after dinner we asked each of them to talk about something risky or daring they'd done. Liz talked about being a flight attendant ferrying troops to and from staging areas in the Philippines during the Vietnam War. Clark had camped in the Himalayas and photographed some of the highest peaks in the world. Ann had dropped out of college for a year to sail to the Galápagos. And Bill had held a summer job with the Forest Service as a firefighter.

We gave them the rest of the evening to digest the results of the first day. The next morning, we split them into pairs—Liz with Bill (the two Thinkers), and Clark with Ann—and gave them the following assignment: If resources weren't a problem, what would the company's goals be? How would the company differ from what it is today?

"Pull out all the stops," we told them. "This was their one chance to reinvent the company." We told them we wanted them to imagine every possible scenario. We asked them to prepare a list of their best ideas for the group. They had two hours.

Then we left the room.

Two hours later, they delivered their reports. Both teams were in high spirits. Liz and Bill had come up with a plan to recast the company as a new company called Disc Doctors. The company would provide on-call emergency repairs for small business computers, regardless of industry or software. Clark and Ann recast the company as a software solutions company serving three related industries: law, accounting, and commercial real estate. Business in one industry would generate leads in the others.

They agreed to spend three intensive weeks analyzing these two alternative visions, plus any other visions that arose during that period. At the end of the three weeks, they would commit to a single vision, and build the company around it.

Four years later, this company is a success story. Clark and Ann's strategy—providing software solutions to related professional industries—has been the key.

More heartening, there's no evidence that the company is about to become saddled with a new organizational culture. Each year, the management team retreats to Lake Tahoe, where the first day's agenda is dominated by one assignment: "Challenge the way we think about our business."

Case Study A Task Force Targets Dwindling Profits

We worked with a midsized law firm in San Francisco that specialized in labor law. The firm had seventy-five attorneys working for it, and fourteen partners. We were called in because the firm wasn't meeting its performance goals. Either the industry was changing or their customers were dissatisfied, they told us, but they didn't know which.

Before we met with the partners, we collected some data on the firm and asked the partners to take the Communication Styles Profile. The Matrix in Chart 26 shows their disbursement of communication styles. The culture was tipped toward the more analytical styles—Directors and Thinkers. That much was clear.

At our first face-to-face meeting, we asked each partner to define the problem as he or she saw it. Here are some of their responses.

"Every one of our competitors is facing the same predicament we are. There's less business to go around. We don't want to lay off attorneys, because labor law is a highly specialized skill, and if the business comes back, we may have to start afresh. But there's little we can do besides attack our competitors."

221

CHART 26: STYLES OF THE PARTNERS

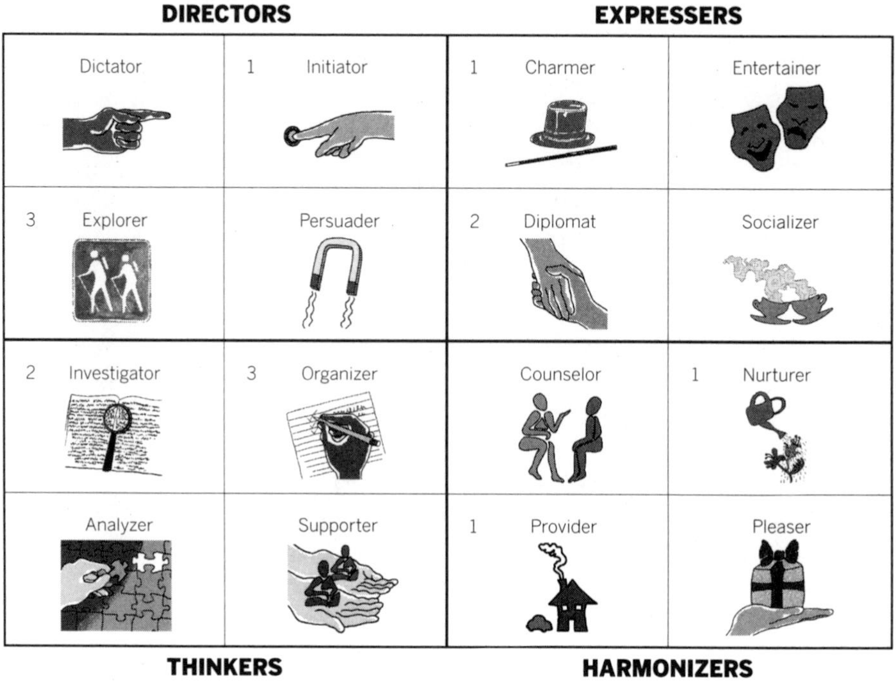

DIRECTORS   EXPRESSERS

Dictator	1 Initiator	1 Charmer	Entertainer
3 Explorer	Persuader	2 Diplomat	Socializer
2 Investigator	3 Organizer	Counselor	1 Nurturer
Analyzer	Supporter	1 Provider	Pleaser

THINKERS   HARMONIZERS

Another partner spoke: "We don't get as much repeat business from our clients as we used to. It's down something like 12 percent as a category. We're making it up to some extent with new clients. But that repeat business is our bread and butter. We need it to survive."

A third partner added: "Not one of us has really focused on getting a new major corporate client. It's all drips and drabs through referrals. We need to beef up our core stable of clients. That's the top priority."

As we listened, we saw an underlying cultural pattern come into focus. No one was asking questions. They were all making strong assertions about the solution. They each assumed that they saw the problem clearly. It reminded us of someone saying "Let me give you some advice" before even knowing the problem. That's how these fourteen lawyers were dealing with a fundamental business problem.

In this case, the cultural style—Directors and Thinkers— was coupled with a professional code of conduct that required high levels of assertive communication. Despite the number of Thinkers and Harmonizers, no one knew how to ask questions.

Our solution was to inject some inquiry into the discussion.

"Each of you has laid out your version of the problem. One of you says the problem is a permanent change in the business—more competition—and the solution is layoffs. A second says the problem is a decline in your repeat business, and the solution is to concentrate on existing clients. And a third says the problem is failing to get new major corporate clients, with the implied solution being to focus there."

We paused and looked around. There were a few heads nodding in agreement, but otherwise no one said a thing. "So what's the correct definition of the problem?"

Someone said: "Actually, we seem to be dancing around the core problem, which is that this year's profits don't equal last year's. That's the problem."

Much head nodding.

"Okay, then let's analyze the underlying causes of that decline. Before we can suggest solutions, let's understand the problem. Okay?"

From that conversation emerged a task force to analyze the underlying causes of the decline. After two weeks, the task force returned with its report. Boiled down, it showed that the cause of the decline in profits was a sharp rise in variable costs over the previous year—postage, outside secretarial work, travel and entertainment. If the firm's variable costs had been the same percentages of revenues as they had the previous year, profits actually would have been higher.

The task force report completely changed the focus of the conversation. Everyone in the firm was shown the evidence. The bonus system was retooled to reward attorneys who met (or exceeded) a specific ratio of revenues to expenses. There was no other way to qualify for the bonus.

The culture changed in a hurry. Everyone started questioning their expenses. They began combining two or three trips into one. Much of the focus was on postage, where overnight delivery charges amounted to $825,000, up from $565,000 the previous year. Documents were sent via regular mail when they could be, and the company contracted with an outside firm for local delivery services—at a fixed cost per day.

The lesson is this: When looking at the problems an organization faces, look first to the problems the culture creates for itself.

In this case, the law firm had a cultural proclivity to jump to conclusions. Had it waited for the data, it might not have squandered valuable billing time.

Conclusion

The managers of every organization imbue its culture with certain habits and tendencies. Over time, however, these habits can become the source of discontent and unresolved conflict. By using the Communication Styles Profile to analyze the styles of top managers, one can discern problems in an organization's culture and isolate possible causes. Finding the right balance of management styles is management's top responsibility—along with ensuring that each style understands its importance to the organization.

EXERCISE: IDENTIFY YOUR ORGANIZATION'S CULTURE

On the Matrix below, place the initials of the senior managers of your organization—the CEO, president, COO, and senior vice presidents or division heads—in the squares corresponding to their respective styles of communicating. If you don't know, make your best guess.

DIRECTORS		**EXPRESSERS**	
Dictator	Initiator	Charmer	Entertainer
Explorer	Persuader	Diplomat	Socializer
Investigator	Organizer	Counselor	Nurturer
Analyzer	Supporter	Provider	Pleaser
THINKERS		**HARMONIZERS**	

Notes:

Next, circle the phrases in the following chart that best describe your organization's culture .

Director Culture	Expresser Culture
Goal oriented	Idea oriented
Emphasis on bottom line	Emphasis on people
Makes quick decisions	Entertaining, fun
Always on the go	Willing to take risks
Willing to take risks	Many meetings
Abrupt, not communicative	Lack of clear priorities
Lack of meeting time	Difficulty with follow-through
Thinker Culture	**Harmonizer Culture**
Fact and process oriented	Relationship oriented
Emphasis on precision	Emphasis on team
Stresses academic credentials	Avoids conflict, change
Lots of quality control	Makes decisions slowly
Unwilling to take risks	Not clear about purpose, goals
Tendency toward missing deadlines	Tendency toward bureaucracy

Notes:

Finally, based on the patterns you detect in the above Matrix and chart, circle your organization's culture. Then, using the material from this chapter, list three ways the weaknesses in your organization's culture could be addressed.

Our Organization's Culture (circle one)

    Director   **Expresser**   **Thinker**   **Harmonizer**

To address the weaknesses in our culture, we should do the following:

1.

2.

3.

Notes:

Chapter Eleven
Solving Organizational Problems

To know that you do not know is the best.
To pretend to know when you do not know is a disease.
— LAO TZU (6TH CENTURY B.C.)

Our firm has several defining pieces of corporate wisdom. They speak to the heart of our business and what we must do to be successful. One of them states: "Eighty percent of solving a problem is defining it correctly." A colleague puts it a little differently: "Solving a problem is not the challenge; it's defining the problem you're trying to solve."

Here's an example.

Our firm was hired to help public television managers sort through the thorny issue of "commercialism" in public television. These 180 senior executives faced a dilemma: On the one hand, federal funding was declining, which meant stations needed to find new sources of revenue; on the other hand, viewers were accustomed to commercial-free fare. Selling commercial time was therefore a risky way to get more money if it meant alienating viewers.

Some managers cited a research project to support their conclusions. In the study, the same programs were aired in comparable markets with and without commercials. After two years, the data showed no significant drop-off in membership support (the money pledged by viewers). Nor was there a detectable decline in ratings (the number of viewers) in markets that ran the commercials. And advertising revenues did increase significantly, especially in larger markets.

Some managers argued, however, that the data were flawed. First, they contended, the study lasted only two years, and therefore neglected any long-term effects—of which, they argued, there could be many. Second, they argued that markets of the same population size weren't actually comparable. Viewers in New Orleans might not be comparable to those in Kansas City. Too many variables were involved to let such important policy decisions be dictated by this one study.

As we conducted our research, we saw a familiar pattern: The television executives often clumped many issues into one—and then reacted in frustration at their failure to resolve the issue. For example, what they branded "commercialism" was really a host of issues: worries about further loss of federal revenues, debates about acceptable advertising, debates about appropriate length of commercials and the time slots when they aired, and the lack of consistency in guidelines from market to market and show to show. Each of these was a separate issue that needed to be tackled on its own.

This phenomenon—lumping many issues into one seemingly intractable one—was not new to us. Yet before any solutions could be reached, the executives needed a way to unravel these issues and determine their relationship to each other. In essence, they needed to learn how to frame issues, much as a doctor needs to know how to isolate the cause of a disease.

Framing Issues

Framing issues in effective ways is the subject of this chapter. It's analogous to what mathematicians do when they search for factors. Take the number 851. At first glance, it appears to be divisible only by itself and 1. But in fact, it has factors of 23 and 37. Similarly, when we tackle a tough business problem, we need to make sure we've identified all the underlying issues before we begin trying to solve it. Otherwise, communication is going to get stuck—and result in a lot of frustration for everyone.

Certain communication styles lend themselves to this part of the problem-solving process. Thinkers will naturally understand the need to reduce an issue to its constituent parts. Expressers will go along with this work as long as they perceive it as requiring creative input—which it does (as we'll see in a moment). And Harmonizers will yearn to do what's best to ensure a positive outcome for the group. But Directors will be impatient with this exercise—and push the group to get on with it—thereby jeopardizing the outcome.

In sum, a group should agree in advance on the importance of framing an issue before trying to solve it. This chapter distills the process down to five steps:

1. Tentatively identify the problem.
2. Discuss related issues.
3. Analyze the relationship of issues.
4. Eliminate issues beyond your control.
5. Brainstorm alternative solutions until you (a) agree on a solution or (b) agree on what evidence or data are necessary in order to resolve the problem.

Step 1: Tentatively identify the problem.

Step 1 simply involves getting the group to tentatively define the problem it seeks to solve. It's not important at this stage that everyone agree. The goal is to get the various definitions on the table. Maybe it's getting profitability back on track. Or deciding whether or not to run commercials. Or finding ways to cut costs. The way the problem is defined will change. But everyone needs to be on record stating: "This is the problem I think we're trying to solve."

Before you start, remind yourselves about the 80 percent rule mentioned earlier. State it this way: "Eighty percent of solving a problem is defining it accurately. Therefore, the time we spend together in defining the problem we're trying to solve is not a preamble to the work we have to do. It *is* the work we have to do."

Kick off the discussion by going around the room and checking with every member of the group. Ask: "How would you define the problem we're trying to solve right now?" Tell the group that the issue will probably change as the conversation develops. But for now, it's important that every voice be heard.

If you're not sure people have had enough time, ask them to think about their answer for a few minutes and write it down on paper. Or break into groups and have each subgroup talk about the issue and then report back. (This latter method actually reduces the time it takes to get everyone's response.)

Here's an example. A Connecticut company, Jensen, Inc.,[1] makes high-quality sailboats. A strategic retreat of its management team is taking place at a resort in New Hampshire. For the first hour, the group

---

1. The name of this company has been changed to protect its privacy.

discusses its communication styles and the tools of straight talk. Then the discussion leader says: "Let's identify the major strategic issue we're trying to solve today. Why don't we each define it as best we can?"

Sally, the marketing director, speaks up first. "We need to figure out how to segment our customers more effectively. Which customers in particular do we want to reach in the next three years? With which products? Do we want customers who have purchased from us before, since they're familiar with the Jensen brand and more likely to buy? Or do we want new customers whose income exceeds $250,000 because they're more likely to buy a new, more expensive and profitable model?"

The next person to take a stab at it is Sherry, the head of information systems. "We don't have a database that tells us accurately who's most likely to purchase, nor do we have demographic data. So one problem is defining what information to collect about our customers. Sally suggested some criteria. But maybe there are other criteria that are more apt to lead to increased profits."

"Like what?" Mike, the president, asks.

"Like whether they already own a boat, or whether they recently took out life insurance, or whether they eat out five times a week. I don't know; it's just that I'm uncomfortable with Sally's analysis. It seems somewhat arbitrary to me."

Mike takes his turn next. "I think Sherry is onto something else. She's saying we need to decide what information we need before we can solve this problem. That gives me something to think about."

"Can you state what you see as the issue before us today, Mike?" the facilitator asks.

"Yeah, more profits," he says. "That's the bottom line."

Step 2: Discuss related issues.

In Step 2, the goal is to redefine the problem to everyone's satisfaction. Everyone needs to discuss the issues related to the problem as it's been tentatively defined. A likely outcome is that the definition of the problem will change—perhaps several times. That's perfectly fine. The purpose of this discussion is to test whether there are other, more primary problems that should be dealt with first.

The wording of the issue, at this point, is not important. It's just a starting point. Begin with your tentative definition of the problem.

Then let people talk about related issues. Tell the group that this is the time to raise any and all related points. Explain that you're all trying to put together a puzzle, but you need all the pieces before you can start. Tell them to make sure all underlying issues are allowed to surface. Say: "This is a time when there are really no bad ideas. Let loose your creativity. Bring up your undiscussables. Tell us what's going on in your Inner Script."

Someone may ask: "What exactly are we trying to do?" Answer it this way: "For now, we want to identify all the issues whose resolution would help resolve this question. We're not concerned with their relationship, just with identifying the issues that are interconnected with this one. Ultimately, our goal is to define the primary issues that must be dealt with first as crisply and clearly as we can."

A word of warning: People will naturally shoot toward the outer ring of the Circle of Assumptions. So it's common for a conversation on "what is the issue?" to veer off into "how do we solve the problem?" Before you know it, the group will be off like a pack of wild horses into a discussion of the merits of a particular suggestion. Caution the group in advance to stay focused on defining the problem. Say: "We don't want to talk about solutions just yet. Keep those thoughts to yourself for now."

If people are reluctant to get going, it's a simple matter to say: "We need everyone to contribute their thoughts. The wackiest suggestion can sometimes lead to the most productive insight. So don't edit yourselves. Let's go around the room and each person will say what he or she thinks." And then proceed to do so.

Let's resume the conversation with the sailboat maker. On a flip chart the discussion leader writes down Mike's tentative definition of the issue: "Profits not high enough."

Sally, the marketing director, says: "I guess a related issue is whether both our fixed and variable costs are under control. For example, our building is not very energy efficient. I've often wondered whether we could save money by making changes in the way it's insulated."

So on the flip chart the discussion leader writes down: "Controls on costs, e.g., heating costs."

Sherry, the information systems manager, says: "A related issue is profit margins versus earnings. Profit margins in our industry average around 8 percent. We're at 8 percent. So are we talking about higher profit margins, or increasing our revenues at the same ratio to our costs and thereby increasing our earnings instead?"

"Profit margins vs. earnings" goes onto the flip chart.

Mike, the president, says: "A third way of looking at it is that we, as a company, don't really have a clear picture of success. We like to hit our financial goals, we like to build good solid boats, but we don't have other ways of defining success. Maybe that's the issue."

"Lack of measures of success" is written on the chart.

The conversation continues in this vein for about an hour until the issues fill three flip chart pages. At that point, the discussion leader asks everyone to switch gears.

Step 3: Analyze the relationship of issues.

A scientist inquiring into the causes of things pursues two separate types of knowledge: function and form. Function concerns itself with the purpose of something, its relationship to other elements; form concerns itself with how each element is made—its materials, its origins, its shape and size. Function has to do with how various elements interact; form with how those pieces are constructed.

People who set out to resolve tough business issues are like scientists. They are inquiring into the causes of things. They are not primarily interested in form, but in function—the dynamics of the system and how to change it for the better. They are interested in influencing future events.

The discussion leader can describe the concept this way: "In the next step, we're going to analyze the relationships of each issue on this list. Some issues are dependent on others. Our goal is to find the primary issues, for which resolution is required before we can successfully tackle others. Let's see if we can reach agreement on this relationship. In the process, we may generate new items for our list—and that's okay. So let's begin discussing the relationship of each item on this list."

Someone might wonder: "But some of these issues we can control, like the quality of our sails, and some are beyond our means to control or influence, such as changes in household income. It seems odd to include them all here."

The discussion leader should say: "That's a good point, and the next step in the process is to decide which of these factors we can control, and which we cannot. If you want to do both steps simultaneously, we can. But I prefer that we don't. Let's just talk about their relationship."

It helps to display the relationship of these issues graphically. The issues map format used in Figures 3 and 4 (see pages 236 and 237) works best for several reasons: (1) You can quickly see how each issue ties into others. (2) You can see the relative importance of issues. (3) It allows for the addition of more issues later on. And (4) you can depict via dotted lines how certain issues loop back on each other. A disadvantage is that it's difficult to read words going in different directions across a page. But that's a relatively small price to pay, given the advantages.

Let's return to the sailboat company. The list of issues generated in Step 2 looks like this:

Related issues:

Profits not high enough

Controls on costs, e.g. heating costs

Profit margins vs. earnings

Lack of measures of success

Lack of database

Unrealistic expectations

Insufficient attention to monthly variances

After passing out blank pieces of paper to everyone, the discussion leader says: "Let's take these issues and map their relationships, with the primary issues at the center and other issues branching off."

Once the group begins, there's spirited discussion about what belongs where. Everyone agrees that "Profits not high enough" is at the center. The results of their work are shown in Figure 3.

Then Sherry speaks up: "I'm seeing 'Lack of measures of success' as more primary than 'Profits not high enough.' It seems to me that if we had clear measures of success, how we perceive our profits would change. So it's more primary."

The discussion leader asks other people for their perspectives.

"I think she's right," Mike says. "It's more central because it affects how we see our performance everywhere."

"I'd also shift the one that says 'Insufficient attention to monthly variances' so that it ties into 'controls on costs,'" Sally says. "It doesn't affect the database. But it certainly affects our ability to control costs."

"Everyone agree?" the discussion leader asks. Heads nod. "Okay." A second chart is drawn, as shown in Figure 4.

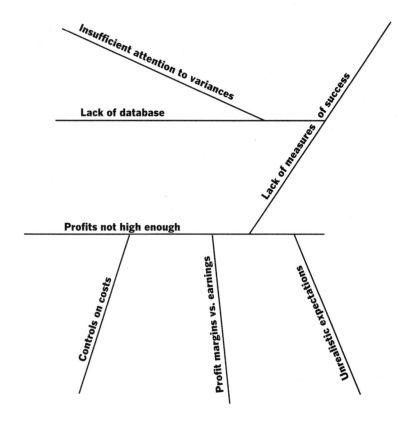

**FIGURE 3. ISSUES MAP: JENSEN, INC.
(FIRST VERSION)**

"Now that we've gone through this exercise," the discussion leader says, "take a moment and write down the issue you feel is most pivotal. We all came here today to help your company. So tell us what problem the company most needs to solve. Another way of looking at it is this: What question, if answered, would result in the most benefit for the company?"

People take about three minutes for this exercise. When they report back, the decision is unanimous: They want to create a set of measurable benchmarks that define success. Each person is asked to explain briefly why this would have the greatest benefit.

"We're too wishy-washy," says Sally. "We need standards we can measure ourselves by."

"Plus," says Sherry, "it would help if we didn't simply accept the industry standard. Maybe our expected profit margins are putting a crimp in our growth. We should look at that."

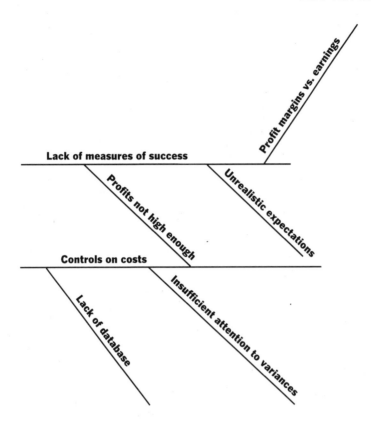

**FIGURE 4. ISSUES MAP: JENSEN, INC.
(REVISED VERSION)**

"As for me," says Mike, "this is not the issue I would have thought to raise right now, given how I was seeing our short-term problems. But I see that it's a very important conversation for us to have. It would enable us to play by a common set of rules, shoot for the same goals, and define winning in ways that we all understood. That would bring more focus to what we're doing."

In this case, the definition of the problem took only a couple of hours. But it can take a day, or even more.

How does a team know when it has redefined the problem successfully? It's up to the people involved. If everyone feels they've pinpointed the issue that will yield the most benefits, then the team is finished. If there are two or three major camps, then the discussion leader has to probe further. Ask each camp to explain its reasoning. Follow the ground rules, give people a chance to test their assumptions, probe for the missing data, and reach agreements. Again, given the 80 percent rule, one cannot spend too much time on this part of the process.

Two different groups might diagram the issues here differently. There's artistry and interpretation involved. Nevertheless, the exercise is invaluable. It illustrates the relationships between issues. It enables a group to appreciate which problems warrant its attention first. And most important, it allows the communication to become highly focused and organized.

Case Study What's the Problem?

Miniature Toys,[2] a maker of replicas of old-fashioned tin toys, had decided it needed to reexamine its sales strategy. It asked us to facilitate a meeting of the management team. After laying out the principles of straight talk, we began helping them define their crucial issue.

"I see us needing to develop a new sales channel through direct mail," said Bill, the sales director. "We're getting chewed up on our discounts to retailers. We should capture 100 percent of our list price, not 40 percent."

"But the problem is we need additional sales right now," said Mary, the marketing director. "We should test direct mail, but I wouldn't want to count on it when retail outlets are our bread and butter. They're going to be hopping mad if we start selling direct."

"I agree with Mary," said Steve, her husband and the company's CEO. He was nearing retirement and starting to let Mary run the show. "We've got to balance short-term and long-term strategies. Focusing on direct mail means a complete reorganization of how we do business."

"When I think about it, I wonder whether the problem isn't the expense side of our sales," said Adam, the young CFO. "That leads to some unpleasant thoughts, but I wonder whether we can continue to sustain overhead that puts our breakeven at 60,000 units per year. All those salespeople cost money."

"I agree," said Bill, the director of sales. "We need to grow in a way that simultaneously lowers our costs of sales and raises sales revenues. Direct mail is the answer."

"How can we define this problem in a way everyone accepts?" we asked. "One perspective, represented by Bill, says that direct

---

2. The name of this company has been changed to protect its privacy.

mail would be a better route to long-term profits. Another perspective, stated by Mary and Steve, says that short-term profits will be jeopardized by a change from the current retail strategy. Does everyone agree?"

No one said anything.

"How far out in the Circle of Assumptions are these two points of view?" we asked.

"Pretty far," someone ventured.

"Then maybe we should hold off accepting those perspectives," we said. "Let's just continue to explore the issue. The question is long-term sales strategy. What are the related issues?"

"I think we have a problem understanding how our business actually works," said Mary. "Bill says direct mail is the way to go, and yet I don't see it that way. If two smart people can disagree on something so fundamental, I wonder whether we really understand our business."

"All right, so let's reframe the issue: You lack knowledge about what drives your business. Let's look now at what some related issues are. We need to test whether we've defined the issue crisply enough."

"Well," said Steve, "we have two sets of customers—our retail outlets and the people who ultimately buy our toys at the store. We know a lot about the former, and not much about the latter. It's sort of an information gap. So we can't help our retail partners figure out how to reach the customers most likely to buy our products."

"Good," we said. "So what's the issue?"

"We can't provide good marketing information to our retail stores. So we're vulnerable on two fronts: to lowballing wheeler-dealers and to competitors who know our customers better than we do."

The conversation proceeded along these lines for another forty-five minutes. Ultimately, the group decided the core issue was the company's inability to be an information company in an information age. The conversation focused on developing a strategy that could continually generate information about customers, which in turn would create leads to additional sales. Customers that could help Miniature Toys fulfill that strategy would be considered priority customers and given special treatment, with such perks as a more expensively produced catalog, first priority on rare or closeout items, and a holiday bonus program. Those that could not would be relegated to a second tier.

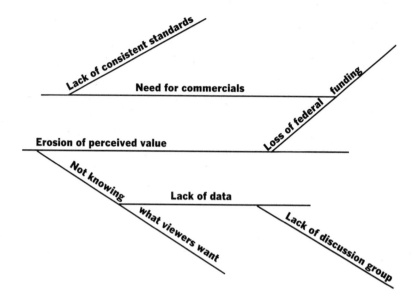

FIGURE 5. ISSUES MAP: PUBLIC TELEVISION

Miniature Toys provides another illustration of how straight talk can lead a group to define its key issue in unexpected ways. The initial problem—"generating long-term profits"—was redefined as "becoming an information-based company." Once the group agreed on the problem, the solution lay within reach.

Step 4: Eliminate issues beyond your control.

Typically, the issues will fall into two categories: those within the group's control and those outside its control. It is self-evident that you cannot control the latter. Therefore, the group should focus on issues it can control.

For example, take the diagram of issues related to commercialism in public television, shown in Figure 5. Which of these issues should station CEOs focus on?

Someone says: "We can't directly control the level of federal funding. That's for Congress to decide." So that issue gets crossed out.

"Nor can we directly control the erosion of perceived value," another person says. "That's tied to what our competitors are doing." It's crossed out.

"We'd like to figure out what our viewers really want," a third person says, "but it's a huge research project. And the stations are too diverse to decide what data they need." A heated debate ensues, but ultimately the issue gets crossed off the list.

Next on the list: "Lack of consistent standards."

"Is that an issue the group can tackle?" the discussion leader asks.

No one says anything for a few seconds. Finally, someone speaks. "You know, we could conduct interesting research on this question. But we lack a representative group that can decide what research will satisfy us all."

Lots of heads nod.

Someone says: "If we had that, we could tackle a host of issues—like what our viewers want."

At this point, the discussion leader recaps what has emerged in the last few minutes of the conversation: "We're saying that the most important issue is the lack of a representative group to decide important industry issues. Isn't that right?"

Heads nod. Everyone agrees. At this point, the discussion leader tests whether the consensus is real. He asks everyone in the group to express their feelings about the conversation to this point. He probes for any possible doubts. He reminds the group that defining the issue correctly is 80 percent of the solution. After thirty minutes of discussion, they agree that the key issue is the lack of a representative group empowered to make decisions for the whole.

There are three different criteria one can use to know whether the primary issue has been correctly identified:

1. Does the group agree that it's the most important problem to solve?
2. Would the resolution of this issue resolve the problem as it was initially stated?
3. Would the resolution of this issue have the greatest benefit to the organization?

If the group is still torn among several possible issues, here's another test: Ask everyone to imagine that each issue will take exactly the same amount of money to resolve. Name a figure, say, $50,000. Then ask the group which issue would be the best investment. If necessary, split the group into two task forces. Nine times out of ten, both groups will report back the same conclusion. At that point, move on to Step 5.

By the way, there's no one correct answer. Two groups might identify different issues as primary. The key is to make sure that everyone in the group agrees and is committed to resolving the issue. Not superficially, but within the heat and substance of straight talk.

If no agreement is reached on what the key issue is, ask the group members why they've reached this impasse. Are certain issues not on the table? Are undiscussables getting in the way? Are the group conflicts such that productive conversations are impossible? (Review Chapter 9 for ways to resolve conflicts.)

Step 5: Brainstorm alternative solutions until you (a) agree on a solution or (b) agree on what evidence or data are necessary in order to resolve the problem.

Your group has taken the time to frame the issue clearly. You all agree that it is an issue within your control, and that it is the most important issue that needs to be resolved.

Most groups are so charged up at this point that they want to dig into the problem right away. If you have time, shift the focus of the conversation to generating possible solutions. Frame it this way: "We've gone 80 percent of the distance now. We're a few yards short of the goal. We may not agree on a solution to this issue today. And that's okay. At minimum, what we will achieve, provided we stick to the ground rules, is agreement on what we need to do to resolve this issue. Let me underscore that point. Our goal is to agree on either a solution or the next steps in gathering information. So let's make that our goal. We will stop once we agree on a solution, or on a series of next steps."

At this point, ask each individual to write down his or her thoughts about possible solutions. If you have more than eight people, it can be helpful to break the group into smaller groups to allow ample time for brainstorming. Regardless of how it's done, ask each individual or group for feedback, and list their ideas on a flip chart. It may be useful to ask someone to serve as scribe, to keep more thorough notes on each idea as it's discussed.

Let's return once more to the sailboat company. We left the conversation with the decision that the central issue was the lack of a set of measurable benchmarks to define success.

At this point, Mike turns to Paul, the CFO, and asks him a question: "What financial benchmarks do we currently use?"

"We look at our ratio of fixed costs to variable costs. We look at our ratio of costs to revenues. Profit margin, of course, both pre- and post-tax."

Sherry speaks: "But aren't I correct? Won't our actual profits double if we increase sales by only a third? Yet since our variable costs are high, our profit margin really won't go up all that much?"

"That's right," says Paul.

"So shouldn't we look at percentage increases in actual profits, as opposed to increases in profit margins, as a key benchmark?" Sherry asks.

"That's a good point," Mike says. "Paul, do you agree?"

"Sure, but we don't have any industry averages then. We'd only be benchmarking against ourselves."

"But that's one of the keys," says Sherry. "Our goal should be continuous improvement of our business—not to compare ourselves to anyone else. That's a much more exciting goal for our team, I think."

"It also means putting the financial data into everyone's hands, however," says Paul. "How comfortable are we doing that?"

"I think we have to," says Mike.

"Even if it means showing our salaries?" says Sally. "How comfortable are you with that?"

"If someone wants to take issue with what I make, let them. It's healthy," says Mike.

As you can see, the group is beginning to identify the elements of a solution to this issue. The conversation will continue in a task force after the retreat. The team ultimately sets forth clear benchmarks in sales, marketing, production, accounting, and customer service. Mike will institute a free flow of information throughout the company and a bonus program tied to the new benchmarks. Ultimately, Jensen, Inc., will report a double-digit increase in profits due, at least in part, to its use of straight talk.

Case Study Sibling Rivalry at the TV Station

One of our clients, a television station affiliated with a major network, created a spin-off news show we'll call Cable One. It was a daring idea—a news show on cable aimed at people with a large appetite for local news.

The company hired a team of producers and reporters to start producing this new show. Company executives explained that people working for it would be paid less than people working for the regular news show, because this show would reach a smaller audience. The staff would be rewarded with experience gained from working in a big television market.

Two years after Cable One was launched, our firm was hired to diagnose the work environment at both the regular news show and Cable One. Not surprisingly, Cable One scored lowest in the area of rewards and compensation—meaning this was the area of lowest employee satisfaction.

As we analyzed the causes, it didn't seem at all surprising that Cable One's pay scales resulted in low levels of satisfaction. On the face of it, the reason seemed obvious: Cable One and the regular news show were both housed in the same building. Cable One personnel kept running into people from the network affiliate who were making twice as much money as they were. It was human nature for Cable One employees to feel dissatisfied.

At the same time, Cable One scored highest in the one area where the affiliate scored lowest. Cable One employees understood their goals and priorities. People at the network affiliate did not. That was interesting.

Our team of four consultants sat down one day to review the case. Our assignment was to identify the key issues and suggest appropriate solutions. We were accustomed to using straight talk, so we first reminded each other of our styles of communicating. Then we tried to define the problem again.

"As I see it," one of my colleagues said, "the problem at Cable One is the shared office. Put them in a separate location, and the salary comparisons will disappear."

"But we know from studies that money is not the most important reward," said another. "I think the problem is the intangible rewards at Cable One. Look at the low score on the question 'I'm rewarded for innovation.' That tells me we've got a different problem."

"Okay," another colleague chimed in, "my interpretation is that Cable One employees are poorly managed. Their average scores across all categories are among the lowest we've seen. Look at all the comments scribbled in the margins. That's pretty unusual. Some talk about management not practicing what they preach; others say they hate working there. I think the problem is the general quality of management."

"Let's clarify our assumptions," I said. "For example, I'm assuming that Cable One doesn't have the resources to undertake major management change. This is a small, start-up operation. Am I right?"

"I think so," said a colleague. "But let me clarify mine. I don't think they're getting enough intangible rewards. They should be taking some pride in this new venture; they should feel excited about coming to work. But I don't see that happening. The data are inconclusive."

"And my assumption," someone else said, "is that the parent company is the root of the problem. We know the management style is old school. They've got shareholders on their minds, nothing else. Managers down the line take their cues from the top. That's my assumption."

We began listing on a flip chart the data we needed to help us define the problem more clearly.

Data We Need:

1. Can our survey data tell us whether some Cable One managers are perceived as doing a relatively good job? What factors make them stand out?
2. To what extent are employees at Cable One rewarded—either tangibly or intangibly—for the show's entrepreneurial success?
3. Do people at Cable One receive accurate information about comparable salaries in similar-sized markets elsewhere?

"So if we had all this information, would we be able to agree on a solution?" we asked.

One colleague shook his head. "No, I'd still want to know about the parent company's influence. It may be an undiscussable. But what if all the problems lead back to them?"

"Can you define a missing piece of data that would help you clarify the problem in your mind?" someone asked.

A colleague walked up to the flip chart and wrote down one more question:

4. To what extent do managers encourage and reward employees for finding problems and implementing solutions on their own?

We agreed that if we had good data on all four questions, we'd be in a position to redefine the problem more accurately. Our data analyst was shown the questions. Here's the summary of her report.

Question 1: We have some data, but it's not conclusive. Two departments, advertising and accounting, appear to have stronger managers. But we can't identify factors as to why. That will require new surveys.

Question 2: The data suggest that employees are not rewarded at all, either tangibly or intangibly, for station successes.

Question 3: No data.

Question 4: No data.

We called the team together to talk through the data analyst's report and decide the next steps.

"I assume that the client doesn't want to pay more money for more surveys," someone said. "Am I right?"

"I think so," another person said. "But I sense that we are closer than we think. What if we hypothesize that managers at Cable One are only looking at revenues to measure their success. We know it's a channel with tiny ratings. Therefore employees aren't going to derive much satisfaction from that. Everything points to the fact that the same benchmarks are being used for the small station as the big one. Cable One is caught in a Catch-22. We've got to shift the way they measure themselves."

"That fits in with what I'm seeing," someone else said. "Their employees aren't getting rewarded, and the reason is that they haven't got a reasonable scale to measure themselves by. That leaves them only the salaries and ratings and revenues of the network affiliate down the hall. I think we're on to something."

Our report back to the client recommended three fundamental changes:

1. A new series of yardsticks and benchmarks at Cable One, tied to material rewards for all employees if the benchmarks were met.
2. Mandatory management training for all managers at the station, with a special emphasis on rewarding innovation.
3. A comparison of salaries in markets with audiences comparable to Cable One's, distributed annually to all employees at Cable One.

We also recommended that Cable One stay in the same build-ing. The new rewards system should make it feel very different from its older sibling.

Conclusion

I hope you've gained an appreciation for how many issues can be embedded in a single "issue"—and how important it is to tease apart the various strands before solutions are discussed. The five steps of framing an issue that were described in this chapter will prevent little snarls from growing into strategic gridlock. There's real excitement when a group defines an issue to everyone's satisfaction. If used in con-junction with straight talk, these steps enable an issue to get framed so that everyone understands it—and so that the solution lies within reach.

We've introduced these tools in dozens of different organizational and corporate settings, and there's one consistent question we're asked. "Can we really do this on our own?"

The answer is: Yes, you can. The group needs to be familiar with the tools, of course. And it helps if you rotate responsibility so that everyone in the group pushes the process forward. When everyone's committed to straight talk, groups can do amazing things.

EXERCISE: DEFINE YOUR ORGANIZATION'S PROBLEM

Assume you're in charge of defining a major problem that needs to be solved by your organization. Write down four issues that come to mind:

Issues our organization needs to solve:

1.

2.

3.

4.

Tentatively identify which issue is most important:

The most important issue is:

On a separate piece of paper, map all the related issues, using the techniques described in this chapter. If your map includes the issues you listed above, that's okay.

Of those issues that lie within your organization's ability to control, which do you now regard as the most important?

The most important issue is:

Finally, list some possible solutions to the issue you've defined. Ask yourself what information you would need in order to decide the best solution.

Possible solutions	Information needed
1.	
2.	
3.	
4.	

Chapter Twelve
Implications for Your Life

I want, by understanding myself, to understand others.
—KATHERINE MANSFIELD (1888–1923)

There's one more power to discover in straight talk—the power to understand what style makes you feel most at ease, most natural, most completely yourself. A colleague of mine refers to this as "authentic communication." She contends that many people, because of their jobs and their desire to succeed, adopt styles of communicating that are not true to their nature. These people don't feel happy—despite outward trappings of success—because they are the victims of a false ideal of appropriate communication.

For example, if you see it as your role to make quick, bold decisions, when you are naturally prone to proceeding cautiously, or if you see it as your role to analyze what everyone says, when you're more comfortable expressing what you feel, then you are already a victim of this false ideal. No one can be happy if the style they have to adopt at work is in conflict with the natural style they desire.

Why do we alter our natural style? As psychologists from Freud onward have pointed out, we carry around an idealized vision of ourselves as powerful beings. Perhaps this is a coping mechanism. No one knows. But the fact is, we like to be successful in our roles. We don't like to admit weakness or failure. So when we accept roles that are thrust upon us, roles that go against our authentic selves, we resolve the contradiction by jettisoning authenticity, by affirming a false ideal of ourselves—and this becomes our downfall.

I call this pattern of self-deluding idealization the "Icarus Syndrome," based on the Greek legend of the boy who escaped from his island prison on wings held together with wax. But because Icarus was drawn by the blinding light of the sun, he flew too high, his wings of wax melted, and he fell into the sea and drowned. His story symbolizes those who are blinded by a compelling vision of themselves as omniscient, which leads to their downfall.

Do you feel the person you are at work is not really you? Do you find yourself communicating or behaving as though someone else were in charge? Do you justify your behavior by saying that you're only doing what's expected of you? If this is a consistent feeling, you may have succumbed to the Icarus Syndrome.

Of course, there's a deep irony in this behavior. We develop an inauthentic style to gain more power and control over our lives. However, the more deeply we deceive ourselves by acting this way, the less in control we really are. People see our defensiveness and instinctively sense that we're communicating falsely. Yet we're caught in a vicious spiral: The closer we fly to the sun, the more we are unable to see our true selves.

Some of us need to fall into the sea. We need what geologists call a "discontinuity"—a time of rapid and disruptive change. We need to leave our jobs. Painful as it may be, we need to come face-to-face with our unsuitability for a given role.

A friend of mine went through this. Handpicked after a nationwide search to be CEO of a major software company, he saw himself as needing to make a series of bold strategic moves. In his first shareholder meeting, he put on a brilliant show, highlighting his company's new direction. In follow-up reports, he assured the board of directors that his strategy was working. He developed the reputation for being brilliant. But among his staff he was also perceived as Machiavellian.

I knew this man to be a sensitive, thoughtful individual. He was naturally cautious and analytical, not bold and decisive. His brilliance allowed him to get away with his act for a time. But he began to suffer from depression. Press reports hinted at major internal debates about the strategy he'd undertaken. He started taking painkillers each day. Soon the press was upbraiding him for "failing to drive his vision for the company."

Fourteen months after he was hired, my friend was fired. Asked why by a reporter, my friend only said that the "board of directors and I differed in our views on the future of the industry."

What my friend neglected to say was that getting fired was a blessing in disguise.

Roots of the Icarus Syndrome

How do we go off track? Why is authentic communication so hard?

Over time, we become bogged down in day-to-day "groupspeak" and lose sight of how important it is to be authentic, honest communicators. We forget that the value we bring to an organization is ourselves and our points of view, not our ability to mimic our boss or say what we think someone wants to hear. Fundamentally, organizations fail to motivate people to do the one thing that can make them truly successful: communicate with each other in honest, authentic ways.

But how do we go wrong in the first place? How do we become inauthentic in communicating with others? Look no further than the role models in today's society. Athletes, celebrities, and rock stars have become the heroes of modern culture. These role models aren't competent communicators. Instead, they perform in media that enable them to be cast as powerful, idealized, more perfect versions of ourselves. Success means making all the right plays, knowing all the right moves, having all the right answers. Success is being perfect—a perfect physique, a perfect report card, a perfect win-loss record. Perfection is the goal.

But perfection is also the poison.

Because perfection is an unattainable goal, the pursuit of perfection undermines what it takes to feel fulfilled. Perfection distracts us from enjoying the journey. Perfection makes it impossible for a group of people to work together to discover their individual fallibility and find their common sense. Idealized models of perfection make people, from executives to file clerks, communicate in a manner that is patently opposed to their natural style.

This book has emphasized that expert communicators are the first to admit their fallibility, their inability to see all the data clearly. Ask yourself whether your role at work prevents you from becoming an expert communicator. Try this technique: Imagine yourself on a beach somewhere, far from the pressures of your job. Imagine a stranger walking up and asking: "What is the one thing you've done that most embarrasses you?"

Would you need to be omnipotent? Would you care whether your ignorance or weakness showed? Or, on the other hand, could you display genuine curiosity about yourself, about the other person, and about the question? Could you find it the most natural thing to say: "You know, I never really thought about it until you asked. That's very interesting. Here's what I think."

Now imagine you're at work. Imagine a colleague walking into your office and asking the same question. Could you respond the same way? Why not? What's stopping you? If it's old baggage, then resolve to talk about it.

"You and I have had a rough time communicating before, and I think it's because I feel defensive around you. I've had a hard time admitting that to myself, but I have. And now I'm admitting it to you. So I'd like to put that behind us now."

Why is that so hard?

Or enlist the help of a friend. Ask him or her to imagine you at your best. Have your friend describe your best self to you—all of your strengths. Then tell your friend that you feel "out of alignment" with that best self. That your natural style and the style you display are sometimes not the same. Ask him or her to describe the difference and when it manifests itself.

You'll be surprised by how much you'll learn.

Case Study A CEO Seeks Feedback

A chief executive of a midwestern bank once sought our help because she felt the day-to-day pressures of her job were making her less effective than she had been in the past. She was worried that she might be affecting the organization in ways she couldn't see. She told us she needed some objective feedback.

Now, most people in high-pressure jobs have enough on their plates without taking on the challenge of a self-examination. Not this woman. She asked us to survey all thirty managers in the organization to determine how the company culture had changed, for better and for worse, since she'd arrived three years earlier.

In the face-to-face interviews, people told us she had brought a new sense of direction to the company, that she'd gotten "everyone pursuing the same goals," and that she was keeping shareholders happy. At the same time, people felt that her expectations were very high, they were afraid to take risks, and they were afraid of her. One manager, widely respected for her creativity, had banged heads with the CEO several times. People knew that there had been "blood spilled," as one person put it.

Our second step was a forty-question survey to analyze changes in the company's culture since her arrival. One question was: "Compared with three years ago, do you enjoy your work more or less?" The results showed that people enjoyed their work less.

Our third step was to analyze and synthesize this information into a set of conclusions to take back to the CEO. Chief among our findings was that people had become more cautious since her arrival. People felt more stifled and more reactive, which was damaging morale.

Fourth, and most important, we moderated an open forum in which the thirty managers got a chance to tell the CEO what they felt, and hear her responses.

One exchange captured the entire event. A midlevel manager asked her: "Since you've been here, I've noticed that people, including myself, spend a lot of time wondering what you're thinking. Why don't you just tell us?"

"I try to," she said. "But there are things I just can't say to you."

"Why not?" came the response.

"Because we're a very visible public company, because I'm supposed to watch after the stock, because the press repeats and distorts what I say."

There was a long silence in the room. Finally, someone said: "We didn't know it was that tough."

She left this meeting feeling very unhappy. We met in her office. She asked whether there was anything she could do to be more responsive to people's need for information. She said she saw her value as setting the overall strategy for the bank as well as acting as the formal liaison between the bank, the board, and the shareholders.

But, she said, "I recognize that what I can do positively in those roles can have a negative impact in other ways. I think I should delegate day-to-day management to someone who can be more responsive."

A month later, she hired a new COO and gave him direct responsibility for managing the bank. She was a good role model—someone who accepted her strengths and limitations—and acted accordingly.

The Role of Role Models

We are a society that needs more role models like that bank CEO. Other societies have given their children role models with weaknesses as well as strengths. In ancient Greece, a young child was given a patron god as a role model. Apollo, the god of war, perhaps; or Aphrodite, the goddess of beauty. But both Apollo and Aphrodite had multiple dimensions. Apollo's quick temper got him into trouble. Aphrodite's vanity made her seem silly.

In certain Native American tribes, when a child is born, he or she is given the name of an animal. The fox signifies cunning, the owl wisdom, the bear warmth, the crow wit and laughter. These symbols become deeply connected to the spiritual growth of the child. And at the same time, the child recognizes that his or her animal spirit is weak as well as strong. The owl cannot fly fast. The bear can be lazy. The fox can be evil. These weaknesses are acknowledged in legends and myths, repeated across generations.

This assigning of role models is a way to link children to society, to give them a sense of who they are, and ultimately to provide a doorway to self-understanding. Even if the child at some point rejects the chosen guide or patron deity, he or she is never without a role model. In choosing who we are not, we are defining who we are. And in knowing that all of us have weaknesses and strengths, these children grow up able to admit fallibility.

But not all cultures or societies do this. In contemporary American culture, we don't assign role models to our children. We let them choose for themselves. We pride ourselves on being a nation of individualists, and as individuals we are sent off to school, to marriage, and to our jobs. Most of us have no other guide than the role models we pick up along the way. Even if our parents are good role models, popular culture makes it awfully hard for their values to stand out.

This is why it's easy for our true selves to become lost along the way. Our guides are not assigned with the same wisdom or understanding that they once were, and therefore our sense of choice, our sense of who we can be, becomes distorted. Parents and educational institutions are at a disadvantage when perfection becomes the model. When what is popular one day quickly vanishes the next, getting connected to our authentic selves is an elusive—if not impossible—goal.

Communicating in Your Authentic Style

When you first took the Communication Styles Profile, back in Chapter I, we asked you to take it in the context of your job. You assessed yourself based on the role you play at work.

Now we want you to take it again.

But this time, assume the role you play at home with your family, or with your friends. Put aside other concerns and remember the person who is most naturally you. Then take the Profile again. This is your authentic style.

When you compare the two results, you'll discover something about yourself. If your working style and your authentic style are the same, then you are living in harmony. Congratulations. You have done well.

However, if your working style and your authentic style are different, then you are out of sync. The style you naturally gravitate toward and the style you are asked to adopt at work are not aligned. The degree to which they are out of alignment can be easily gauged by their distance from one another on the Matrix.

In the following example, a woman in her forties who managed a chain of retail clothing stores discovered that her authentic style was Socializer, whereas her working style was Organizer, as shown in the Matrix in Chart 27.

When she found this out, she was dismayed. She had wondered why she didn't like her work. Now she knew. Despite the good salary and the esteem of an important job, she wasn't enjoying it. She used to be selling clothes and meeting with customers, which she loved. But now, because of promotions, she was in an office most of the time. "I'm a well-compensated schizophrenic," she said to me, only half-jokingly.

There's no magic solution, other than self-awareness. This woman eventually quit her job to become a buyer for another chain. While it didn't put her back on the floor selling clothes, it at least gave her contact with new people each day. Which is exactly what she needed.

The American philosopher William James put it this way in one of his letters: "I have often thought that the best way to define a man's character would be to seek out the particular mental or moral attitude in which, when it came upon him, he felt himself most deeply and intensely active and alive." At such moments there is a voice inside that speaks and says: "This is the real me!"

CHART 27: AUTHENTIC STYLE VERSUS WORKING STYLE

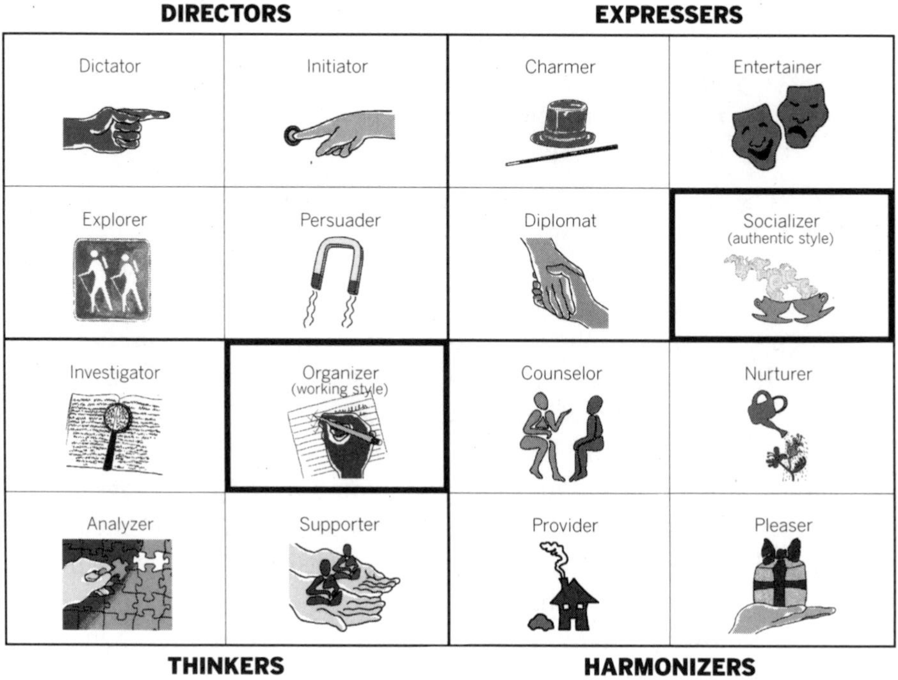

DIRECTORS   **EXPRESSERS**

Dictator	Initiator	Charmer	Entertainer
Explorer	Persuader	Diplomat	Socializer (authentic style)
Investigator	Organizer (working style)	Counselor	Nurturer
Analyzer	Supporter	Provider	Pleaser

THINKERS   **HARMONIZERS**

Conclusion

Much as we try to find careers suited to our skills, our working roles can wrench us far from the style of communicating that is most natural and comfortable to us. Eventually, we may wind up in a working role that requires us to communicate and behave in ways exactly contrary to our authentic style.

When this happens, we may notice that we feel tense or edgy. But lacking any hard evidence or objective way to understand what's going on, we typically try to muddle through, continuing to accept our role and responsibilities without question. In so doing, we devalue our natural style of communicating and deny ourselves a source of deep personal fulfillment.

As skilled as we become at modifying our style, we are not infinitely elastic. People can tolerate a lot of stress and conflict. But eventually, like a rubber band, we may snap.

People who are genuinely happy in their jobs are those whose working style mirrors their authentic style. The Communication Styles Profile can help you discern whether you're suffering a fundamental conflict between your working and authentic styles.

EXERCISE: DISCOVER YOUR AUTHENTIC STYLE

Circle the communication style you use at work on the Matrix below. Next, if you haven't already done so, take the Communication Styles Profile a second time to discover your authentic style. When you are finished, mark down your authentic style on the Matrix.

DIRECTORS   **EXPRESSERS**

Dictator	Initiator	Charmer	Entertainer
Explorer	Persuader	Diplomat	Socializer
Investigator	Organizer	Counselor	Nurturer
Analyzer	Supporter	Provider	Pleaser

THINKERS   **HARMONIZERS**

If the two styles are not the same, write down three specific career steps or goals that would enable you to reinforce your authentic style. List those goals below.

Career goals that would reinforce my authentic style:

1.

2.

3.

Finally, write down three things you could do in the next month that would help you attain the goals listed above—people to call, letters to write, journals to read, and so forth. When you're finished, ask yourself what would prevent you from doing these things.

Things to do in the next thirty days:

1.

2.

3.

Epilogue

Everything has changed—
except the way we think.
—ALBERT EINSTEIN (1879-1955)

We said at the outset that this book would flip some traditional ideas on their head. Particularly, the notion of competence. With all the attention placed by business writers and managers on core competency, this book argues that a learning organization's most important core competency is the ability to admit fallibility.

This ability to admit what we don't know is the start of "double-loop learning," according to Chris Argyris, one of the pioneers in the field of organizational learning. It is the key to becoming engaged in the learning process.

Our society, and our world, are evolving into an interconnected network where people increasingly need to learn more quickly and effectively. People need tools that can help them manage not just their communications software, but their communications "humanware." Through this book you've begun to use these tools, to learn how people can interact and communicate with maximum results.

Ideally, these tools have helped you improve the *process* of communicating—by learning the critical principles and tools that facilitate that process. And they've helped you improve the *content* of what is communicated, by learning how to untangle the assumptions embedded in what is said and to focus on the missing data.

The tools of straight talk give us the power to change, to transcend, to go beyond what we are and to evolve into something new. Ultimately, straight talk gives us the ability to challenge ourselves, to frame ourselves, and to change. Through straight talk we learn how to change our way of thinking—and thereby change everything. Yet so subtle is straight talk that we often overlook it. We pass from day to day, forgetting that we have it within our reach, to do our bidding if only we summon it.

If this book has a larger purpose, it is about living a more conscious life, about being more aware of our behavior with each other. As writer Terrence McKenna puts it:

> Our crisis as a culture is a crisis of insufficient consciousness. . . . If our problem is a lack of consciousness, then any technique or thing that increases consciousness is part of the solution and should be looked at.

The value of straight talk—and its power—lies in its ability to raise our consciousness about how we communicate. This is a paradoxical power, because most people seem not to want it. Even our culture seems not to value it, valuing instead people who talk in one dimension only—issuing opinions and asserting their omniscient ability to see things clearly.

The paradox we have observed, after guiding and watching straight talk prevail in many organizations, is why this should be so. Why should our software-based information tools be so much more advanced than our brain-based communication tools? Could our culture be somehow complicit in perpetuating poor communicators? Is there some reason why we haven't made straight talk pervasive in our classrooms, our legislatures, and our society?

I don't know the answers to these questions. All I know is that straight talk is a powerful tool. And as more organizations discover it, I trust in its power to transform our society.

What do you think?

Case Study Straight Talk in Action

Let's examine the transcript from an actual conversation in which participants were trained in using straight talk. The players are all CEOs of public television stations. They are members of a special team handpicked to address tough issues. Each station they manage is individually owned and operated. But each belongs to the PBS network, which provides a prime-time schedule and pays the stations to carry it.

These executives represent the widest possible diversity of viewpoints: small stations, large stations, rich stations, and poor stations. Note how these very different viewpoints are tempered by the tools of straight talk.

The issue of the day is a deal that PBS has cut to distribute programming via satellite to dishes at homes. This means that the stations may no longer have absolute control over "the last mile" to the home. This new deal could bypass them altogether and threaten their existence.

The conversation picks up after a moderator has laid out the ground rules and everyone has identified their communication styles.

Moderator: Who wants to give me a definition of the issue before us today?

James: Let me try. The issue is whether the stations should continue to affiliate only with PBS, or whether stations need multiple programming partners.

Moderator: Good. Who else has a definition?

Colleen: One might say the issue is roles: In essence, the role of PBS versus the role of the station. But as I say that, I realize I'm not sure what problem I'm trying to solve.

Moderator: That's okay. Let's just get as many definitions as we can.

Cary: I think we're being challenged to change the way we think about our system. We're being forced to face a fundamental question by virtue of the PBS deal: What is the source of our long-term economic strength?

Beth: For a long time we've considered our business to be aggregating eyeballs. The more eyeballs that tune in, the higher our ratings, and thus the higher our underwriting revenues.

Cary: But I would challenge that thinking. I think we can argue that that model is founded on an unproved premise: that more products and services are sold because an advertising message reaches more eyeballs. That argument says nothing about the quality or demographics of the audience.

Dennis: That makes me think about the issue before us in a different way. If we derive our economic strength today from one model—the eyeball model—then how long will that model last? What scenarios can we imagine that might change that model?

Stan: Let me build on that idea. We've got PBS making a deal with DIRECTV. Let's assume that within five years, DIRECTV will be able to reach every household with a television set via a satellite dish. Furthermore, let's assume that PBS will focus its programming based on maximizing its revenues and profits. What are the economic models that would induce PBS to concentrate its resources on the DIRECTV network over our station-based network?

Moderator: Good question. Before we start answering it, does anyone have any other ways to define the issue in front of us?

Beth: No, I'm intrigued by Stan's definition. Because if we can envision an economic model that will lure PBS away from creating programming in partnership with us, and toward DIRECTV, then that allows us to prepare for one vision of the future—one in which PBS abandons us. However, if we see no scenario that leads to that event, then it allows us to prepare for another vision of the future—one in which PBS needs us.

Moderator: Everyone agree?

Group: Yes.

Moderator: Okay, then let's begin with a conversation about this issue Stan has posed. Who wants to start?

James: First, let's state the issue as I see it now. Are there scenarios that make it more attractive for PBS to go it alone with DIRECTV and no longer with the stations?

Stan: I think that's pretty close. And it's concise, which is good.

Moderator: So, what do you think about this issue?

Cary: What data do we need in order to establish that the scenario in which PBS abandons us is a real possibility?

Colleen: What data do we need to establish whether PBS would bypass us all, or only some of us? In other words, what data do we need to assess the distribution options PBS will have in five years?

Beth: I think we can make pretty good guesses about those options. Then we might see how to substantiate them with data.

Moderator: Before we go there, let's see what other people have to say about the issue as James and Stan have defined it.

Dennis: I have an undiscussable. PBS has a deal with DIRECTV. But why does that matter? Why couldn't there be a third scenario, in which we stations leave PBS and band together in our own programming alliance that results in just-as-widespread distribution as we currently enjoy?

Cary: Can you explain your reasoning more clearly?

Dennis: Sure. Here's what I'm thinking. And help me if I'm assuming too much. In the digital era, there'll be plenty of opportunities for us to create multiple networks. The word "network" won't mean anything. What's a network when each station can slice its channel into four or eight or twelve separate broadcasting streams, and each slice can belong to a different network? There may be anywhere from four to forty new alliances. Gone will be the network brand, and in its place will be microbrands, managed by a combination of local stations, telecommunications companies, and so forth. I don't want to frame the debate around two options only.

Beth: But let's challenge your thinking for just a moment. Is there anything you're missing? You're assuming, for example, that the digital era will result in access for all of us to more channels in our local markets. But we don't control that. The FCC does. And ultimately, it's Congress's decision.

Dennis: Good point. But isn't it likely that we will retain our full spectrum, which we can then carve into at least four or eight separate channels?

Beth: I think you're right, but it's an assumption.

Moderator: Let's follow the money. What economic model might induce PBS to abandon the stations?

Cary: If DIRECTV can sell something other than eyeballs to advertisers, then they might have a competitive advantage we don't.

James: What might that be?

Stan: Well, one possibility is that they'd have so much consumer information that the relative value of those eyeballs would be considerably higher than what it is today.

Dennis: Or technology could enable them to send individual messages to each receiver.

Cary: But I doubt the economics are there, when you're aggregating a million viewers, to send individual messages.

Beth: That's an assumption.

Cary: Okay. Here's a question. What form of programming could PBS offer that an alliance with DIRECTV would enable them to purvey, and that an alliance with us would not?

Beth: It would have to hinge on some proprietary piece of software that DIRECTV has.

Stan: Good point. And how likely is proprietary software to stay in one company's hands? We certainly haven't seen that so far. It's been the case that companies have been able to quickly rip off ideas and clone them.

Cary: If we accept that premise, then there's no programming that an alliance between PBS and DIRECTV could develop that would be unique—and thus challenge us.

Beth: Is that true? Have we already reached that conclusion? Help me challenge your thinking.

Cary: Okay. We just said that DIRECTV could not develop proprietary software that would enable them to translate a programming alliance with PBS into some competitive advantage. I could challenge that by saying: Sure there is. DIRECTV could own the operating system for all these digital televisions. And if so, then no one could send programming to a digital television set unless it had DIRECTV code. And DIRECTV's partners would have easier access to that code than anyone else.

Beth: I'm seeing antitrust violation written all over that scenario.

Cary: Yeah, but think of what happens in antitrust cases. They take several years to develop. By the time they get decided, much of the opportunity has been lost.

Stan: This says to me that there are ways this alliance could damage us. But only if DIRECTV gets control of the digital television operating system.

James: I think that's right. And so this points out both a defensive strategy and an offensive strategy. Defensively, we want to block DIRECTV, both in Congress and in the Justice Department. Unfortunately, our lobbying organization represents both us and PBS. So we're going to need a separate lobbying effort on this one. Offensively, we stations can form our own programming alliances and begin doing our own thing. We'll push PBS to see whether it values our relationship more than DIRECTV's, or less.

James: I think that's a good end point for this issue. We don't need to resolve it any further. But we need to take action to collect data about these future scenarios, and we need to begin exploring other partnerships. I suggest we fund a special task force, with consulting help, to do it.

Beth: I agree.

Stan: I'm in.

Cary: Me, too.

Glossary

Advocacy: A statement asserting something. For example, "John is becoming very effective in his job."

Circle of Assumptions: The various circles of interpretation that ripple outward from data to conclusions. A person far out on the Circle is asserting conclusions. A person at the center of the Circle is reciting data. Depicted as a series of concentric circles (see Figure 1).

Communication style: A person's typical manner of talking and listening to others. A person's style is measured through the Communication Styles Profile. The four basic styles are Director, Expresser, Thinker, and Harmonizer.

Communication Styles Profile: A questionnaire, with accompanying scoring instructions, that determines a person's style of communicating. It can be found in Chapter 1.

Conclusion: A decision based on interpretation or evaluation of data.

Data: Information generally accepted to be fact.

Director: One of the four styles of interacting with others, characterized by focusing on tasks.

Expresser: One of the four styles of interacting with others, characterized by focusing on ideas.

Frame: How a person interprets a situation. Determined by looking at how one views oneself, others, and the activity or task.

Goal(s): What an organization hopes to accomplish.

Harmonizer: One of the four styles of interacting with others, characterized by focusing on people's needs.

Inner script: What people say to themselves, but not to others, about a particular issue.It is used to uncover hidden assumptions.

Inquiry: A question, such as "Can you clarify what you mean?" Contrast with advocacy. Sometimes what appears to be an inquiry is actually advocacy, such as: "Isn't that a great idea?"

Issue: A problem that needs to be resolved; a question that needs to be answered.

Issues map: A way to illustrate issues that shows their relationship to each other. Used to sort out issues.

Matrix of Communication Styles: A chart showing the relationship of the sixteen mixtures of primary and secondary styles.

Prevailing styles: The two communication styles a person uses most often.

Primary style: A person's most frequent style of communicating with others. Either Director, Expresser, Thinker, or Harmonizer.

Productive conversation: A discussion of an issue in which participants challenge their thinking in nondefensive ways, identify underlying assumptions, and reach agreements about missing data.

Secondary style: A person's second most frequent style of communicating with others. Either Director, Expresser, Thinker, or Harmonizer.

Table of missing data: A tool to help people reach concensus by focusing them on what they don't know—but would like to know—about a particular issue.

Thinker: One of the four styles of interacting with others, characterized by focusing on facts.

Research into the Douglas Communication Styles

Lisa Bohon, Ph.D.
Associate Professor of Psychology,
California State University, Sacramento

In order to deepen the understanding of interpersonal communication, I asked the faculty of the psychology department at California State University, Sacramento, to conduct research into the Douglas Communication Styles and the underlying theory of human communication contained in Straight Talk. *The resulting research was led by Dr. Lisa Bohon, associate professor of psychology, whose efforts yielded much in the way of fruitful results.*

Further research is under way as Straight Talk *goes to press. That research will be published on the* Straight Talk *web site (Straight-Talk-Now.com) when it is complete.*

—Eric F. Douglas

The goal of the first phase of our research[1] was to construct a survey that could reliably measure the Douglas Communication Styles. The research focused on developing a tool to measure the Director, Expresser, Harmonizer and Thinker communication styles. We considered both what Eric Douglas's theory told us about the different communication styles, as well as the responses of participants in the study. It was important to consider both the theory and the data, because using one without the other could increase the probability that chance alone would affect the final choice of statements.

We knew that we wanted to end up with a final survey—or inventory—consisting of between 30 and 40 statements. With this goal in mind, we developed 98 statements that we thought could diagnose the four different communication styles. A quarter of these statements would measure the Director style, a quarter would measure the Expresser style, and so forth. After we had randomized these 98 statements and

---

1. Thanks to Linda Kelley, Lisa Garner, and Tiffiny Schmid for assistance in data collection and data entry.

compiled them into a survey, we gave it to 237 individuals to complete on their own.[2]

After we collected the data, we summed the individual response items for each style. Next, we correlated each of the 98 items with all four of the styles to see which statements were most strongly related to each communicaton style (Jackson, 1970). We then chose the 12 items for each of the four styles that had the highest correlation with each style and were at least .05 different from correlations with the other three styles. In addition, any item that had a high correlation with a communication style for which it was not intended was discarded. Thus, our second generation inventory was winnowed down to 48 statements.

The next step was to subject this refined inventory to a factor analysis. This would allow us to measure the underlying traits responsible for the ways that people respond to the statements on the inventory. (Tabchnik & Fidell, 1996). Factor analysis also ensures that each statement is measuring the same underlying trait, and that the statements are maximally related to a single subscale while being minimally related to the other subscales.[3]

A scree plot of the results showed us that four factors (or communication styles) had eigenvalues[4] greater than one (2.88 to 13.26). This confirmed that the data are best explained by four communication styles, rather than, say, three or five.[5]

Based on this preliminary factor analysis, we narrowed our survey to eight statements for each communication style. We conducted a final factor analysis, which showed that each of these eight statements "loaded" on its relevant style with a score of .3 or above, and loaded lower than .3 on the other three styles. We were very pleased with these results, because they confirmed that our survey instrument was meeting established professional standards. (See Chart 27).

---

2. Participants in the first phase were all college students. The majority were female (70.5 percent) and young (85.2 percent were between the ages of 18 and 27). The ethnic mix of the sample was 1.7 percent African American/Black; 5.1 percent Asian Amercian; 7.4 percent European American/White; 10.2 percent Hispanic American/Latino; and 8.9 percent other.

3. We chose to use the Promax rotation, because the theory says that the communication styles are somewhat related. For example, an individual who is high in the Director style is often also high in the Expresser style.

4. Eigenvalue is a measure that shows how much variance in response scores is explained by common features, e.g., communication styles.

5. The chi-square test for number of factors suggested that more than four were needed (chi-square = 679.152 (374), p = .0001). We placed more weight on the scree plot, however, because the chi-square test tends to inflate the number of factors needed (Gorsuch, 1993).

CHART 27: FINAL ITEM-SUBSCALE LOADINGS OF THE DOUGLAS COMMUNICATION STYLES INVENTORY (ROTATED FACTOR PATTERN)

Item #	Director	Expresser	Thinker	Harmonizer
14-E	−.08	.80	.06	−.09
8-E	−.07	.75	−.07	.23
2-E	−.04	.68	−.03	−.09
29-E	−.01	.64	.04	.29
16-E	.21	.62	−.12	−.24
10-E	.13	.62	−.03	.14
19-E	.12	.61	.08	−.14
32-E	.12	.59	−.05	.10
17-T	.07	−.05	.81	−.07
7-T	.06	.06	.79	−.10
1-T	−.01	.06	.61	−.07
25-T	.19	−.07	.60	.10
12-T	.02	−.04	.50	.04
20-T	−.06	−.10	.46	.16
30-T	−.24	.02	.45	.07
5-T	−.16	.04	.44	.10
9-H	.19	−.08	−.11	.69
13-H	−.10	.21	.16	.64
4-H	−.10	.08	.01	.64
26-H	.08	−.27	.08	.57
21-H	.17	.00	−.05	.54
31-H	−.18	.10	−.08	.53
23-H	.05	.09	.09	.47
28-H	.07	−.12	.13	.42
24-D	.78	.01	−.13	−.06
27-D	.67	−.02	−.24	.05
6-D	.56	−.02	.06	.14
11-D	.50	.08	.24	.11
18-D	.48	.08	−.07	−.06
15-D	.42	.20	.25	−.12
3-D	.37	−.01	.20	.13
22-D	.34	.11	.05	.25

Note: Letters after items indicate the communication style for which they were created: E = Expresser, T = Thinker, H = Harmonizer, D = Director.

CHART 28: CORRELATIONS AMONG THE DOUGLAS COMMUNICATION STYLES INVENTORY AND THE SOCIAL DESIRABILITY SCALE

	SDS	Director	Expresser	Thinker	Harmonizer
SDS	1.00				
Director	−.08	1.00			
Expresser	.17*	.44*	1.00		
Harmonizer	.60*	.23*	.27*	1.00	
Thinker	.37*	.18	.05	.34*	1.00

Note: * denotes significance at the .001 level. $N = 237$.

CHART 29: ALPHA RELIABILITY COEFFICIENTS FOR THE DOUGLAS COMMUNICATION STYLES INVENTORY SUBSCALES

Subscale	Reliability Coefficients
Director	.77
Expresser	.88
Harmonizer	.79
Thinker	.81

We then conducted correlation analyses of the four subscales and the Social Desirability Scale (SDS; Crowne & Marlowe, 1964). We focused on the Social Desirability Scale because we were interested to see how the four subscales related to a scale that measured the tendency to present oneself in a favorable or socially desirable light. We found that the SDS was meaningfully related to the Harmonizer ($r = .60$) and the Thinker ($r = .37$) styles (see Chart 28). These relationships were predicted by the theory. Furthermore, we found strong relationships between the Expresser and Director subscales ($r = .44$) and the Thinker and Harmonizer subscales ($r = .34$) These relationships are also predicted by Douglas's theory.

The purpose of the next set of analyses was to investigate the internal consistency of the Douglas Communication Styles Inventory (DCSI). This would confirm that each item within the same subscale measures the same underlying communication style. Alpha reliability coefficients of .70 and above are considered acceptable. Our results revealed that the DCSI subscales showed good internal consistency (see Chart 29).

---

6. These surveys were counterbalanced when they were given to the same pool of subjects.

CHART 30: TEST RETEST RELIABILITY CORRELATION COEFFICIENTS

Subscale	Correlation Coefficients
Director	.85
Expresser	.93
Harmonizer	.70
Thinker	.84

CHART 31: COMPARISONS OF AVERAGE SUBSCALE SCORES FROM TIME 1 TO TIME 2

Variable	Mean	SD	t	df	Significance
Director (T1)	26.56	4.75	.48	63	.63
Director (T2)	26.41	4.89			
Expresser (T1)	25.25	6.93	–.15	63	.88
Expresser (T2)	25.30	6.60			
Harmonizer (T1)	29.48	3.46	.88	63	.38
Harmonizer (T2)	29.19	3.47			
Thinker (T1)	31.39	4.59			
Thinker (T2)	31.33	4.52	.19	63	.85

Note: Significance levels equal to or less than .05 are considered meaningful.

T1 = Time 1; T2 = Time 2; sd = standard deviation; df = degrees of freedom.

We next investigated the stability of the Douglas Communication Style Inventory subscales. We gave the DCSI to 64 college students to fill out. Two weeks later our volunteer participants completed the DCSI once again. We conducted correlations of each of the DCSI subscales from time one to time two (see Chart 30).

The Director, Expresser, Harmonizer, and Thinker subscales showed excellent test-retest reliability (acceptable coefficients are equal to or greater than .70). Overall, the DCSI had an average test-retest reliability of .83, which indicates that this scale is stable across time.

We also conducted t-tests for correlated groups to see if average subscales changes significantly from Time 1 to Time 2 (see Chart 31).

7. The demographic characteristics of this sample matched those of the sample in Phase 1.

CHART 32: CORRELATIONS AMONG THE DOUGLAS COMMUNICATION STYLES INVENTORY SUBSCALES

	Director	Expresser	Harmonizer	Thinker
Director	1.00			
Expresser	.62*	1.00.		
Harmonizer	.24	.42*	1.00	
Thinker	.38*	.46*	.22	1.00

Note: * denotes significance at the .001 level. N = 237.

CHART 33: ALPHA RELIABILITY COEFFICIENTS FOR THE DOUGLAS COMMUNICATION STYLES INVENTORY SUBSCALES

Subscale	Reliability Coefficients
Director	.81
Expresser	.90
Harmonizer	.61
Thinker	.82

These analyses showed that average scores did not change from Time 1 to Time 2. This was added confirmation that the subscales are stable across time.

Next we correlated each of the DCSI subscales to determine their inter-relationships (see Chart 32).

Again, we found the expected high relationship between scores on the Expresser and Director subscales (r = .62), but not the Thinker and Harmonizer subscales (r = .22). We also found significant relationships between the Thinker and Director subscales (.38), the Harmonizer and Expresser subscales (.42), and the Thinker and the Expresser subscales (.46). We believe, however, that the correlations from the first phase more accurately reflect the relationships among variables because they are based on a larger number of people (237 vs. 64), and therefore are more reliable.

The purpose of the final set of analyses was to confirm the internal consistency of the DCSI subscales. Our results revealed that the DCSI subscales were internally consistent (see Chart 33) with the exception of the Harmonizer subscale. As before, the alpha reliability coefficients from Phase 1 were given more weight because they were based on a larger sample.

In summary, we were very pleased with the results of the first phase of the research. The Douglas Communication Styles Inventory showed an ideal factor analysis pattern and good internal consistency. Moreover, the expected relationships among the DCSI subscales and the Social Desirability Scale were found. We were also pleased with the reliability of the survey instrument. The DCSI showed a good average test retest reliably (.83) and good internal consistency. Together, these results confirmed that the DCSI was a reliable instrument for measuring the four discrete styles of communication.

References

Crowne, D. & Marlowe, D. (1964). *The Appraisal Motive*. New York: Wiley.

Gorsuch, R. L. (1983). *Factor Analysis* (2nd ed.). Hillsdale, N.J.: Lawrence Erlbaum Associates.

Jackson, D. N. (1970). A sequential system of personality scale development. In C. D. Spielberger (Ed.), Vol. 2, *Current Topics in Clinical and Community Psychology*. New York: Academic Press.

Tabachnik, B. G., & Fidell, L. S. (1996) *Using Multivariate Statistics* (3rd ed.). New York: Harper Collins.

Bibliography

Argyris, C., Putnam, R., and Smith, D. M. *Action Science.* San Francisco: Jossey-Bass, 1985.

Borgatta, E. F. "The Structure of Personality Characteristics." *Behavioral Science,* 1964, *12,* 8–17.

Chalmers, D. *The Conscious Mind.* Oxford, England: Oxford University Press, 1995.

Chalmers, D. "The Puzzle of Conscious Experience." *Scientific American,* December 1995.

Crowne, D., & Marlowe, D. (1964). *The Appraisal Motive.* New York: Wiley.

Drucker, P. F. *Managing the Future.* New York: Penguin Books, 1993.

Eliot, J. *Models of Psychological Space: Psychometric, Developmental, and Experimental Approaches.* New York: Springer-Verlag, 1987.

Fromm, E. *Escape from Freedom.* New York: Holt, Rinehart and Winston, 1941.

Goleman, D. *Emotional Intelligence.* New York: Bantam Books, 1997.

Gorsuch, R. L. (1983). *Factor Analysis* (2nd ed.). Hillsdale, NJ: Erlbaum.

Gould, S. J. *Full House: The Spread of Excellence from Plato to Darwin.* New York: Three Rivers Press, 1997.

Hauser, M. D. *The Evolution of Communication.* Cambridge, Mass.: MIT Press, 1996.

Henderson, J. L. *Cultural Attitudes in Psychological Perspective.* Toronto: Inner City Books, 1984.

Humphrey, N. *A History of the Mind: Evolution and the Birth of Consciousness.* New York: Simon & Schuster, 1992.

Jackson, D. N. (1970). A sequential system of personality scale development. In C. D. Spielberger (Ed.), *Current Topics in Clinical and Community Psychology,* Vol. 2. New York: Academic Press.

Jung, C. G. *Psychological Types.* New York: Harcourt Brace, 1923.

Minsky, M. *The Society of Mind.* New York: Simon & Schuster, 1986.

Mintzberg, H. "Planning on the Left Side and Managing on the Right." *Harvard Business Review,* July 1976.

Pinker, S. *How the Mind Works.* New York: Norton, 1997.

Senge, P. *The Fifth Discipline.* New York: Doubleday/Currency, 1990.

Sheldon, W. H. *Varieties of Temperament: A Psychology of Constitutional Differences.* New York: HarperCollins, 1942.

Smith, M. *The Theory of Evolution.* New York: Cambridge University Press, 1993.

Tabachnik, B. G., & Fidell, L. S. (1996) *Using Multivariate Statistics* (3rd ed.). New York: HarperCollins.

Thorne, A. *Portraits of Type: An MBTI Research Compendium.* Palo Alto, Calif.: Consulting Psychologists Press, 1991.

About the Author

Eric F. Douglas entered the publishing business as a journalist, beginning in 1973 with the *Pasadena* (California) *Star-News* and later, from 1976 to 1981, with the *San Francisco Chronicle.*

In 1981 he and his family left San Francisco to live on a farm in Virginia. Douglas became managing editor of the *Charlottesville* (Virginia) *Daily Progress,* where his work led to numerous awards for editorial excellence. In 1984 he became executive editor of *Baltimore Magazine,* which he guided to two National Magazine Awards, the highest honor in the industry. During this time, Douglas also began developing tools to improve organizational communication and decision making.

In 1989, Douglas moved to the *Sacramento Bee,* flagship of the McClatchy newspaper chain, as vice president of marketing. Among other accomplishments, he launched several electronic media ventures, including an on-line educational service and a fax-on-demand service. He was recognized by the industry in 1991 as a pioneer in electronic publishing.

In 1993 Douglas left the *Bee* and joined BMR Associates, a management consulting firm in Marin County, California. Douglas continued to refine his communications learning tools, including the Invision Communication Styles Profile. As his success grew, so did the demand for his tools and teaching methods. Today his philosophy of communication is the core of a management training program used by clients throughout the United States, including the University of California and America's Public Television Stations.

Douglas graduated with honors from Harvard University with a degree in government and did postgraduate work at the Kellogg School of Management. He lives with his family in Sacramento.

Index